Marketing in Nonprofit Organizations

Marketing in Nonprofit Organizations

edited by

Patrick J. Montana

amacom

A Division of American Management Associations

1978

HF
5415
.M2985

Library of Congress Cataloging in Publication Data
Main entry under title:

Marketing in nonprofit organizations.

   Bibliography: p.
   Includes index.
   1. Marketing—Addresses, essays, lectures.
2. Corporations, Nonprofit—Addresses, essays, lectures.
I. Montana, Patrick J.
HF5415.M2985   658.8   78-18322
ISBN 0-8144-5494-1

First Printing

Preface

The concept for this book developed from my long-time interest in the application of marketing concepts, considerations, and techniques to nonprofit organizations. Between the publication by AMACOM in 1967 of my first book, *The Marketing Executive of the Future* and *Managing Nonprofit Organizations* (with Diane Borst) in 1977, I have received repeated requests from executives in nonprofit organizations for a comprehensive source of information on marketing in nonprofit organizations. This need became even more evident between 1974 and 1976 when I served as president of the Professional Institute of the American Management Associations and directed the AMA overall efforts in the public sector of the business community to fill the management needs of such nonprofit areas as education, government, health care, associations, religious and charitable organizations, and quasi-public corporations. The need was further accentuated by many requests from students and faculty in schools of public and business administration and by the paucity of information on the subject.

Most of the material available at the time consisted of articles in periodicals. These were widely scattered throughout the professional literature and served as points of reference in compiling this book.

The articles were culled from a variety of sources for their applicability and relevance to the marketing process, their ease of reading, and their understandability. All the articles are intended to reflect state-of-the-art information. With a few exceptions, they were published between 1974 and 1978.

Part I features a chapter on a viewpoint of the subject based on the results of an interview I held with two practitioners of the art and science of marketing with whom I have worked and regard highly, Mr. Merrell M. Clark and Dr. Paul A. Wagner.

Many other persons deserve credit for their contribution to this book. Those who wrote the original articles deserve special credit, for the book would be impossible without them. Special thanks are due to Bob Zenowich for sharing thoughts and ideas on the basic thrust and organization of the book and to Deslie Lawrence for editorial assistance. My thanks go also to Gertrude L. Anderson, who oversaw all the details of obtaining permissions, typing, and proofing.

PATRICK J. MONTANA

Contents

Introduction

According to estimates in the recent report of the Commission on Private Philanthropy and Public Needs, one out of every ten service workers and one out of six professionals in the United States is employed by a nonprofit organization. The Commission maintains further that there may be as many as six million private organizations in America's voluntary sector alone. The core group includes 350,000 religious organizations, 37,000 human services organizations, 6,000 museums, 5,500 private libraries, 4,600 secondary schools, 3,500 hospitals, 1,500 colleges and universities, and 1,100 symphony orchestras.

The growth of nonprofit organizations and public service institutions in recent years has been astounding. In 1970, general government employed 14.3 million persons—or 17 percent of the labor force. Health expenditures of $126 billion comprised 12 percent of the U.S. gross national product. Total educational services for the same year were $76 billion—or 5 percent of the total gross national product. Even allowing for overlaps and possible double counting, these three sectors alone accounted for nearly 25 percent of this country's total GNP. This represents a phenomenal trend away from the manufacturing and production-oriented economy that characterizes the growth periods of the first half of the twentieth century. Continued growth is forecast for these sectors as well as for other nonprofit sectors, such as associations. Thus, the nonprofit sector is becoming a major portion of modern society and of the economy. These organizations must perform satisfactorily if society and the economy are to function efficiently and effectively.

Yet the evidence for satisfactory performance in the nonprofit fields is not impressive. Government, education, health care, associations, foundations, religious and charitable organizations, as well as quasi-governmental institutions, are all huge beyond the imagination of an earlier generation. Many dispose of astronomical budgets. Almost everywhere they are in crisis. Cities are leaning toward the brink of economic collapse; pressures for cost containment in the health-care field can be read daily in newspapers and periodicals; education has come under heavy public criticism; tuition fees continually increase, and the gap between income and expense continues to widen in many private educational institutions; some foundations have been forced to curtail their grants severely; and government continues to be generally distrusted. Nonprofit organizations appear to be attacked on all sides for lack of performance. People are complaining louder and louder of "bureaucracy" and mismanagement in these institutions. "What are we getting for our dollars?" is a common question.

One of the clearest responses to these criticisms has been for the nonprofit sector to become more marketing conscious. In all nonprofit organizations, concepts and tools of business management and marketing are becoming increasingly popular. These are wide in range and include marketing training and development, marketing analysis and planning, marketing strategy formulation and implementation (including market segmentation and marketing mix development), marketing operations, and services (including sales, marketing research, and promotion). This is a healthy sign, but it is no more than that. It does not mean that the nonprofit organizations understand the problems of marketing, nor does it mean that techniques that are well-proved in industry can be applied without modification. The increased interest in marketing does mean that executives of nonprofit organizations have begun to realize that at present, they may not be marketing as effectively as they could be.

The purpose of this volume is to assemble selected articles from periodicals and viewpoints on marketing in nonprofit organizations. The book is intended to provide the reader with information on various marketing considerations, techniques, and tools now being applied in a variety of nonprofit organizations. The theme emerging from this selection of articles is that of marketing under the marketing management concept. Expressed in its most basic terms, marketing is the performance of business activities that *directs* the flow of goods and services from producer to consumer (or user) in order to satisfy customers and accomplish the organization's objectives.

The marketing concept is the recognition on the part of management that all business decisions of an organization must be made in the light of customer needs and wants. In effect, all marketing activities must be under one supervision and all activities of an organization must be coordinated at the top, in terms of market requirements.

The first and most important step in applying the concept is acceptance of a wholehearted customer orientation. Without acceptance of this concept at least by top management, any change in organizational structure will be purely mechanical. It requires a change of mind within an organization.

The marketing manager's job consists of trying to satisfy a particular group of customers—the target group—with a particular good or service, while satisfying the objectives of the organization and operating within the resources and constraints imposed by the organization.

To succeed in his or her job, let us remember that the marketing manager is first a *manager*. Consequently, the marketing manager generally has three basic tasks: to set up a general plan or strategy; to direct the execution of this plan; and finally to evaluate, analyze, and control the plan. For simplicity, this might be condensed to planning, execution, and control.

First, the marketing executive must evolve a plan—or as I will call it, a "marketing strategy"—aimed at a given group of customers. Developing a marketing strategy consists of two distinct, yet interrelated, steps: (1) selection of the market target—the particular groups of customers to whom the organization wishes to appeal (the market grid idea or market segmentation is applicable here); and (2) development of a marketing mix—the choice of the elements the organization intends to combine in order to satisfy this target group (the 4P's: product, place, promotion, and price, as well as the uncontrollable factors affecting the organization's market are applicable here). The development of a marketing strategy is of primary interest. Without a well-defined master plan, there are no guidelines for execution, control, or evaluation. Only after the basic marketing strategy is developed can management concern itself with the implementation of that strategy. Control, too, should be emphasized, since it provides the feedback that leads to the modification of marketing strategies. The process and its links may be viewed this way:

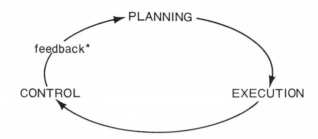

*In the form of information concerning results of marketing planning.

These elements of the marketing management process are rather widely accepted in the business world and, in fact, some very sophisticated techniques have been developed in each of the areas. This book is not addressed to these fairly advanced techniques, but rather to elements of the marketing and management process as they are currently being applied in the nonprofit sector.

The manager in a nonprofit organization may have an immediate and predictable reaction to applying generally accepted marketing techniques in a nonprofit setting, ranging from "it's impossible" to "nonprofits are different and cannot be marketed like a business." Undoubtedly, there are significant differences between profitmaking and nonprofitmaking businesses—just as there are significant differences among industries within the profit sector. For example, marketing strategies and techniques in the farm equipment sector are clearly different from those applied in the retailing sector. Yet they both use elements of the same marketing process.

In the nonprofit organization, there *is* a uniqueness; however, the point is to regard the uniqueness not as a stand-alone, single unit, but as a part of a larger process. Not *all* marketing techniques will work in the nonprofit sector, but some marketing techniques are working very well in a variety of organizations within the nonprofit sector. The first section of this book addresses the question of whether or not nonprofits can, in fact, be marketed.

The contributions in succeeding sections on the Nature and Structure of the Market; Marketing Strategy; and Marketing Planning, Operations, and Services show how these marketing concepts are now being applied in specific nonprofit sectors and organizations. Each section in itself can be viewed as a way to apply the marketing concept in a nonprofit organization. While reading each of these sections, the reader is encouraged to bear in mind the basic elements of the marketing management process—planning, execution, and control—so as to be able to apply these ap-

proaches conceptually to his or her own nonprofit organization. The closing section of the book addresses itself to marketing the performing arts;
the museum; and the City of New York.

The articles in each section were chosen from as many sectors as
possible so as to be of interest to marketers of a variety of nonprofit
organizations. A wide scope of sources was used to provide the reader
with a broad perspective on marketing in nonprofit organizations.

Part 1

**MARKETING
THE NONPROFIT ORGANIZATION**

Can It Be Done?

BEFORE ADDRESSING THE "HOW TO" of any problem, it is always wise to step back and ask a question about whether the problem can be solved at all, given the state of resources and technology. This notion is particularly important in addressing the question of marketing the non-profit organization. One of the most frequently heard comments has to do with the "uniqueness myth" propagated by many nonprofit organizations. It takes the form of: "We're different from business—we don't make a profit," or "We don't have any objectives," or "We don't have any accountability," or "We don't have any shareholders or stockholders." Any or all of these may be true in varying degrees throughout the non-profit sector but, as shown in the contributions in this section, these attributes of the uniqueness myth can be used in a positive sense in determining which kinds of marketing techniques are applicable and which can be used successfully.

The matrix below shows the titles and authors of the articles as well as the nonprofit sectors they address.

	Government	Education	Health	Religious and Charitable	Associations and Others
Broadening the Concept of Marketing Philip Kotler and Sidney Levy	X	X	X	X	X
Marketing for Nonprofit Organizations Benson P. Shapiro	X	X	X	X	X
Marketing for Profits and Nonprofits George Wasem	X	X	X	X	X
Marketing for NPOs — From a Practitioner's Point of View Paul Wagner	X	X	X	X	X

Broadening the Concept of Marketing

Philip Kotler
Sidney J. Levy

The term "marketing" connotes to most people a function peculiar to business firms. Marketing is seen as the task of finding and stimulating buyers for the firm's output. It involves product development, pricing, distribution, and communication; and in the more progressive firms, continuous attention to the changing needs of customers and the development of new products, with product modifications and services to meet these needs. But whether marketing is viewed in the old sense of "pushing" products or in the new sense of "customer satisfaction engineering," it is almost always viewed and discussed as a business activity.

It is the authors' contention that marketing is a pervasive societal activity that goes considerably beyond the selling of toothpaste, soap, and steel. Political contests remind us that candidates are marketed as well as soap; student recruitment by colleges reminds us that higher education is marketed; and fund raising reminds us that "causes" are marketed. Yet

Reprinted with permission from *Journal of Marketing,* January 1969.

these areas of marketing are typically ignored by the student of marketing. Or they are treated cursorily as public relations or publicity activities. No attempt is made to incorporate these phenomena in the body proper of marketing thought and theory. No attempt is made to redefine the meaning of product development, pricing, distribution, and communication in these newer contexts to see if they have a useful meaning. No attempt is made to examine whether the principles of "good" marketing in traditional product areas are transferable to the marketing of services, persons, and ideas.

The authors see a great opportunity for marketing people to expand their thinking and to apply their skills to an increasingly interesting range of social activity. The challenge depends on the attention given to it: marketing will either take on a broader social meaning or remain a narrowly defined business activity.

THE RISE OF ORGANIZATIONAL MARKETING

One of the most striking trends in the United States is the increasing amount of society's work being performed by organizations other than business firms. As a society moves beyond the stage where shortages of food, clothing, and shelter are the major problems, it begins to organize to meet other social needs that formerly had been put aside. Business enterprises remain a dominant type of organization, but other types of organizations gain in conspicuousness and in influence. Many of these organizations become enormous and require the same rarefied management skills as traditional business organizations. Managing the United Auto Workers, Defense Department, Ford Foundation, World Bank, Catholic church, and University of California has become every bit as challenging as managing Procter and Gamble, General Motors, and General Electric. These nonbusiness organizations have an increasing range of influence, affect as many livelihoods, and occupy as much media prominence as major business firms.

All of these organizations perform the classic business functions. Every organization must perform a financial function insofar as money must be raised, managed, and budgeted according to sound business principles. Every organization must perform a production function in that it must conceive of the best way of arranging inputs to produce the outputs of the organization. Every organization must perform a personnel function in that people must be hired, trained, assigned, and promoted in the course of the organization's work. Every organization must perform a purchasing function in that it must acquire materials in an efficient way through comparing and selecting sources of supply.

When we come to the marketing function, it is also clear that every organization performs marketing-like activities whether or not they are recognized as such. Several examples can be given.

The police department of a major U.S. city, concerned with the poor image it has among an important segment of its population, developed a campaign to "win friends and influence people." One highlight of this campaign is a "visit your police station" day in which tours are conducted to show citizens the daily operations of the police department, including the crime laboratories, police lineups, and cells. The police department also sends officers to speak at public schools and carries out a number of other activities to improve its community relations.

Most museum directors interpret their primary responsibility as "the proper preservation of an artistic heritage for posterity."[1] As a result, for many people museums are cold marble mausoleums that house miles of relics that soon give way to yawns and tired feet. Although museum attendance in the United States advances each year, a large number of citizens are uninterested in museums. Is this indifference due to failure in the manner of presenting what museums have to offer? This nagging question led the new director of the Metropolitan Museum of Art to broaden the museum's appeal through sponsoring contemporary art shows and "happenings." His marketing philosophy of museum management led to substantial increases in the Met's attendance.

The public school system in Oklahoma City sorely needed more public support and funds to prevent a deterioration of facilities and exodus of teachers. It recently resorted to television programming to dramatize the work the public schools were doing to fight the high school dropout problem, to develop new teaching techniques, and to enrich the children. Although an expensive medium, television quickly reached large numbers of parents whose response and interest were tremendous.

Nations also resort to international marketing campaigns to get across important points about themselves to the citizens of other countries. The junta of Greek colonels who seized power in Greece in 1967 found the international publicity surrounding their cause to be extremely unfavorable and potentially disruptive of international recognition. They hired a major New York public relations firm and soon full-page newspaper ads appeared carrying the headline "Greece Was Saved From Communism," detailing in small print why the takeover was necessary for the stability of Greece and the world.[2]

An anticigarette group in Canada is trying to press the Canadian legislature to ban cigarettes on the grounds that they are harmful to health. There is widespread support for this cause but the organization's funds are limited, particularly measured against the huge advertising resources of the cigarette industry. The group's problem is to find effective ways to make a little money go a long way in persuading influential legislators of the need for discouraging cigarette consumption. This group has come up with several ideas for marketing antismoking to Canadians, including television spots, a paperback book featuring pictures of cancer and heart disease patients, and legal research on company liability for the smoker's loss of health.

What concepts are common to these and many other possible illustrations of organizational marketing? All of these organizations are concerned about their "product" in the eyes of certain "consumers" and are seeking to find "tools" for furthering their acceptance. Let us consider each of these concepts in general organizational terms.

Products

Every organization produces a "product" of at least one of the following types:

Physical products. "Product" first brings to mind everyday items like soap, clothes, and food, and extends to cover millions of *tangible* items that have a market value and are available for purchase.

Services. Services are *intangible* goods that are subject to market transaction, such as tours, insurance, consultation, hairdos, and banking.

Persons. Personal marketing is an endemic *human* activity, from the employee trying to impress his boss to the statesman trying to win the support of the public. With the advent of mass communications, the marketing of persons has been turned over to professionals. Hollywood stars have their press agents, political candidates their advertising agencies, and so on.

Organizations. Many organizations spend a great deal of time marketing themselves. The Republican Party has invested considerable thought and resources in trying to develop a modern look. The American Medical Association decided recently that it needed to launch a campaign to improve the image of the American doctor.[3] Many charitable organizations and universities see selling their *organization* as their primary responsibility.

Ideas. Many organizations are mainly in the business of selling *ideas* to the larger society. Population organizations are trying to sell the idea of birth control, and the Women's Christian Temperance Union is still trying to sell the idea of prohibition.

Thus the "product" can take many forms, and this is the first crucial point in the case for broadening the concept of marketing.

Consumers

The second crucial point is that organizations must deal with many groups that are interested in their products and can make a difference in its success. It is vitally important to the organization's success that it be sensitive to, serve, and satisfy these groups. One set of groups can be called the *suppliers*. *Suppliers* are those who provide the management group with the inputs necessary to perform its work and develop its product effectively. Suppliers include employees, vendors of the materials, banks, advertising agencies, and consultants.

The other set of groups are the *consumers* of the organization's product, of which four subgroups can be distinguished. The *clients* are those who are the immediate consumers of the organization's product. The clients of a business firm are its buyers and potential buyers; of a service organization those receiving the services, such as the needy (from the Salvation Army) or the sick (from County Hospital); and of a protective or a primary organization, the members themselves. The second group is the *trustees* or *directors*, those who are vested with the legal authority and responsibility for the organization, oversee the management, and enjoy a variety of benefits from the "product." The third group is the active *publics* that take a specific interest in the organization. For a business firm, the active publics include consumer rating groups, governmental agencies, and pressure groups of various kinds. For a university, the active publics include alumni and friends of the university, foundations, and city fathers. Finally, the fourth consumer group is the *general public*. These are all the people who might develop attitudes toward the organization that might affect its conduct in some way. Organizational marketing concerns the programs designed by management to create satisfactions and favorable attitudes in the organization's four consuming groups: clients, trustees, active publics, and general public.

Marketing Tools

Students of business firms spend much time studying the various tools under the firm's control that affect product acceptance: product improvement, pricing, distribution, and communication. All of these tools have counterpart applications to nonbusiness organizational activity.

Nonbusiness organizations to various degrees engage in product improvement, especially when they recognize the competition they face from other organizations. Thus, over the years churches have added a host of nonreligious activities to their basic religious activities to satisfy members seeking other bases of human fellowship. Universities keep updating their curricula and adding new student services in an attempt to make the educational experience relevant to the students. Where they have failed to do this, students have sometimes organized their own courses and publications, or have expressed their dissatisfaction in organized protest. Government agencies such as license bureaus, police forces, and taxing bodies are often not responsive to the public because of monopoly status; but even here citizens have shown an increasing readiness to protest mediocre services, and more alert bureaucracies have shown a growing interest in reading the user's needs and developing the required product services.

All organizations face the problem of pricing their products and services to cover costs. Churches charge dues, universities charge tuition, governmental agencies charge fees, and fund-raising organizations send out bills. Very often specific product charges are not sufficient to meet the organization's budget, and it must rely on gifts and surcharges to make up the difference. Opinions vary as to how much the users should be charged for the individual services and how much should be made up through general collection. If the university increases its tuition, it will have to face losing some students and putting more students on scholarship. If the hospital raises its charges to cover rising costs and additional services, it may provoke a reaction from the community. All organizations face complex pricing issues, although not all of them understand good pricing practice.

Distribution is a central concern to the manufacturer seeking to make his goods conveniently accessible to buyers. Distribution also can be an important marketing decision area for nonbusiness organizations. A city's public library has to consider the best means of making its books available to the public. Should it establish one large library with an extensive collection of books, or several neighborhood branch libraries with duplication of books? Should it use bookmobiles that bring the books to the customers instead of relying exclusively on the customers coming to the books? Should it distribute through school libraries? Similarly the police department of a city must think through the problem of distributing its protective services efficiently through the community. It has to determine how much protective service to allocate to different neighborhoods; the respective merits of squad cars, motorcycles, and foot patrolmen; and the positioning of emergency phones.

Customer communication is an essential activity of all organizations, although many nonmarketing organizations often fail to accord it the importance it deserves. Managements of many organizations think they have fully met their communication responsibilities by setting up advertising and/or public relations departments. They fail to realize that *everything about an organization talks.* Customers form impressions of an organization from its physical facilities, employees, officers, stationery, and a hundred other company surrogates. Only when this is appreciated do the members of the organization recognize that they all are in marketing, whatever else they do. With this understanding they can assess realistically the impact of their activities on the consumers.

CONCEPTS FOR EFFECTIVE MARKETING MANAGEMENT IN NONBUSINESS ORGANIZATIONS

Although all organizations have products, markets, and marketing tools, the art and science of effective marketing management have reached their highest state of development in the business type of organization. Business organizations depend on customer goodwill for survival and have generally learned how to sense and cater to their needs effectively. As other types of organizations recognize their marketing roles, they will turn increasingly to the body of marketing principles worked out by business organizations and adapt them to their own situations.

What are the main principles of effective marketing management as they appear in most forward-looking business organizations? Nine concepts stand out as crucial in guiding the marketing effort of a business organization.

Generic Product Definition

Business organizations have increasingly recognized the value of placing a broad definition on their products, one that emphasizes the basic customer need(s) being served. A modern soap company recognizes that its basic product is cleaning, not soap; a cosmetics company sees its basic product as beauty or hope, not lipsticks and makeup; a publishing company sees its basic product as information, not books.

The same need for a broader definition of its business is incumbent upon nonbusiness organizations if they are to survive and grow. Churches at one time tended to define their product narrowly as that of producing religious services for members. Recently, most churchmen have decided that their basic product is human fellowship. There was a time when educators said that their product was the three R's. Now most of them define their product as education for the whole man. They try to serve the social, emotional, and political needs of young people in addition to intellectual needs.

Target Groups Definition

A generic product definition usually results in defining a very wide market, and it is then necessary for the organization, because of limited resources, to limit its product offering to certain clearly defined groups within the market. Although the generic product of an automobile company is transportation, the company typically sticks to cars, trucks, and buses, and stays away from bicycles, airplanes, and steamships. Furthermore, the manufacturer does not produce every size and shape of car but concentrates on producing a few major types to satisfy certain substantial and specific parts of the market.

In the same way, nonbusiness organizations have to define their target groups carefully. For example, in Chicago the YMCA defines its target groups as men, women, and children who want recreational opportunities and are willing to pay $20 or more a year for them. The Chicago Boys Club, on the other hand, defines its target group as poorer boys within the city boundaries who are in want of recreational facilities and can pay $1 a year.

Differentiated Marketing

When a business organization sets out to serve more than one target group, it will be maximally effective by differentiating its product offerings and communications. This is also true for nonbusiness organizations. Fund-raising organizations have recognized the advantage of treating clients, trustees, and various publics in different ways. These groups require differentiated appeals and frequency of solicitation. Labor unions find that they must address different messages to different parties rather than one message to all parties. To the company they may seem unyielding, to the conciliator they may appear willing to compromise, and to the public they seek to appear economically exploited.

Customer Behavior Analysis

Business organizations are increasingly recognizing that customer needs and behavior are not obvious without formal research and analysis: they cannot rely on impressionistic evidence. Soap companies spend hundreds of thousands of dollars each year researching how Mrs. Housewife feels about her laundry; how, when, and where she does her laundry; and what she desires of a detergent.

Fund raising illustrates how an industry has benefited by replacing stereotypes of donors with studies of why people contribute to causes. Fund raisers have learned that people give because they are getting something. Many give to community chests to relieve a sense of guilt because of their elevated state compared to the needy. Many give to medical charities to relieve a sense of fear that they may be struck by a disease whose cure has not yet been found. Some give to feel pride. Fund raisers have stressed the importance of identifying the motives operating in the marketplace of givers as a basis for planning drives.

Differential Advantages

In considering different ways of reaching target groups, an organization is advised to think in terms of seeking a differential advantage. It should consider what elements in its reputation or resources can be exploited to create a special value in the minds of its potential customers. In the same way that Zenith has built a reputation for quality and International Harvester a reputation for service, a nonbusiness organization should base its case on some dramatic value that competitive organizations lack. The small island of Nassau can compete against Miami for the tourist trade by advertising the greater dependability of its weather; the American Heart Association can compete for funds against the American Cancer Society by advertising the amazing strides made in cardiac research.

Multiple Marketing Tools

The modern business firm relies on a multitude of tools to sell its product, including product improvement, consumer and dealer advertising, salesman incentive programs, sales promotions, contests, multiple-size offerings, and so forth. Likewise nonbusiness organizations also can reach their audiences in a variety of ways. A church can sustain the interest of its members through discussion groups, newsletters, news releases, campaign drives, annual reports, and retreats. Its "salesmen" include the religious head, the board members, and the present members in terms of attracting potential members. Its advertising includes announcements of weddings, births and deaths, religious pronouncements, and newsworthy developments.

Integrated Marketing Planning

The multiplicity of available marketing tools suggests the desirability of overall coordination so that these tools do not work at cross-purposes. Over time, business firms have placed under a marketing vice-president activities that were previously managed in a semi-autonomous fashion, such as sales, advertising, and marketing research. Nonbusiness organizations typically have not integrated their marketing activities. Thus, no single officer in the typical university is given total responsibility for studying the needs and attitudes of clients, trustees, and publics, and undertaking the necessary product development and communication programs to serve these groups. The university administration instead includes a variety of "marketing" positions such as dean of students, director of alumni affairs, director of public relations, and director of development; coordination is often poor.

Continuous Marketing Feedback

Business organizations gather continuous information about changes in the environment and about their own performance. They use their salesmen, research department, specialized research services, and other means to check on the movement of goods, actions of competitors, and feelings of customers to make sure they are progressing along satisfactory lines. Nonbusiness organizations typically are more casual about collecting vital information on how they are doing and what is happening in the marketplace. Universities have been caught off guard by underestimating the magnitude of student grievance and unrest, and so have major cities underestimated the degree to which they were failing to meet the needs of important minority constituencies.

Marketing Audit

Change is a fact of life, although it may proceed almost invisibly on a day-to-day basis. Over a long stretch of time it might be so fundamental as to threaten organizations that have not provided for periodic reexaminations of their purposes. Organizations can grow set in their ways and unresponsive to new opportunities or problems. Some great American companies are no longer with us because they did not change the definitions of their businesses, and their products lost relevance in a changing world. Political parties become unresponsive after they enjoy power for a while, and every so often experience a major upset. Many union leaders grow insensitive to new needs and problems until one day they find themselves out of office. For an organization to remain viable, its management must provide for periodic audits of its objectives, resources, and opportunities. It must reexamine its basic business, target groups, differential advantage, communication channels, and messages in the light of current trends and needs. It might recognize when change is needed, and make it before it is too late.

IS ORGANIZATIONAL MARKETING A SOCIALLY USEFUL ACTIVITY?

Modern marketing has two different meanings in the minds of people who use the term. One meaning of marketing conjures up the terms selling, influencing, persuading. Marketing is seen as a huge and increasingly dangerous technology, making it possible to sell persons on buying things, propositions, and causes they either do not want or which are bad for them. This was the indictment in Vance Packard's *Hidden Persuaders* and numerous other social criticisms, with the net effect that a large number of persons think of marketing as immoral or entirely self-seeking in its fundamental premises. They can be counted on to resist the idea of organizational marketing as so much "Madison Avenue."

The other meaning of marketing unfortunately is weaker in the public mind: it is the concept of sensitively *serving and satisfying human needs*. This was the great contribution of the marketing concept that was promulgated in the 1950s, and that concept now counts many business firms as its practitioners. The marketing concept holds that the problem of all business firms in an age of abundance is to develop customer loyalties and satisfaction, and the key to this problem is to focus on the customer's needs.[4] Perhaps the short-run problem of business firms is to sell people on buying the existing products, but the long-run problem is clearly to create the products that people need. By this recognition that effective marketing requires a consumer orientation instead of a product orientation, marketing has taken a new lease on life and tied its economic activity to a higher social purpose.

It is this second side of marketing that provides a useful concept for all organizations. All organizations are formed to serve the interest of particular groups: hospitals serve the sick, schools serve the students, governments serve the citizens, and labor unions serve the members. In the course of evolving, many organizations lose sight of their original mandate, grow hard, and become self-serving. The bureaucratic mentality begins to dominate the original service mentality. Hospitals may become perfunctory in their handling of patients, schools treat their students as nuisances, city bureaucrats behave like petty tyrants toward the citizens, and labor unions try to run instead of serve their members. All of these actions tend to build frustration in the consuming groups. As a result some withdraw meekly from these organizations, accept frustration as part of their condition, and find their satisfactions elsewhere. This used to be the common reaction of ghetto and college students in the face of indifferent city and university bureaucracies. But new possibilities have arisen, and now the same consumers refuse to withdraw so readily. Organized dissent and protest are seen to be an answer, and many organizations thinking of themselves as responsible have been stunned into recognizing that they have lost touch with their constituencies. They had grown unresponsive.

Where does marketing fit into this picture? Marketing is that function of the organization that can keep in constant touch with the organization's consumers, read their needs, develop "products" that meet these needs, and build a program of communications to express the organization's purposes. Certainly selling and influencing will be large parts of organizational marketing; but, properly seen, selling follows rather than precedes the organization's drive to create products to satisfy its consumers.

CONCLUSION

It has been argued here that the modern marketing concept serves very naturally to describe an important facet of all organizational activity. All organizations must develop appropriate products to serve their sundry consuming groups, and must use modern tools of communication to reach their consuming publics. The business heritage of marketing provides a useful set of concepts for guiding all organizations.

The choice facing those who manage nonbusiness organizations is not whether to market or not to market, for no organization can avoid marketing. The choice is whether to do it well or poorly, and on this necessity the case for organizational marketing is basically founded.

REFERENCES

1. This is the view of Sherman Lee, director of the Cleveland Museum, quoted in *Newsweek,* April 1, 1968, p. 55.

2. "PR for the Colonels," *Newsweek,* March 18, 1968, p. 70.

3. "Doctors Try an Image Transplant," *Business Week,* June 22, 1968, p. 64.

4. Theodore Levitt, "Marketing Myopia," *Harvard Business Review,* July/Aug., 1960, pp. 45–46.

Marketing for Nonprofit Organizations

Benson P. Shapiro

For years, certain successful marketing techniques that were once considered to belong almost exclusively to profit-motivated business enterprises have been used advantageously by alert managers in private
nonprofit organizations. However, many other managers of nonprofit
organizations have failed to recognize that marketing is as intrinsic to
the nonprofit sector as it is to the business community.

There are four key business concepts that provide the basis for marketing thought and action in the nonprofit environment. Consider:

1. The *self-interest* aspect of the transaction or exchange, in which
   both the buyer and the seller believe they are receiving greater
   value than they are giving up.
2. The *marketing task,* which stresses the importance of satisfying
   customer needs.

3. The *marketing mix,* the elements of which are the tools that marketers use, such as advertising and public relations, channels of distribution, pricing, and product policies.

4. The idea of *distinctive competence,* in which the company concentrates on what it does best because doing so maximizes profits.

These four marketing concepts are closely related. Self-interest forces the consumer to search out the best way to fulfill his needs and the company to search out the most efficient way to satisfy the consumer. Thus the marketing task is based on the idea of a transaction. The marketing mix merely enumerates the tools the marketer has for satisfying the consumer. And distinctive competence makes sense because any company, with its limited competence and resources, can most profitably serve only those consumer needs which it can most efficiently serve.

In this article, I shall show how the last three of these business concepts apply to marketing in private nonprofit organizations and provide examples of their successful application (I shall not bother discussing the concept of self-interest; it can be taken for granted).

THE MARKETING TASK

As we have just seen, the marketing task in the business sector is based on the idea that good company management leads to satisfied consumers which, in turn, leads to company profitability. This works because the company has but one primary constituency to which it provides products and from which it receives funds. The typical private nonprofit organization, however, operates in a more complex manner. It has two constituencies: clients to whom it provides goods and/or services, and donors from whom it receives resources.

Thus the profit-motivated company has one marketing function—namely, to facilitate a direct two-way exchange—which simultaneously includes both resource allocation (providing goods and services) and resource attraction (obtaining revenue). By contrast, the nonprofit organization must approach these two tasks separately because they involve separate constituencies.

This dichotomization gives the nonprofit organization flexibility. The approach it uses for clients need not be the same as the one it uses for donors, provided the managers of the "nonprofit" believe that this is both ethical and effective. Along with flexibility, however, the nonprofit's dual constituency makes the marketing task more complex, since there are two different functions to perform and two different "consumers" to satisfy. If the organization is to be successful, it must satisfy both parties.

It is relatively easy to measure marketing success in the business community. One can look at a company's profit growth or profitability relative to that of competitors, or at sales growth or sales volume relative to that of competitors. Although consumer satisfaction with a product or service, or with some particular aspect of a product or service, can also be measured in other ways, sales volume and profits are the key criteria in the final analysis.

The success measurement of the nonprofit organization's resource attraction is analogous: if the donors contribute, they are satisfied; if they do not, they are not. This measure is not, however, a valid measure of the success of the total organization. While the profit-motivated company is judged to be successful when it accomplishes its primary objective (making money), the nonprofit organization which receives large donations can be considered successful in attracting contributions but not necessarily in satisfying its clients. Father Flanagan's Boys Town, for example, appears to be considerably better at fund raising than at child raising.[1] The overall success of the nonprofit organization can be measured only in terms of the attainment of goals related to client satisfaction.

To complicate the nonprofit's situation further, activities which lead to the satisfaction of client needs may meet with the disapproval of the donor. This is especially likely to occur in an organization which is changing its objectives. The United Methodist Church, to illustrate, found that many of its members (donors who provide much of its financial support) were not pleased by its growing interest in helping blacks who were not parishioners.

For nonprofit organizations whose donors and clients are identical—such as country clubs or consumer cooperatives—the classic measure of business success, financial viability, is also a valid measure of overall success.

Let us now look more closely at the nature of the marketing task in the nonprofit organization—specifically, how it is derived from resource attraction, resource allocation, and persuasion.

Resource Attraction

Some private nonprofit organizations, such as The Ford Foundation and The Rockefeller Foundation, raise operating funds by investing the contributions made by their family sponsors. Thus such organizations are in the enviable position of not having to seek contributions.

But

Most nonprofits, however, must find contributors. Some organizations do this on their own; others join forces. Joint fund-raising organizations can be based on geography (for example, United Fund and Community Chest) or on some other common tie (for example, the United Negro College Fund). Resource attraction is often carried out by professional fund raisers, and it is typically the nonprofit organization's most sophisticated marketing function.

While those who give to nonprofit organizations are inevitably getting something in return, the quid pro quo varies considerably. As Philip Kotler noted: "Many give to community chests to relieve a sense of guilt because of their elevated state compared to the needy. Many give to medical charities to relieve a sense of fear that they may be struck by a disease whose cure has not yet been found. Some give to feel pride."[2] Undoubtedly, others give to "insure a place in Heaven," to show the extent of their financial resources, or in response to personal pressure.[3]

Resource attraction typically takes one of two approaches, advertising or personal selling. Generally, the advertising campaign is used when an organization is attempting to generate many relatively small contributions from a large number of potential donors; personal selling, to obtain larger contributions from a more limited but highly identifiable group of potential donors. If the organization has broad appeal and can attract enough volunteers, it can use a personal selling approach to a mass campaign, such as the Mothers' March on Polio and the annual Halloween UNICEF drive.

Personal selling to potential large donors is often thought to be most effective when the solicitor can make a direct exchange with the donor. The exchange need not be explicit. For example, retailers may be particularly successful in soliciting donations from suppliers, because the suppliers are pleased to be able to win goodwill in an ethical manner. The flattery involved in being solicited by a prominent member of the community is another inducement, often sufficient to prompt a large donation.

Resource attraction is a highly sophisticated marketing task which includes all the basic elements of business-oriented marketing. The first assignment is a dual one of segmenting the donor "market" into homogeneous groups and of determining which appeal or "product" position will be most effective for that segment. Different segments are amenable to different approaches.

For example, a state university might appeal to alumni on the basis of their loyalty and emotional attachment, to parents of students on pride in their children, to individuals on state pride and lower taxes, and to businesses on the basis that the university improves the economy of the state and produces well-trained employees.

Once the different approaches are developed, nonprofits must take care to ensure that the appeals are congruent but can be kept separate. The emphasis is consistently on providing the donor with a reason for giving and on making it easy for him or her to give.

An important aspect of resource attraction is the determination of the amount to be raised from fees for goods and services. In this way, clients may actually be donors. For example, most universities raise part of their money from tuition and other student fees. Hospitals charge most of their patients for services rendered. But some nonprofit organizations expect their clients to pay nothing. Typically, such organizations either cater to the needs of the poverty-stricken or they provide relatively small services, often advisory (such as Travelers Aid).

Resource attraction is more than just fund raising. In addition, it includes obtaining volunteer labor, services, and goods such as raw materials. Goodwill Industries' appeals for repairable merchandise are resource attraction.

Resource Allocation

In the nonprofit organization, resource allocation is somewhat analogous to product policy in the business company. In a company, the key product-policy question is: "What business are we in?" The answer defines the products to be offered and the consumers to be served. Often, even determines the communications and distribution policy. Similarly, the nonprofit organization must determine its basic function or mission.[4] It must decide who its clients are and what it will provide them. This task is obviously much easier for the single-purpose organization than for the multimission organization. The United Fund of Greater New York, for example, provides funds to 425 community agencies and thus has a very long and complex "product line."

Nondonor Persuasion

Only a comparatively few nonprofit organizations involve themselves in the third marketing function—that is, persuading people to do something which the organization desires but which makes no direct contribution to the organization itself. Examples include antilitter campaigns, voter-registration campaigns, and health campaigns encouraging people to have themselves examined for various diseases.

For some organizations, persuasion is the central task. The Student

Vote campaign, for example, was organized solely to get young people to register after the minimum voting age was changed from 21 to 18. Campaigns of this type are distinguished from resource attraction in that they do not ask the individual to interact with the organization. The individual contributes to the achievement of the goal of the organization by changing his or her attitude and behavior, not by contributing funds or by accepting goods or services as a client.

THE MARKETING MIX

In this section, I shall discuss each major element of the marketing mix—communications program, distribution channels, pricing, and product policy—with reference to the three functions of nonprofit marketing: resource attraction, resource allocation, and persuasion.

Communications Program

This element of the marketing mix, which includes advertising and personal selling, is relevant to both resource attraction and persuasion. Persuasion is, in fact, solely a communications function.

Advertising Activities. Fund raising depends heavily on advertising, which is generally intended to produce relatively small donations from a large number of donors. Some organizations utilize general mass media for advertising because their managers believe that they can effectively appeal to many different types of people. The United Fund in Boston, for example, received contributions from 400,000 donors in its 1971–1972 campaign, largely through persuasive mass media advertising. Obviously, this was a very effective means of reaching large numbers of people with a relatively complex message concerning the community needs to which the United Fund addresses itself.

Other organizations use a more focused approach, with the conviction that their appeals are most attractive to a particular segment of the donor population. Colleges and universities have traditionally emphasized the alumni in fund raising and have relied on direct mail and advertising in their magazines. The alumni magazine, in fact, serves two important fund-raising purposes: (1) it helps create a positive attitude toward the institution and toward the idea of "belonging" among active alumni supporters, and (2) it delivers the actual appeal.

Furthermore, ethnic related charities often use media which appeal to the particular ethnic group. The United Jewish Philanthropies in Boston, for example, depends heavily on the newspaper *The Jewish Advocate* for both editorial support and advertising space.

Previous donors are another important market segment on which advertising can focus. CARE uses direct mail advertising to past givers and appears to keep detailed records of the results. Past contributors are obviously a good potential pool because they are aware of the organization and have, or did at one time have, reason to support it. Political campaign organizers are becoming increasingly aware that a list of past donors is a valuable asset, and are spending substantial sums to generate such lists.

Still other organizations have taken a third approach to segmenting the "market" of potential donors: they use mass media in an attempt to reach segments of the population that are able to give more than average. The United Negro College Fund, for example, has advertised in *Business Week,* undoubtedly because its readers are both wealthier and better educated than the average citizen. The organization probably reasoned that better-educated people are more anxious than others to support education.

Whatever the approach to the market, the nonprofit's advertising message is generally designed to provide the potential donor with a reason to give. In essence, the organization exchanges its product for the donor's money.

Usually, the persuasion function in the nonprofit organization is also based on advertising, which sometimes is tied in with fund raising. Probably the best known campaign of this nature is the American Cancer Society's "Fight Cancer With a Check-Up and a Check" approach.

Conservation and ecology groups have been quite active communicators in alerting the public to the problems they perceive and in obtaining active support for their causes. Some of these campaigns have stressed the importance of nonmonetary contributions (for example, the Smokey the Bear program against forest fires).

Advertising is also used with respect to resource allocation—that is, in communicating with potential clients of the organization.[5] Sometimes the communication is a by-product of fund-raising activities. One organization which provided training for blind people found that its fund-raising campaign also informed blind people of its services.

More often, however, the communications program is especially designed to attract clients. Museums, symphonies, and other cultural organizations put a great deal of effort into attracting audiences. In cases like these, the cost structure of the organization makes such efforts worthwhile. Most of the costs are fixed—that is, they do not vary with the number of clients. Thus, if a symphony attracts one additional spectator to a performance, the price of the ticket is almost all added "profit" because the cost of servicing the spectator is very little—the orchestra and the hall cost just as much without the additional spectator.

Alcoholism and drug rehabilitation centers find it especially difficult to attract the clients whom they are designed to serve. In fact, the communication decision sometimes becomes a crucial resource allocation issue: How much to spend communicating to prospective clients and how much to spend serving clients? The previously mentioned training organization for the blind, for example, found that it has to devote a substantial portion of its efforts to attracting clients.

Personal Selling. This important means of communication, used primarily in fund raising, is most effective when the audience is small and the message complex. Often, the message is especially tailored for a particular listener, such as when large donations are sought from a few people. One United Fund, for example, raises over 10 percent of its funds from 850 large individual contributors, who represent less than 1 percent of the total number of contributors. Nearly 30 percent of its contributions are made by another 1,500 company contributors. Since fund-raising drives usually produce such a pattern, the personal selling approach is justified. The size of the gift is worth the cost of the sales call.

Some fund-raising drives rely on mass personal selling campaigns. Although the sales people are volunteers, with little or no training, the approach often succeeds because (1) it ensures that the population is informed of the drive, and (2) it uses person-to-person contract to encourage the potential donor to give.

The mass personal selling campaign is really a two-step proposition: attracting the volunteer salesmen and sales managers, and the actual fund raising. Obtaining the volunteers is often a mixture of advertising and personal selling; recruitment efforts focus on people who have participated before.

Fund raising itself can also be looked on as a two-stage operation: getting donors to make an initial contribution, and then attempting periodically to raise that contribution. Once the donor has made an identifiable contribution (one which can be traced back to him), he can be approached by special direct mail and personal selling campaigns. (Before the initial contribution, it is often so difficult to identify good prospects that expensive, focused direct mail and personal selling campaigns are not warranted.)

Personal selling can also be a means of attracting clients. It is particularly useful when a would-be client has indicated some interest in an organization but is unsure of what action to take. Outreach programs designed to inform potential clients about birth control methods are used in many clinics. Drug and alcoholic rehabilitation centers often use ex-addicts and alcoholics to explain their experiences to potential clients. Alcoholics Anonymous, for example, has made extensive use of this approach. Many neighborhood health clinics have outreach programs in which professional and nonprofessional community personnel spread the clinic's message to the surrounding area.[6]

Religious organizations often use missionaries and evangelists to explain their points of view. In the industrialized countries, the professional evangelism of organizations such as the Billy Graham Crusade and the Campus Crusade for Christ are prime examples. Other religious organizations, such as the Mormons and the Jehovah Witnesses, use volunteer "salesmen" who sometimes are well-trained but who "sell" for only a limited time.

Many colleges endeavor to attract top students using recruiting teams, which are usually combinations of full-time administrators and part-time alumni salesmen.[7] These recruitment programs sometimes focus on special types of potential clients (outstanding athletes, for example).

Distribution Channels

All nonprofit organizations must be concerned with communications, but relatively few of them deal with channels of distribution. For those which do, life's growing complexity—particularly in sprawling metropolitan areas—has increased the importance of their choice of distribution channels.

In profit-motivated companies, channels of distribution perform two primary functions: they provide location utility and information. The retailer or wholesaler distribution channel is valuable to the manufacturer both because it provides a place to sell the product and also because it transmits information about it. In addition, the channel often offers ancillary services, such as credit and post-sales service.

In the nonprofit environment, the importance of distribution channels is location, which is relevant to resource attraction in three ways:

1. Location can make donation easier. Some fund-raising drives place collection tins in high-traffic locations, such as stores and movie theaters. Location performs the same function in mass personal selling campaigns. The donation is either collected directly or by means of a preaddressed envelope, relieving the donor of some work. The ubiquitous Salvation Army collectors who solicit

funds between Thanksgiving and Christmas are a particularly conspicuous example of location policy easing the donor's job.
2. Location can provide a base for local fund raising and operations. It is easier to get volunteers to work near their homes rather than far away.
3. Location can provide credibility and show the organization's interest in an area, both of which facilitate fund raising. When the local businessman asks why he should give to the organization, the fund raiser can respond, "We have a convenient clinic (or campus or museum) right here where your family and employees can use it."

More important, however, is the role of location in resource allocation. The location becomes a part of the product. In Michigan, students who live too far from Ann Arbor to attend classes on the University of Michigan's main campus can attend classes on its Flint or Dearborn campuses.

Location is especially crucial to potential clients who live in ethnic neighborhoods and who fear the outside world. Often, transportation and language barriers aggravate the problem. Crusades for immunization against various diseases and distribution of birth-control information have both, on occasion, been impeded by poor location.

Pricing Considerations

In a profit-motivated company, pricing links resource allocation to resource attraction. The company charges a price which exceeds its costs for goods and services. Thus by attracting more funds than it spends, it creates a profit and financial viability.

As noted earlier, many nonprofit organizations also charge fees for their services. In some, such as consumer cooperatives, the fees equal the costs and the organization operates at the breakeven point; it does not have to generate additional funds from nonclient donors.

There are several reasons why other nonprofit organizations might want to move toward "self-sufficiency" through a single constituency system in which client fees are the sole source of financial support. First, it simplifies the marketing function because the organization deals with only one constituency. Second, if management satisfies the clients (through judicious resource allocation), it can expect financial viability. In other words, the financial fate of the organization rests on its actual ability to meet client needs, not on its ability to convince donors that it meets client needs. Third is the apparent "justice" of a system in which the users are also the payers.

Many nonprofit organizations recognize the attractiveness of moving toward a single-constituency system. Some nonprofit organizations, however, cannot charge sufficient fees for their services. This is particularly true of welfare and charitable organizations whose primary purpose is to help those without the ability to pay.

Once a nonprofit organization becomes a self-sufficient, single-constituency operation, it is a close analogue of the profit-oriented company. Therefore, traditional business concepts and techniques can be applied to its marketing needs. However, a nonprofit organization whose charter or mission prohibits a client-supported system must operate with two constituencies—donors and clients—and this presents two pricing considerations.

One consideration is monetary. As we have seen, symphonies and museums have admission fees, hospitals charge for services, and universities charge tuition.

But the price can also be nonmonetary. Thus it can include many things more personal than money, such as time, effort, love, power, prestige, pride, friendship, and the like. Alcoholics Anonymous, for example, charges a very high price—commitment not to drink and public admission of one's problem. The Third Nail, a drug rehabilitation center, expects its clients to abstain from drugs and to contribute time and effort toward the maintenance of the center.

One reason for the intangible part of the price is the thought that commitment makes a more willing client. The higher the price, presumably, the more value the client places on the services he receives and the harder he works to take advantage of those services.

All clients are not necessarily charged the same price—at the symphony, seat locations are priced differently. Sometimes different categories of clients (for example, students or the elderly) are charged lower fees. Volume discounts may be offered. Health clinics often charge a patient less proportionately for extensive care than for a minor service.

It is difficult to provide equity in pricing, however, because the value provided to the nonprofit organization by the donor (price) or to the client by the organization (product) varies among individuals. Even if the same price is asked for all, it is never as easy for some people to give or pay as for others.

Some members of Alcoholics Anonymous undoubtedly find it easier than others to announce their problems publicly. This type of inequity is also found in monetary prices: money is dearer to some people than to others, both because of the person's resources and because of his or her subjective attitude toward money.

Donors are charged differing prices of many types. In the purely monetary transaction, contributors give different amounts. Thus they are paying different prices. Donors also provide time and effort in varying amounts, as workers, managers, or trustees. For both donors and clients, a minimum price may be set or implied. Membership fees are a typical means of establishing a minimum price.

Product Policy

This element is at the very core of business marketing. It determines the products a company offers and, implicitly, the consumers to whom it will offer these products.

A nonprofit organization must have two sets of product policies, one for donors and the other for clients. The definition of product is probably more important in the nonprofit environment than in the business sector because the nonprofit's product is more elusive than just goods and services. Broadly defined, the organization's product includes intangibles such as personal satisfaction, pride, a feeling of belonging, and a "warm feeling inside."[8]

The complexity of product policy varies from one organization to the next. Some nonprofits have a relatively simple policy because their charter or mission is limited. Certain organizations specialize in providing warm lunches for the elderly or toys for poor children at Christmas. If resources are limited, a crucial decision is the trade-off among the quality of the product, the number of clients served, and the quantity of the product. Still, the decision is relatively simple and well-defined.

Product policy is more complex in an organization with a tightly focused mission but with many ways of accomplishing that mission. Health organizations provide good examples. The American Cancer Society, for one, has a number of ways of fighting this disease, such as research, treatment, informing the public, working with government regulating agencies, and so forth. Furthermore, the American Cancer Society must assign priorities among the various types of cancer and among various regions of the country. It can emphasize prevention, detection, or treatment.

Probably the most complex product policies are those of umbrella-type organizations, such as the United Fund and large foundations. The United Fund of Greater New York, as cited earlier, provides support for more than 425 services, ranging from the Boy Scouts and Girl Scouts to hospitals and health organizations. The needs of their various clients must be carefully balanced.

It is clear that product-policy decisions are resource-allocation decisions. The organization has a limited amount of resources to allocate to various activities. It is difficult, and often impossible, to assess the actual benefits of current products; it is even more difficult to assess the benefits of prospective products. The problem of assessing benefits is further aggravated when different groups of clients are involved.

Product policy is also related to resource attraction. But the donor's benefits are elusive; therefore, they are often difficult to sell. In recognition of this fact, some organizations have attempted to lower the price to the donor through various techniques, such as tax benefits, and to increase the value of their products.

Many nonprofit organizations believe that it is important to supplement their intangible products with more concrete goods, even if with only token or symbolic gifts. Thus a minimum donation to CARE gets a Mother's Day greeting sent to people of the donor's choice. The donors undoubtedly realize that the minimum contribution necessary to obtain the gift substantially exceeds its actual monetary value. Nevertheless, the concrete nature of the gift makes the transaction more attractive. Even a certificate of giving can make a transaction concrete.

A more complex product-policy approach involves double sets of donors. In such a system, the organization solicits one set of donors (sometimes individuals and sometimes businesses) for donations of goods or services which it then sells (often by auction) to another set of donors.

DISTINCTIVE COMPETENCE

The private business sector of the U.S. economy operates on a competitive basis. That is, companies compete with one another for the consumer's support, and those whose efforts are successful are rewarded with a strong sales performance and financial viability. The competitive system may not work quite so smoothly and sharply in actuality as it does in theory, but it is generally self-correcting: companies prosper when they meet consumer needs successfully; they fail when they do not.

This self-correcting mechanism is not found in the nonprofit sector for two reasons. First, many of the needs served by nonprofits are so great that clients cannot choose between "competing" organizations—they have to settle for what they can get. Whereas competition is greatest in any business environment where supply exceeds demand, in the nonprofit sector demand often exceeds supply. Clients have little choice, and all organizations can survive. Second, the financial viability of the organization depends on resource attraction rather than on resource allocation. Thus, poor servicing of clients does not ensure financial doom.

The imbalance between supply and demand may be temporary, but the discontinuity between resource allocation and financial viability is built into the system's structure.

The situation might be corrected by creating a quasi-market in which the clients control the financial viability of the organization. Several ideas have been advanced for creating markets in certain nonprofit industries, particularly in those which receive large amounts of government funds, such as education and housing. One proposal that has been discussed at length is to give parents chits with which to pay for their children's education at any of a variety of private educational institutions.

Competition forces a profit-motivated company to do what it does best, and to do it efficiently. If the structure of nonprofit markets cannot be altered to allow for the introduction of competition, the benefits of competition might instead be realized through changes in the organization's attitude toward itself and toward other organizations which provide the same or similar services.

Much could be accomplished through interorganizational cooperation, especially in education and health care. If jealousies could be put aside, individual organizations could voluntarily restrict their activities to providing the services they are best able to provide. They would band together for those tasks which are more efficiently performed through joint effort than through individual action.

Many nonprofit organizations are beginning to evaluate their roles in terms of the consumers they serve, the products they offer, and their own distinctive competence—those things that they do better than anyone else. Thus there may be an opportunity to use cooperation for the same purpose as competition.

CONCLUDING NOTE

In this article, I have sought to demonstrate that there is a definite marketing function in private nonprofit organizations, and that the managers of such organizations should attempt to improve their understanding of the exchange process and their ability to define their product. Realistic marketing analysis and planning can enable private organizations to substantially improve their operations.

I have purposely omitted from my discussion any mention of government nonprofit organizations up to this point. That is because private and government nonprofit organizations differ from one another in the nature of the donor's responsibility: taxpayers are required to contribute the funds needed by government organizations; donations to private organizations are usually voluntary.

The difference becomes blurred when private organizations are partially financed by government funds (for example, the college and university building programs financed by the federal government) or when government organizations are partially financed by voluntary contributions (for example, state universities and the Smithsonian Institution).

ACKNOWLEDGMENTS

I wish to thank the Marketing Science Institute and the Division of Research of the Harvard Business School for their support of the study from which this article is drawn.

REFERENCES

1. "Boys Town Bonanza," *Time*, April 10, 1972, p. 17.
2. Philip Kotler, *Marketing Management: Analysis, Planning, and Control* (Englewood Cliffs, N.J., Prentice-Hall, 1972), p. 875.
3. See Steven E. Diamond, "Multiple Sclerosis Society: Fund Raising Strategy" (Boston: Division of Research, Harvard Business School, 1970), No. 9-571-020; see also Sidney J. Levy, "Humanized Appeals in Fund Raising," *Public Relations Journal*, July 1960.
4. See Seymour Tilles, "Strategies for Allocating Funds," *Harvard Business Review*, January/February 1966, p. 72; see also L. Richard Meeth, "Innovative Admissions Practices for the Liberal Arts College," *Journal of Higher Education*, October 1970, p. 535.
5. For a good analysis of client communication, see Gerald Zaltman and Alan Vertinsky, "Health Service Marketing: A Suggested Model," *Journal of Marketing*, July 1970, p. 19 (this volume).
6. Ibid., p. 27.
7. For a description of a proposed program, see L. Richard Meeth, op. cit., pp. 537–538.
8. For an outstanding description of the nature of a product in a political campaign, see Joe McGinnis, *The Selling of the President 1968* (New York: Trident Press, 1969).

Marketing for Profits and Nonprofits

George Wasem

Why can't you sell brotherhood like you sell soap? was the question asked by G. D. Wiebe in 1952. (*Merchandising Commodities and Citizenship on Television*, Public Relations Quarterly, winter issue 1951–1952).

He wrote that marketers of soap usually were effective while marketers of social causes usually were inept.

He based his conclusion on his research of several social campaigns in which he determined the reasons for their success or failure. He found social campaigns that used the elements of business marketing were more successful than those that disregarded those techniques.

His message: It's possible to combine marketing and sociology.

Two years later, Peter Drucker gave his answer in his *Practice of Management:* "Marketing is the distinguishing, the unique function of the business. A business is set apart from all other human organizations by the fact that it markets a product or a service. Neither church, nor army, nor school, nor state does that. Any organization that fulfills itself through

Reprinted with permission from *Bankers Monthly Magazine,* March 1975.

marketing a product or a service is a business. Any organization in which marketing is either absent or incidental is not a business and should never run as if it were one.''

His message: Marketing is strictly an entrepreneurial function.

What Drucker said will surprise a lot of bank marketers who are advising their churches on how to attract new members, charitable organizations on how to raise money, and symphonies on how to broaden their base of patrons.

We think there's a connection between the art of marketing services for profit and the art of marketing a nonprofit's services for social good.

The purpose of this chapter is to discuss that connection.

INTERFACE

During rare moments of chutzpah and machismo, we suggest to managers and boards of nonprofits that marketing isn't an occult pursuit. Rather, they would gain if their efforts were conducted within the framework of the same elements of, say, a bank marketing program.

"That's very nice," they sniff as if recalling the funeral of a distant relative.

After the weeping stops, they attack, with tongues sharp enough to splice tape, on the basis of the business-social difference in profit goals.

Also, to some people the idea of using such crass commercialism shows a lack of taste. It's like putting whipped cream on a hot dog, they say.

Like a football coach who builds character on the side, both of us are trying to attract money, to run successful enterprises, and to gain acceptance among the same people in the same community. The major objectives are the same.

Less tastefully, we add that they should accept the logic to implement marketing methods, because they're recommended by businessmen who successfully use them.

On second thought, don't use that last comment. It's nasty cracks like that that brought down the czar.

The fact is, many nonprofit causes are in need of marketing techniques. It's also a fact that some marketing concepts are being used effectively by nonbusiness organizations.

If we were to poll the readership, as we do in class, on the opinion of the most successful marketing program in the community during the past year, there's no doubt that the winner would be the United Fund (Community Chest). It wins every time in class votes.

DIFFERENCES

It requires hard study to sort out the profit and nonprofit strands in this tangled question, but we'll try. Ready?

There are differences, of course, in the marketing tasks for business and nonbusiness groups.

Bank marketing is based on the idea that good marketing management leads to satisfied customers, who, in turn, lead to bank profitability.

This works, because a bank has only one primary market segment to which it provides services and from which it receives deposits. That's the customer.

The typical nonprofit has two primary market segments to consider: people to whom it provides services, and people who provide it with the funds to operate.

So, a bank's marketing job is easier. The exchange is direct and simultaneous. It provides services and receives deposits from only one segment.

The nonprofits, by contrast, must approach both jobs separately, because they involve different segments. The job is more complex. There are two distinct functions and two distinct "customers" to satisfy. The organization isn't successful if it doesn't satisfy both.

Another difference is the measurement of success. A bank is considered successful if its profit and sales growths are better than its competition. There are other tests, but profits and growth combined are a key criterion. That measurement continually is made.

The success of a nonprofit is more involved. Let's assume, to illustrate, that every year it reaches its campaign's dollar goal. Is that a valid measure of success? Hardly. It proves only that it's successful in raising money. It doesn't prove that it's satisfying the needs of the people it serves.

It's true total success must include a measurement in terms of reaching the goals that are related to satisfying the requirements of people. That measurement seldom is made.

Financial viability, as a single measure of success, is applicable only to those nonprofits whose supporters and clients are identical, such as clubs and cooperatives.

A third difference is that the operating funds of a private nonprofit usually are limited. The deficiency is overcome by hard work. Do you recognize the difference between a bank and, say, a Boys' Club?

Exceed the marketing budget in a bank and somebody shrugs as we go to deficit financing. Exceed the agency's budget and it's out of business.

Do they ever happen? Does a rabbit have a sex life?

SIMILARITIES

There are similarities in the marketing jobs.

For one example, it's our experience that most nonprofits don't have an organized public information program. The same is true of many banks and their marketing programs.

A need for both is a written plan. It's as rare as Howard Cosell's silences.

For another, both possess research data. Nonprofits have important primary information. They know, for instance, the "big givers." They know names, addresses, salary ranges, pledges, and how the pledges will be paid.

That's all. As banks, they should know a great deal more about the people who keep them in business.

The demographics should be supplemented by a knowledge of the motivation for giving or not giving. Some surprises may be in store for those brave enough to do the psychographics.

The information may expose the following:

* These people are apathetic toward the organization and its program. They contribute for very different reasons, including arm-twisting and pressure. They're generally uninformed about how their money is used. They're not interested enough to find out.
* Some of these big givers are familiar with the objectives and the work, but aren't interested enough to contribute their time.
* Some feel the nonprofits is too interested in big organization charts and not interested enough in charting the benefits they should offer people.

The study, on the other hand, may uncover positive factors, such as:

* A large percentage of these people do identify with the nonprofit and its program.
* They're a strong nucleus of dedicated dependence.
* They welcome receiving information periodically about the work being done.

The point is that many, probably most, nonprofit groups, like banks, don't have the necessary research information in organized form for maximum use.

MORE SIMILARITIES

In some ways, the social marketing approach corresponds to that used by profit-oriented companies.

The goals of both types require the same coordination of marketing mix with service mix. Let's take a closer look.

Every seasoned marketer between the polar caps knows about the four Ps of marketing, the simple line that goes: "Develop the right *product*, support it with the right *promotion*, put it in the right *place*, and at the right *price*."

In bank marketing, we're supposed to study the needs and wants of our customers and prospects and then design new services (*product*) and/or innovate old ones in order to satisfy those customers and prospects. (We won't discuss the fact that many banks don't practice the theory.)

Nonprofits could do the same thing: they could study their present and prospective publics and then design the services so attractively that one segment would use them and the other segment would finance the work.

Designing services is a special challenge in the social area. How do you market blood-giving? The social objective is clear, but how do you design the service to reach the objective?

There's public education and information, of course, and special appeals, and mobile units, and recognition awards to donors. But blood-giving isn't easy to market.

The same is true of bank services. In both cases, the organization is aware of the service—blood-giving and savings accounts—and then tries to create appeals that do two things: attract support and reach the objective.

The marketing tossed salad also includes *promotion* which, in turn, includes advertising, personal selling, publicity and sales promotion. Both banks and social institutions use these and other promotional activities.

Some assume that promotion means "hard sell," which some banks and nonprofits give an aura of illegitimacy.

Nobody sells harder than the volunteer who believes in the social cause for which he or she is ringing doorbells.

Promotion includes some hard sell. It also includes grace, sensitivity, and ethics. It's the state of promotion that may be subject to criticism, not promotion the activity.

The third element of the marketing approach, *place*, means simply that people know where they can give their support or receive the benefits of services, financial and social. Most banks and nonprofits successfully practice this strategy. But it's not free of problems.

For instance, how do interested people do something about the energy and pollution problems? People are aware of them, are interested in doing their share to solve them, but there's little or nothing tangible to support, such as an energy candidate or a pollution machine.

The same is true of health, education, and welfare issues of particular interest to local nonprofits. There are always committees conducting hearings on these programs, but they lack coordination and often are at cross-purposes. Usually, it's impossible for the average person to find a place, in Washington, in the state capitol, or even locally, to which to respond.

Then, there's *price,* which includes monetary and nonmonetary. For both, profits and nonprofits, there are always money costs, time costs, and charges including admissions to the local symphony, hospital fees, and university tuition. In all cases, the buyer must accept price before he gives his support.

We must assume that patrons do make a cost versus benefit analysis when considering their contribution of money or time or both. Thus, price is an important motivation.

In social marketing, as in bank marketing, the problem is to market services on the basis of benefit and cost and then to go one step further by asking: "How do we increase the benefits of the services in relation to the cost of buying or maintaining them?" Better still: "How do we increase the benefits and reduce the costs?"

Competition is another condition both groups must face. We know about bank competition. The nonprofit group is becoming increasingly competitive.

There are more and more campaigns being staged with brio, dayglo, and noise, even where the United Fund umbrella approach is used. Some agencies are independent and conduct their own fund-raising activities. Some groups within the United Fund conduct special campaigns for new buildings. This adds up to more competition for interest and backing.

It's quite possible that because of competition some independent nonprofits are in the process of failing. They're not flourishing; rather, they're having more and more difficulty raising the necessary funds to operate and attracting volunteer help.

Competition isn't limited to the private sector. Nonprofits also operate in a very competitive environment.

STRATEGIES

Market segmentation is equally applicable to social marketing. It's our impression that it's used to a limited degree by some agencies.

For example, donors are designated into homogeneous groups such as advance gifts from business, fair share from individuals, industrial and commercial units, and so on.

The "heavy user" concept is an axiom widely accepted by banks. We know of no bank that has ever taken the trouble to prove it, but there's some truth to the truism.

The advance gift and fair-share segments are prime targets under the same premise. To put it another way, when you have a big cannon, shoot it!

The rich are different than you and me—they have more money. That's why one key to any bank sales program and to any social cause is to isolate the "heavy user" and the "big giver" and the other segments rather than marketing to an undifferentiated mass.

. The other strategy for bank marketing—differentiation—isn't being used very well by nonprofits. They seem to have an uneasy grasp of it.

There's a failure to appreciate that different communities are amenable to different appeals or to determine what appeal would have the best reception in a particular community.

Instead, in the case of national campaigns, the local group usually adopts the nationally prepared materials. Sometimes little consideration is given to the question of whether or not they apply to the local situation.

By local standards, the materials may be too naive or too sophisticated. And, they may be too broad for practical use at the local level.

The problem is the additional cost of tailor-making the strategic materials. The other side of the issue must be considered, and that's the possibility of greater appeal because of the local tie-in. It may increase the cost of raising money, but it may also succeed in raising more money, net.

Bank marketers can have exactly the same problem with canned advertising programs.

Our conclusion is that marketing is as intrinsic to the nonprofit sector as it is to banking.

Bank marketers are in excellent position to help. They understand needs, communications, promotion, and other techniques important also to the social marketing being done in their commentaries.

Marketing for NPOs— from a Practitioner's Point of View

Paul A. Wagner

More and more nonprofit organizations are coming to the realization that they must begin to apply marketing strategies and techniques to their special fields of activity, if they are to succeed in serving the society that is supporting them. Few NPOs are without their financial problems; many are in great need of expanding the base of their support. But with these financial pressures has come the understanding that marketing presents a disciplined way of managing resources to meet the real needs of their clients—the "consumers" of their valuable services. Ironically, such discipline is even more necessary in the nonprofit than in profit-centered fields, because of the added responsibility that comes with the proper utilization of tax-exempt resources. This is true whether the NPO is a university, a foundation, or a professional organization.

Up to this time, nonprofit administrators have been reluctant to entertain the idea of marketing, partly out of fear of being criticized for using "strange language," and partly out of the fear that marketing activities would somehow affect their programs adversely.

Actually, the marketing concepts, however expressed, that have created successful corporate entities, can be readily adapted to the world of philanthropy, with the same success rate. The difference between marketing for nonprofit and profitmaking organizations does not involve programming. The *products* of a nonprofit enterprise are similar to those of a corporation: they both fulfill a *consumer* need. Once nonprofit administrators realize that business terminology is not demeaning to their professional cause but rather brings a new and valuable discipline to the promotion of that cause, they begin to use the marketing language with the same facility and in the same way that any corporate manager would.

THE GROWING IMPORTANCE OF MARKETING

Even in the business community, modern marketing is only now reaching a point where it is generally accepted as a key discipline within the business environment. Fifty years ago, one rarely saw a chief executive of a corporation who was also a marketing man. Now they take their place along with the financial people as chief executive officers. This represents the recognition that more than financial management and efficient production are necessary to move an enterprise forward in a dynamic economy.

The same thing has happened in the NPO world, because the boards of trustees are demanding of organization managements the same performance they would demand of their corporate managers.

DEFINING THE MARKETING FUNCTION

Marketing has been identified as the cutting edge for growth and profit in a dynamic economy because it has a way of recasting the shape of corporate resources to meet new developments in the marketplace. The same dynamism is even more needed in those organizations that deal with social change. For the elevation of the marketing function in a nonprofit organization is not intended merely for self-interest or self-preservation, but rather as a way of ensuring that the services of the NPO will be most relevant to the actual needs of a fast-changing society. (In 1978, it would be a waste of human and financial resources to promote the building of an orphanage. Unlike the early decades of this century, America has virtually no true orphans. The new drive is for the proper care of children whose families need to be repaired before the youngsters can return home. And the new "consumer need," if you will, requires an entirely new "marketing analysis.")

If the marketing strategy is arrived at in a professional manner, society will reward the organization with greater resources.

The problem, then, is to find nonprofit managers and trustees who are willing to learn the marketing language, or conversely for those who already possess marketing expertise to learn the specialized language of the nonprofit organization so that the marketing missions of the latter can be reinterpreted to management in terms it will understand and can act upon.

COMMON ERRORS IN MARKETING

Self-interest is not the prime mover here, for marketing begins with consumer needs—not producer needs. Professor Theodore Levitt of the Harvard University Graduate School of Business Administration gives us many case studies of corporate enterprises that started with an *assumption* that there was a need, without determining whether or not there was a *real need*. A prime example: the computer people stated confidently that there was a need for their computers in the nation's classrooms. This constituted an expensive misuse of the concept of marketing, because it started with *self*-interest: "We have computers, we produce computers, we want to sell computers—therefore, we know how good they are for you."

And, of course, we all know what a tremendous fiasco such thinking proved to be for all the giant computer concerns. What should have been said was: "Let's build a bridge from the opposite side of the river; let's build it from *real* consumer needs."

If those real consumer needs do *not* exist, we can begin with the first links of the marketing chain by educating the consumer as to its advantages, but not by starting out immediately to sell the product or service. Again the case in point: Teachers did not believe there was a need for computers in the classroom. Naturally, when the computers were brought to the classrooms, they became playthings for the children and not the valid teaching tools they could have been. An upfront marketing campaign would have shown teachers how computers could fit in with curricular needs and with the methodology then in effect. Following Ted Levitt's reasoning, it is always wise to make certain you are dealing with real needs and not evanescent ones of self-interest.

Furthermore, most of the professional groups who tend to dominate a not-for-profit organization are vulnerable to the attitude that they are a priesthood of sorts. Because of the special knowledge they have, they feel that only they can provide people with something of special worth. What it comes down to is: "We've got the honey, but you must bring the cups." The marketing attitude is clearly quite the opposite: The provider requires nothing more than the ingenuity to come up with the resources that the customer indicates he needs.

Thus, effective marketing by nonprofit organizations truly serves the public. They are not merely "sold a bill of goods." They are provided with services they truly need and want and recognize as such.

THE KEY PROBLEMS OF MARKETING IN NONPROFITS

The first and most important problem of marketing—for profit as well as for service—is the lack of adequate funds for effective market research. Market research is fairly expensive, if it is done properly. (Of course, this doesn't apply to the mother-in-law type of survey done on the commuter train by an executive who turns to his next-door neighbor and asks, "What do you think so and so needs?" To which the friend replies, "Well my mother-in-law says . . .")

Only truly valid research can produce data that can be the keystone for valid programs. Marketing research provides the road map for the most efficient, effective, and direct route. Without it, an NPO will be retracing the old trial-and-error route employed by corporations 50 years ago. The design of a proper research program is the province of professionals. Although such expertise can be developed within the organization, far more objectivity can be achieved by employing an outside firm. (One large advertising agency hired an outside firm to do marketing research on how to market itself to new prospects because it did not feel its own research people would be objective enough!)

It is very important to get outside the "priesthood" in order to obtain a clear picture of the marketplace. What consultants lack in terms of the esoteric information involving a given field or project, they more than make up for by their problem-solving approach.

Experience with several hundred nonprofit organizations leads to the conclusion that the most conspicuous problem is either the total lack of marketing expertise within the organization or the low status of those staff members who do have that function. Historically, executives who have the responsibility for "production" in not-for-profits are so dominant that those who have the marketing responsibility have little leverage.

Returning to the central issue of financing, it is difficult to determine whether the problem of marketing in nonprofit organizations is a question of basic economics or professional status. Is it a given in nonprofit enter-

prise that in order to provide a service at all one must put so much into
payroll of the service providers, that there is simply not enough left
to do an effective marketing job—or is it closer to the truth to say
those assigned marketing functions are not high on the organizatio
totem pole?

In this connection, there is a semantic hurdle that many people in
nonprofit organization must surmount before they can accept the bas
concept of marketing. Perhaps it stems from the rather low status held b
advertising in our community. Even though survey after survey show
that people respond to advertising, consider it a necessary informatio
process, and prefer newspapers or magazines that include it, many
idealistic citizens have a fear of such activity as being mere hucksterism.
And idealists tend to gravitate to the nonprofit world.

A recent survey indicated that in every age group in our society—
from the youngest to the oldest—there were substantial numbers of respondents who had grave misgivings about advertising. (Was the advertiser telling only part of the story? Was he gilding the truth? Of course, the
advertiser always retorts: "What do you want me to do? Pay my money
to tell you the worst part of my story?")

There is such widespread mistrust of any kind of promotion—public
affairs, marketing, public relations—that the nonprofit administrator at
first puts out a hand and says: "Stand back, my members won't like it."
When a prominent national professional organization first asked the NPO
Task Force, Inc., to study a marketing problem, the stipulation was made
that the term "marketing" was to be struck from the vocabulary. But the
consultants refused to be handcuffed. They talked in the language that is
part of their professional set of tools, while taking care always to explain
the concepts in terms of the needs of the organization and its members.
Lecturing around the country to the local units of the association over a
period of two years, and generating constant feedback, the consultants
have found that this strategy has gained fairly wide acceptance. Now even
the members are using the marketing terms without apology.

Nevertheless, consultants still come up against some resistance. Several of the most prestigious professional organizations consider it undig-
nified and lacking in professional ethics to market their services. Such
groups feel that they are highly professional and simon-pure, and do not
want to "get down into the marketplace." One of the contributions that
some marketing experts who are interested in the nonprofit field have
made is to allow people to feel more at home with marketing terminology
by applying it in a dignified manner. The old semantic gaps are slowly
disappearing.

SETTING REASONABLE MARKETING TIMEFRAMES

The longer one works with organizations—and this is both in the for-profit and nonprofit sectors—the more aware one becomes of the reluctance of people to do long-term planning. It is characteristic in the venture field, for example, to cut off an operation that has not paid off within 36 months. When Procter and Gamble (held up to marketing students as the *sine qua non*) plans to market a product, it knows that certain levels of public awareness can be achieved in a certain time by investing $20 million or $40 million, as opposed to $8 million. They know it would take much longer to feed the pipeline and pull the product through if they were to invest a lower amount. But an organization that doesn't have $20 million to spend in marketing, but can swing $2 million, has to construct a longer timeframe to achieve a somewhat similar effect. And finally, an organization with only $200,000 to invest in national marketing activities must think in much longer terms.

Unfortunately, too many NPO administrators think only in short-run terms—the mythical "36 months" of the large corporations. Even when a marketing plan has been written, and new materials produced, the Board members will wait only 12 or 14 months before asking: "Where are those results?" So they may discontinue a program after 24 or 36 months which, in the first place, would have taken 60 months to mature. Granted, if the organization is a marginal one, it cannot afford to think in terms of 60 months. On the other hand, if one is considering some of our great educational, cultural, and health resources, one cannot focus myopically on every plan in terms of what it produces in a single year. A decade or more of a sustained campaign may be required before a legitimate objective can be achieved.

THE DANGER OF OVERSIMPLIFYING THE MARKETING APPROACH

It is not fair to single out the nonprofit administrator or director for lack of marketing foresight. It is also necessary to look at the marketing professionals who go into the nonprofit world in an attempt to serve, yet fail to realize a fundamental difference between the profit and the nonprofit fields. The average marketing person does not do a thorough enough job of preliminary research to become familiarized with what must be many times the complexity of the average consumer product. A consumer product or service may have a great deal of complexity, yet may hardly compare with any of the societal problems that the nonprofit or national professional organizations are attacking, with their attendant sociological, political, and economic implications. In the nonprofit area, you may even be attempting to change ingrained attitudes toward race and life-style and religion—far more difficult than marketing a candy bar, a car, or some other consumer product.

Too few marketing professionals appreciate that the veterans of the nonprofit sector have studied the nuances of the problem and come up with new terms to explain its subtleties. Anyone who talks to a lawyer about the difficulties in a given case is impressed with the fact that lawyers have come up with legalese because they need precise, accurate definitions. A professional marketing executive must also learn the language of his or her client.

The nonprofit responsibility operates in a larger societal context, as against the relatively simple needs being met by consumer products. For instance, a chair is a product required in almost every room. A simple set of mathematical parameters can be obtained quickly. You know that it should be in the neighborhood of 17 inches high, and that the market for chairs serving different purposes can be determined in a statistical manner. But a new people-oriented strategy has been introduced even in such a standard business line.

Manufacturers have begun to think of chairs, not as things to sit on, but as things to make people comfortable while they are seated at various tasks. Humans have different measurements from knee to heel, as well as different ways of sitting. The sophisticated marketer of chairs copes with these factors and creates a much more detailed marketing plan.

Marketing chairs is obviously nowhere near as complex as the problem facing a major foundation—that of convincing people on the Island of Leyte in the Philippines that it is to their own well-being that fecal matter be collected and examined by scientists for certain parasitic diseases. The inhabitants of that island have an entirely different view of life and death from that of the scientist, and they oppose him. The marketing of health education plans under such conditions requires sociological and psychological understandings far more complex than the chair manufacturer's most sophisticated marketing grid.

SELLING SERVICES

Administrators have complained that marketing experts fail to reach the appropriate market. One nonprofit organization invested $30,000 for a marketing campaign. It brought in two firms, the first of which failed completely and was dismissed within several months. The second firm used the big business technique of taking large mailing lists, producing brochures, and sending them out broadcast—a big shotgun blast. Unfortunately, the message in the brochure was not on target—and the mailing lists represented the wrong targets. Clearly a lack of knowledge of the demographics and complexities was involved.

To be fair to the marketers, many of the people who work for non-profit organizations are trained in the scholarly tradition and relish digging into complex problems. What eludes them is a definition of their competition—the misconceptions and predilections of the specific consumers of their services and information. Once they are made aware of the large number of publics that comprises their market—in short, the segmentation that is inevitable in a pluralistic society such as ours—they begin to think in terms of rifling their messages, instead of employing shotgun techniques. By working in close collaboration with their NPO clients, professional marketers can avoid the disasters that inevitably come from using textbook approaches.

EFFECTIVE MARKETING CAMPAIGNS

There is a long list of successful marketing campaigns in the association field. NPO managers have been sophisticated in their list management, while some association pricing and planning techniques are among the finest to be found in American marketing. For instance, the work of the American Management Associations has included building a membership, providing educational services, moving people through the process of learning, and using a network of merchandising for thousands of products which people have used in developing their own skills in a very wholesome way.

Two of the greatest cultural institutions in the world—the Smithsonian Institution in Washington, D.C., and the Metropolitan Museum of Art in New York City—suffered considerable agony before they finally recognized their function as merchandisers of culture to society. The merchandising effort paid off by increasing their audiences. Furthermore, not only were they generating revenue, but they were also returning a greater volume of service to the public.

Still another example of a successful marketing strategy is the U.S. Army, a tax-supported institution that performs many functions in our society besides defense. Over the last several years, we have witnessed the conversion from universal military conscription to a voluntary army, the result of sound market planning, and an excellent promotional campaign executed by the J. Walter Thompson Co. It is to be hoped that the strategy will be noted by other departments of government that need to serve the public through much greater public persuasion.

The American Association of Retired People (AARP) is successful in its marketing strategy because it has tapped a very real need of a large group of people. The United States has the greatest number of retirees in the world, who are better educated and healthier than any other group of retirees—past or present. These people are interested in certain life-styles, yet they also have certain fears. Whoever laid out the marketing plan for the AARP played on all those deeper human emotions and brought about a successful plan for marketing insurance and membership. It is not hard to plan a marketing strategy when you have a clear consumer need.

MEASURING MARKET SHARE IN NONPROFIT ORGANIZATIONS

Any universe consists of many smaller populations that have particular characteristics. If you are addressing one of these subgroups, your objective is simply to increase the percentage of the total population displaying the desired characteristics. Share of market is always a function of a percentage of one population against another, whether the subject is product usage or living conditions. The statistics and the mathematical formulas always come down to a simple computation involving people who share characteristics or usage patterns as a percentage of the total population.

This analysis may appear simplistic in the light of our "measured society," where government is constantly studying the various publics, and statistics constantly pour out of Washington. But the truth is that most of the fields we are working in lack the statistics we need. Determining market share is far from the precise operation enjoyed by the corporate marketing executive.

Take the field of adoption. We do not know how many children in the United States are in foster homes or in residential group care, or in institutions. We do not know how many are available for adoption. Without such knowledge, it is very difficult to measure the success of a national organization attempting to help these children. If it has succeeded in getting 200 handicapped children adopted, or if it raises the educational level for 200 children in small group homes, there is still no basis of comparison with other types of child care.

Often we have to resort to making our own surveys, admittedly less detailed than an extensive government survey might be, but absolutely necessary to establish rough benchmarks. For instance, in the field of the elderly, with x million members of AARP as against x thousand from another organization, one can get a fair measure of marketing success. Granted, obtaining the needed information can be difficult and expensive—a high expense is attached to developing a baseline and updating the data in order to judge performance in a given market.

Many a well-funded service institution does not even base its operations on increasing its market share in terms of the end product. For example, public school districts all over the country are seeing market erosion—as far as its student population is concerned—but in major urban areas there is a share loss in another sense. The market share of those have the competency levels normally expected from secondary school training is actually diminishing. Consequently, although a lower number of young people is going to school, even a lower percentage has achieved the objectives those institutions were designed to fulfill.

The fundamental lack of marketing thinking and long-range marketing planning is obvious. Educators were so concerned with the day-to-day operation that they failed to consider what was happening to their "market." As a result, the performance of schools in serving these children, as well as the taxpayers, is seen to be at a low ebb by the American public.

MEASUREMENT OF PERFORMANCE EFFICIENCY

Nonprofit organizations have a reputation for being run less efficiently than their profit-making counterparts. For one thing, nonprofit organizations tend to be smaller and do not feel they can allocate as much to management as do many larger corporations.

Also, the two worlds generally attract different personalities. As a rule, the financial incentives of working in business attract the most competitive people in our society. People who are able to live within firm disciplines and work at a high level of performance for which they will be substantially rewarded tend to be attracted to business organizations. In contrast, the kinds of people who gravitate to nonprofits tend to be interested in more complex issues in our society and less willing to have their interests sidetracked in the name of pragmatic, "hard-nosed" objectives. Thus, the executive personalities and the *raison d'être* of the nonprofit group generally make for a less efficiently run operation than that of their peers in the profit-oriented world.

However, nonprofit managers are not intrinsically less efficient. They want to be efficient, many know how to be efficient, but most feel that their organizations cannot afford efficiency. The financial factor has a direct bearing on the measure of efficiency. Many a nonprofit organization has a small staff that is overworked and underfunded. They work almost to the point of exhaustion, hence "inefficiently." If the same organization's resources increase—either because their membership has grown or because they have received grants—they turn more and more to computerized operations, similar to their corporate neighbors. The latter then perceive the former as "efficient."

But operating efficiency within an organization is not always the most important measure. Nonprofit organizations provide an indispensable service to society. They meet needs that no other organization in the community is willing to meet, and by virtue of their service and availability—however inefficiently it may be provided—are an extremely functional operation in a broad social setting.

FINANCIAL PERFORMANCE AND THE MARKETING FUNCTION

One of the classic problems in managing profitmaking organizations is determining the appropriate incentive compensation for high performance in the marketing function. How does one explain why the marketer from the sixth most productive area (who was considered mediocre at best) turned out to be a marketing hero when asked to take over the most productive area? And conversely, when the acknowledged star of the marketing force fails to improve sales in the least productive area, who or what is to blame?

Organizations operating in the right time and the right place may be superproductive for a variety of reasons—and tend to reward their marketing executives well. Those that are in trouble tend to penalize the marketing function. The job of evaluation is a tough one. And if it is difficult in a profitmaking situation, it is almost impossible in some nonprofit activities. Nevertheless, an attempt must be made if any efficient system of accountability is to be employed.

USING ROI IN NONPROFIT ORGANIZATIONS

Return on investment is difficult for NPOs to measure, but a rough approximation can be helpful. Say you have only $200,000, out of which

$175,000 has to be allotted to ongoing programs. With $25,000 left, you are expected to make certain returns, even though the resource allocation usually is minimal and the expectations are unrealistically high. Thus, the concept of ROI clearly exists, but it lacks a logical structure.

Certainly one cannot simply follow a standard formula for developing ROI, but if a basic model of viewing the inputs is used, with investments in an aggregate leading to a more substantial leverage of additional investments in social improvement, the pyramiding theory can become operative and have a significant impact on how financial resources are used in nonprofit institutions. Admittedly, the techniques for assigning values to the societal changes that take place are highly subjective, but thoughtful marketing executives can quantify the results in a way that most fair-minded Board members would find acceptable.

Sometimes a corporate leader on the board of a foundation is annoyed that the foundation has not used ROI. A clash often ensues. For example, when Henry Ford resigned from the board of the Ford Foundation, the dialog that took place was healthy. Mr. Ford probably learned that you can't graft a standard formula onto every foundation situation, and management came to the conclusion that they had to do more to grapple with a basic marketing problem.

THE MARKETING MIX

As mentioned previously in this chapter, the concept of market segmentation can be borrowed from industry and adapted to the needs of the nonprofit organization. The first step is to appreciate the pluralism of our society and to identify the segments involved in the NPO's sphere of activity.

Two cases will underline the importance of this basic marketing concept. An organization in a large Eastern metropolis took out full-page ads in the local newspapers urging people to step forward and volunteer their time to help in the city's many institutions. Only four inquiries were received—two from people who had misread the ads thinking they were for a paying job. One person finally volunteered. The total cost of recruiting that one volunteer was astronomical.

Yet, in another city, where an organization began to think in terms of market segmentation, a call was put out for people who would teach chess to children in hospitals, or gardening to children in elementary schools, or knitting to girls in mental institutions. They were flooded with volunteers. In short, without identifying such market segments, an organization can spin wheels and spend an enormous amount of money trying to appeal to a diverse and ill-defined general public.

There is nothing *in principle* that differentiates nonprofits from profits in terms of the characteristics of such a mix. However, among the profit organizations, the picture is somewhat complicated by the fact that many of the marketing resources in this country are allocated to the mass marketing of packaged goods. Accordingly, the kinds of media and planning and distribution systems used by giant corporations seem too complex to the average nonprofit marketing executive.

But nonprofit organizations can operate like the smaller business services in their marketing mix. They can rely more heavily on personal contact and personalized service in a relatively limited "trading area." Other than that, any distinction between the way profits and not-for-profits use the marketing mix is meaningless. The disciplines are the same, and the traditional approach to product, promotion, price, and place (distribution) applies in both contexts.

PUBLIC RELATIONS: THE MARKETING SUPPORT ARM

In the nonprofit field, virtually everything one does involves promotion. All the services rendered and the way in which they are rendered constitutes promotion in terms of the public. Here the fields of public relations and marketing coincide.

There is a marvelous home for boys in northern Florida that illustrates this point. As you come up to the gate of the Florida Sheriff's Boys Ranch, you are struck by the way the entry is planned, by the roadside signs, by the care with which the fields are tended, and by the friendliness of the people you meet. The total picture is one of careful planning—the brochures, the annual report, the films—all reflect a basic understanding of what it takes to appeal to contributors. And to no one's surprise, the ranch is one of the most popular and successful agencies in the state.

The equation is simple: A successful marketing campaign will create a larger budget that will allow for larger expenditures for public relations—thereby helping to spiral the marketing process.

Public relations people can ensure the success of a marketing program—*if* they understand the marketing objectives in detail. After all, both public relations and marketing require an understanding of the publics involved, of the messages these publics respond to, and the media to which they are most receptive. When these two forces are synchronized and given full rein, the goals of an NPO are sure to be met.

THE EDUCATION OF A BOARD MEMBER

Although some nonmarketing businesspeople do have a knowledge of marketing, most boards of trustees of nonprofit organizations are composed of people who do not understand the basic elements of modern marketing. Even someone who has been in the legal profession or in a financial institution may not be familiar with marketing strategies. But one thing they will have in common, and that is the ability to measure cost-effectiveness. When the funds at their disposal are not producing the results they have come to expect, someone on that governing body invariably calls for "better promotion" of the program. It may be difficult to sell—or even to explain—the marketing concept prior to that stage, but when storm clouds hover, all hands suddenly realize that marketing is indeed an integral part of the effective management of a nonprofit organization.

And when the problems are analyzed in marketing terms, the required actions are clear. Everything the organization does or proclaims must be tailored to the consumer's needs: what the service accomplishes, how it is packaged, how it is sold, and when and where it is presented. Each operation must be aimed at a single, discrete target, and all the operations must be geared to creating "satisfied customers."

In a profit center, the executive who watches the bottom line knows when a firm is successful. In a nonprofit situation, the executive who watches for social change knows when his or her organization has fulfilled its public trust.

SUMMARY

Marketing is not a foreign or a fancy pseudoscience that needs to be tacked on at great expense and at tremendous risk to a nonprofit organization's standard operation. Marketing provides a point of view about the place of that organization in society. It helps determine when an organization is providing effective service and how it can renew itself in order to improve the delivery of that service. There is nothing contrary to the finest standards or ethical principles of any profession. Indeed, it may be the way to redeem the public reputation of some professions. For the nonprofit organization, marketing is a burgeoning field. Only a few books now deal with this area, but as more and more NPOs become involved, the language and the concepts of modern marketing will find their way into virtually every significant nonprofit endeavor.

Part 2

NATURE AND STRUCTURE OF THE MARKET

Customers and Uncontrollable Considerations

WITHIN THE MARKETING PROCESS, the nature and structure of the market are vitally important and should receive increasing attention from the standpoint of customers and uncontrollable considerations. An analysis of the market should question who the customers are or could be; when they buy, where, and how; and what essential aspects of the nature of the market are. The types and number of competitors and their share of market form the structure of the market.

	Government	Education	Health	Religious and Charitable	Associations and Others
Special Demands on Non-profit PR Don Bates	X	X	X	X	X
The Marketing of Public Goods Leo Bogart	X				
The Blood Business Seymour Lusterman	X		X	X	X
The Pleasures of Non-profitability *Forbes Magazine*		X			X

Special Demands on Nonprofit PR

Don Bates

According to estimates in the recent report of the Commission on Private Philanthropy and Public Needs, also known as the Filer Commission after its chairman, John Filer of Aetna Life & Casualty Co., one out of every ten service workers and one out of six professionals in the United States is employed by a nonprofit organization.

By nonprofit we mean the gestalt in which national and local organizations operate as tax-exempt, voluntary associations of people who have banded together in common pursuits for the public good. These organizations, some 20 categories in all, qualify for tax exemption under Internal Revenue Service code 501(c)(3) through 501(c)(18) and section 501(d). They are granted tax-free operation in exchange for their promise to act apolitically in endeavors where helping people, not profit, is the goal. Typically, this "agreement" is in the form of written statements upon incorporation, and annual tax and activity reports to the IRS and numerous state regulatory agencies.

There are many types of nonprofits, including chambers of commerce, labor unions, credit unions, and foundations, each of which is guided by distinct state and Federal legal requirements affecting its financing and the limits of permissible activities. The Filer Commission maintains that there may be as many as six million private organizations in America's voluntary sector. The core group includes 350,000 religious organizations, 37,000 human services organizations, 6,000 museums, 5,500 private libraries, 4,600 secondary schools, 3,500 hospitals, 1,500 colleges and universities, and 1,100 symphony orchestras.

Here, however, we are limiting the discussion to health and social welfare groups, organizations that fall almost wholly within the 501(c)(3) category, principally in the human services. Their aim is helping people through research, information, education, and direct services. No part of their net income can inure to the benefit of private individuals, and they cannot attempt to influence legislation by traditional lobbying practices, or participate in political campaigns for or against candidates for public office. They can, of course, enlist support for their causes and points of view through information and wide-ranging education programs.

These organizations include giants in the health field like the American Cancer Society, the American Heart Association, and the National Foundation/March of Dimes, each of which has well-staffed units in most states and major cities. In social welfare, there are equivalents like the National Urban League, the Salvation Army and the American National Red Cross. They also encompass thousands of local, but no less essential agencies—hospitals, mental health associations, drug abuse clinics, camps, and so forth—that provide social and rehabilitative assistance to the homeless, the handicapped, the poor, and to millions of others, regardless of class or income. These agencies can be best understood by thinking of the groups served by the more than 2,200 "umbrella" funding units of the United Way.

To appreciate the importance of 501(c)(3) to health and welfare organizations, large or small, one has only to consider the amounts of money they annually raise from charitable solicitations. According to the American Association of Fund-Raising Counsel, of the more than $26.88 billion raised in 1975 for all of philanthropy—79.7 percent from individuals, 7.5 percent from foundations, 8.3 percent from bequests and 4.5 percent from corporations—health and social welfare were two of the major beneficiaries. They received $4.01 and $2.46 billion, respectively. Of the remainder, religion got the lion's share—$11.68 billion. Next in order were education ($3.59 billion), arts and humanities ($1.94 billion), and civic and public affairs ($0.82 billion). The final $2.38 billion was for an assortment of causes, including citizen aid for drought stricken areas of the world. Besides charitable contributions, voluntary organizations received an additional $20 billion in government funds for various public service projects and services.

Besides focusing attention on the acceptability and desirability of these organizations, the sums also suggest the importance of public relations in helping to manage and publicize nonprofit efforts. No organization operating with and in behalf of the popular will can function without an abiding concern for its publics—government officials and private citizens in particular. Without providing information on and interpretation of its purposes and activities, the organization would perish from lack of public attention and support—a fate experienced by too many nonprofits in the past.

PR PRACTICE IS SIGNIFICANT

How big the public relations force is that serves the health and social welfare fields is a difficult statistic to determine. The number is considerably less than in the profit sector, but it is not nearly as small as some might think. When you consider that there are more than 300 national nonprofit organizations in these fields, a majority of whom have at least one public relations person on staff, many with several, some with a dozen or more, the force immediately approaches several hundred. Added to this are the more than 2,000 to 3,000 public relations people in America's hospitals and medical centers. Finally, there are the ranks of the estimated 36,000 local agencies cooperating with the United Way, a sizable portion of which employ public relations professionals, many doubling as fund raisers.

Certainly, there are several thousand practitioners, perhaps as many as 10,000, in these pursuits, several hundred working in part-time capacities. Serving them are membership associations such as the National Communication Council for Human Services, which has provided publications, consultation and education since 1922. There is also an assortment of related national groups, including the Academy of Hospital Public Relations, the American Society for Hospital Public Relations, the Religious Public Relations Council, the Mental Health Materials Center, the National Association of Government Communicators, and the Public Relations Society of America. Equally important are organizations in fund raising such as the National Society of Fund Raisers, the Direct Mail Fundraisers Association, the National Catholic Development Conference and the American Society of Association Executives in Management.

Their efforts and the efforts of their members have resulted in many advances within and outside of their immediate areas of concern, including contributions to the public relations literature summarized in the comprehensive bibliographies of Scott Cutlip and Robert Bishop (available from the Public Relations Society of America), and books such as the 1966 text from Columbia University, *Public Relations in Health and Welfare,* edited by Harold Weiner and Frances Schmidt in cooperation with the National Communication Council for Human Services.

Organizations such as the American Cancer Society and the American Heart Association have public relations staffs—often referred to by the term "public information" or "communications"—of 20 or more in their headquarters offices. The directors of departments like these often earn upwards of $30,000; their assistants as much as $18,000 to $20,000 and more. Around the nation, there are many public relations people, particularly in the larger cities, who earn comparable salaries with equally sophisticated staffs and budgets.

In a 1975 survey of salaries and personnel policies among national nonprofit groups, undertaken by the National Assembly of National Voluntary Health and Social Welfare Organizations, the public relations directors among the 50 national agencies reporting earned from $19,520 to $29,112. In addition, many of these directors used management consultants, film and videomakers, fund raising firms, opinion pollsters, free lance writers and graphics designers, and other experts.

In sum, the public relations practice in health and social welfare is substantial, growing and challenging. Writing in *Public Relations Journal* in January, well-known author Allen Center predicted that health, welfare, government, and education would be the fastest areas of growth for public relations and public affairs activity.

Nonprofit public relations is an impressive picture, but like all things impressive it is not without problems.

UNIQUE DIFFERENCES

The difficulties faced by nonprofit practitioners have mainly to do with limitations on resources to do the job. Their responsibilities vary, depending on the nature of their resources and priorities, but most handle publicity, press relations, membership promotion, conferences, annual reports, and special events. They are also advisors and counselors to management on the full range of internal and external communication concerns and projects.

Despite nonprofit public relations growth, most departments in this field lack adequate budgets to handle these tasks. This means limitations on staff, as well as project funds. For example, most national health and social welfare organizations, with the exception of the 20 or so giants, have only a handful of public relations professionals, and between them they probably share one or two secretaries or grudgingly cooperate in an overburdened information-processing center or secretarial pool. Actual budgets, salaries and overhead excluded, range around $50,000 to $100,000 annually, although they probably spend substantially more, two or three times more in some instances, for expenses incurred on behalf of other departments for purchases of printing, graphics, press mailings, and the like.

OTHER DISTINCTIONS

Besides budget and staff limitations, nonprofit public relations people are dependent on public service time and space—as opposed to paid advertising—to gain media attention. Radio and TV spots are produced by the public relations departments of the nonprofit organizations, sometimes with the donated services—principally creative—of commercial ad agencies and public relations firms, sometimes the stations themselves.

In addition to ads and announcements, non-profit public relations people also place guests on talk and news shows and provide facts and research for documentaries. Often, they answer inquiries from reporters for other kinds of information, including quotes from their executive or volunteer leadership for editorials or features requiring comment and interpretation. Finally, many organizations have begun to work with cable television to reach deeper into their communities.

Although not required by law to do so, the print media carries public service announcements and stories about nonprofit organizations. Newspapers, in particular, are known for writing, designing and printing Sunday supplements on hospital open houses and anniversaries. Major publications may also have periodic editorial conferences with the staff and leadership of important organizations to discuss current social issues and prepare special features.

Incidentally, the departments of most of the large non-profit agencies produce films and public relations materials that their field units use to reach the local press and other communication mediums. These include finished ad mechanicals, slide presentations, brochures, and photographs available at minimal cost or free.

Many national organizations—the United Way is a good example—obtain millions of dollars of public service time and space under the auspices of the Advertising Council which develops campaigns for regularized distribution to the national media. The Council, which is funded by corporate contributions, arranges for ad agencies to provide the creative talent needed to develop first-rate professional campaigns. The nonprofit groups provide the out-of-pocket expenses, often privately raised from donors, of $150,000 or more, to complete a year-long package.

Unfortunately, the work of the Council and much of the advertising community is constrained to noncontroversial accounts whose objectives do not threaten the interests of corporate contributors such as the tobacco industry and other publicly sensitive businesses. As a result, organizations such as the American Cancer Society and American Lung Association have to arrange for their own campaigns, working independently with agencies of their own choosing. Nonetheless, the Advertising Council's contributions are extremely important in generating public service time and space for private and public agencies of human care. The major public relations counselors have yet to imitate, let alone match, this involvement for the public good.

Another difference for the non-profit practitioner is dependency on the organization's volunteers to gain visibility, press attention, and communication support. Volunteers—there are 40 to 60 million in the United States, contributing an estimated six billion hours of work—are the backbone of community support for nonprofit health and social welfare groups. Besides serving as unpaid backup for budget-pressed staff, they also act as ambassadors of good will, spreading the gospel of their organization's crusade.

DIFFERENT ISSUES

In addition to differences in practice, there are also several important issues that weigh more heavily on the nonprofit sector, perhaps, than on the profit area. Central among these is the question of accountability and credibility. Various segments of the public, the press most conspicuously in recent months, want to know more about what charities are doing with the money they raise. A few writers and reporters have legitimate questions based on the abuses of a minority of organizations over the years. Others, unfortunately, are ignorant or misguided.

The government is also scrutinizing the credibility of nonprofit organizations. Currently, there are at least three bills before Congress aimed at regulating the public information and fund-raising requirements of charities. Although none is likely to be seriously acted upon soon, perhaps two or three years hence the day will come when federal regulation will be a fact of life. This will be in addition to the current obligation of all nonprofit organizations to report their income and expenses to the IRS, and current fund-raising regulations in at least 38 states, 25 of which require bonding.

Constraints on funding and traditional ways of doing business also mean that non-profit organizations have to develop greater sophistication in the art of marketing their purposes. This requires ingenuity and imagination. Already, for example, organizations such as the United Way, YMCA, and the National Multiple Sclerosis Society are using the voluntary services of professional athletes to aid in their public relations/public education campaigns. This past winter, the United Way arranged with the NFL and network TV to have public service announcements aired during every game of the regular season, reaching an estimated 75 million viewers each weekend.

There is a greater appreciation within and among nonprofit health and social welfare organizations for the need to exploit new public relations techniques, new relationships, and new ideas in order to overcome the deficiencies of a static economy and the recent trend among a few influential members of the press and Congress to call into question the nation's traditional "hands-off" approach to the regulation and monitoring of the voluntary sector.

The Marketing
of Public Goods

Leo Bogart

The title of this paper represents, at first glance, a contradiction in terms. The term "marketing" derives from the word "market," a place where individuals negotiate the transfer of specific goods and services. Each buyer and seller competes not only with all others buying and selling the same items, but with all those buying and selling a great variety of possible substitutes that might otherwise attract equivalent purchasing power or productive effort and skill.

In contrast, public or social goods are indivisible by definition. They cannot be itemized and auctioned off in varying quantities under the classical laws of supply and demand, and thus there is, strictly speaking, no "market" for them. True enough, in many cases public goods have at least some competition from the private sector. Essential services like police and fire protection are augmented by private security systems. In the supermarkets, bottled water provides an alternative to the murky fluids provided by the municipality. Private delivery services supplement

Reprinted with permission of *The Conference Board Record,* November 1975.

the faltering postal system. In England, some physicians continue flourishing private practices while the National Health Service remains free to all. But these exceptions do not change the rule: Multipartite bargaining is central to the concept of the market, but does not exist in the case of public goods and services. By definition, public goods are accessible to all, and depend on resources that no individual could muster for private use.

Yet even if we can deny the existence of a *market* for public goods, we must confront the question of *marketing* them. This apparent contradiction exists simply because the term "marketing" has acquired an autonomous meaning quite apart from its origins. Marketing is the discipline of analyzing demand, designing products to fit maximum profitable demand, and developing promotional and selling methods to activate demand. That definition covers public goods, no less than private ones. The marketer's professional armory consists of diagnostic, organizational, and persuasive skills that can and should be applied to purposes broader than those of the private corporation.

As we enter the last quarter of the century, a confluence of great problems makes it especially urgent to consider how the marketer's talents might be applied in the public sector.

THE PUBLIC/PRIVATE TRADE-OFF

For the first time in history Americans are being forced to realize that our resources are finite, that our appetites for the "good life" cannot be indefinitely satisfied, and that there are severe imbalances between the consumption needs fostered by our mass communications system and our ability to sustain them in a world we cannot control.

We have suddenly been hit by the necessity for choices or, in the vogue term, "trade-offs," among such values as abundant energy, convenience, clean surroundings, and health. We are slowly beginning to learn that we cannot have everything at the same time. This discovery is in direct contradiction to the whole ideology of consumption that marketers have been promoting, each selling his own product in the glorious faith that that mysterious invisible hand would guide him and his competitors toward the common benefit.

In our new view of economic reality, demand may turn out to be bad and not good.[1] The marketer may be called upon to use his talents to motivate consumers to buy less rather than more (animal protein or lawn conditioner, for instance), to pay extra for what he doesn't think he needs (in a car equipped with automatic safety features and a catalytic converter), to inconvenience himself (by using returnable bottles or public transportation instead of his car), to exert himself (by turning off the lights and the air conditioning), to control unnecessary acts (by dropping refuse in receptacles instead of on someone else's front lawn).

Implicit in all such pressures is a redistribution of the present allocation of resources between public and private goods. We cannot all ride the bus to save energy and expect Detroit to sell the same number of cars each year. As we enlarge the public sector and increase the amenities available to all (including national defense) we must pay the price in the form of higher taxation or accelerated inflation—in either case, by reducing consumption of private goods.

Actually, we have been doing just that. Since the Second World War, through the combination of taxes and debt, an increasing share of the gross national product has been expended on the public sector and less on consumer goods. In 1947, the first year of the postwar economy, government accounted for 12.2 percent of GNP. In 1974, it was 22.1 percent. As the public sector is enlarged, marketers must confront the question of whether and how our professional skills can be put to work there, of whether we can have marketing without a market in the traditional sense.

MARKETING WITHOUT A MARKET

In the domain of public goods the marketer is deprived of two familiar instruments of his art: competitive pricing and a ready calculation of return on investment.

Public agencies are no more apt than private companies to experiment radically with the prices of their goods and services. In the private sector some motion picture theaters have found it profitable to cut the price of tickets drastically. In a comparable fixed-cost operation in the public sector, offering a two-for-one New York subway or bus ride on Sunday has brought increased patronage, though not the added revenues required to make the change more profitable. But this is looking at the balance sheet in the conventional way. Under the new concept of social accounting, the public interest in clean air and unclogged highways must also be assigned values in the calculation of profit and loss.

In Europe it has long been recognized that cultural activities (orchestras, operas, theaters) belong in the category of public goods and that the collective interest requires that they be maintained at government expense to achieve the widest possible audience, even if they cannot cover their costs in the open marketplace.

The U.S. Postal Service reports that third class advertising mail pays its way, while second class mail for publications is run at a loss to preserve the public interest. Yet spokesmen for the magazine industry contend (I believe with good reason) that a rise in second class postal rates would entail a much greater ultimate social cost, by reducing information flow, than the dollars and cents' savings in the federal budget.

In the case of both public and private goods, market price is often deceptive because of hidden subsidies not directly apparent to the consumer. In 1974 the federal government subsidized the nation's railroads by under $300 million, and the highway system by nearly $5 billion. Yet the enormous cost of highway construction and maintenance is invisible to the motorist who compares his out-of-pocket expense for a drive with the price of a railroad ticket. As one newspaper reported: "The high school cafeteria serves a splendid hot meal for 50¢ without any cost to the taxpayers, thanks to a Federal government subsidy."

These kinds of delicate measurement issues perplex the social account.[2] They also represent critical questions for the marketer of public goods. Evaluations of social costs and benefits can be quantified by techniques of consumer research that replace subjective evaluations with reports of public preferences. But it is also possible to make enormous errors by literally accepting the ranking of social priorities or the ranking of social values as these emerge from public opinion polls.

The theoretical choices that are made in survey responses are not necessarily translated into actions when the time comes for an actual test. Moreover, the priority that people give to different goods and services (public *and* private) is susceptible to rapid change, particularly at times when normal distribution channels are disrupted. During the energy crisis of early 1974, it appeared that mobility had become such a necessity to most Americans that they were willing to forego spending on food, clothing, and shelter in order to continue the habit of using the family car. In total contradiction of economic theory, the demand for gasoline has proved to be remarkably inelastic in spite of a doubling of the retail price. B. Bruce-Briggs estimates that demand would continue to hold fairly steady even if the price of crude oil doubled again.[3]

PRESENT/FUTURE TRADE-OFFS

For many Americans, critical consumption choices can be postponed, because we have for so long been accustomed to eating our cake and having it, too. Quite apart from the use of credit cards and charge accounts, a fifth of all consumer goods are bought on installment credit.

Indeed, much of the expansion of the American economy in the last two decades has been made possible by this vastly increased use and active promotion of credit buying.* The prevailing assumption that one can fly now and pay later has held equally for the individual planning a flight to Las Vegas and the U.S. Air Force planning one to Hanoi. In both instances the resultant debt has contributed to the rate of inflation. High interest rates and high prices do not necessarily deter consumption (as the Brazilian experience has shown), so long as consumers expect both to keep rising. Can this inflationary spiral be broken if marketers persuade the public *not* to consume?

The objectives of ending inflation, maintaining economic growth, and enhancing the quality of life are not mutually incompatible, but they may have to be met sequentially. This means that the necessary trade-offs are political in character. The voices of the environmentalists were suddenly overwhelmed when the energy crisis made it imperative to open up the fields of the Alaska North Slope. A similar reversal of policy on strip mining may be inevitable. In both these instances the market mechanism was incapable of resolving the public issues involved.

THE POLITICS OF MARKETING

The promotion of public goods is at an intersection point of politics and marketing. Although American business fosters the myth of the free market economy, demand is a function of price for most goods and services, and increasingly price is a function of government policies formed in the crucible of politics. A widening proportion of all business decisions are mandated by government, either directly (as with package goods labeling) or indirectly by taxes, tariffs, interest rates, import quotas, subsidies, and procurement policies. These political elements are most visible in the case of a commodity like gasoline, in whose pricing formula the depletion allowance has long been an ingredient. Crop subsidies, stockpiling, and foreign aid have for years significantly affected the pricing of agricultural commodities. Considerations of ideology or military strategy limiting trade with areas like Cuba or Rhodesia have affected the price of sugar and chrome, while the political strategy of détente led to the 1973 Soviet wheat deal, with its inflationary trigger effect on grain prices.

The marketer's focus of concern is always the market of the moment.

---

* In September 1974 installment debt amounted to $155 billion, or about $2,200 per household. Interest and repayments of that debt amounted to about 17 percent of take-home income.

But almost every public policy decision that involves money balances present and deferred consumption. Any investment in the future carries a price tag. When the government anticipates future drought by stockpiling grain, this drives up the current price. If the oil companies are expected to invest earnings in exploration and technology to find new fuels, they cannot be asked to reduce the present price of gasoline to a point where no reserves are available for new development.

SELLING THE FUTURE

Prudent and rational policies in the public interest usually require the consumer to defer immediate gratifications in return for future benefits. But these future benefits are less appealing as they are more remote. Savings for oneself are in a different category from savings for one's children, one's eventual descendants, or for remote coming generations. Despite the self-evident difficulty of selling shares in the future, every unit of government engages in this practice when it borrows from the public for needed long-term capital projects to benefit all—schools and sewers, subways, and incinerators.

The case of public borrowing has not always depended strictly on straight economics, as represented by interest rates and tax laws. In World War II, war bonds were sold as warrants of patriotism rather than as investments. Are there circumstances less emotionally engaging than those of wartime which can summon up this kind of "altruistic" enthusiasm?

The difficulty of generating such a mood is that no action by any individual makes a perceptible difference on behalf of social goals. Yet there is no way in which social goals can be achieved except through individual actions, voluntary or coerced. Taxes that transfer the society's productive capacities from private to public goods are inevitably perceived by the individual consumer as a deprivation: they reduce his span of direct control over what he consumes, even though his aggregate consumption is not necessarily reduced at all.

Who else but the marketer can answer the long-standing question of how to move people across the gap from attitudes that are favorable in the abstract to specific socially beneficial acts that require some sacrifice? This question is not getting any easier to answer, in spite of the tremendous changes that have taken place in public attitudes and values. Even the generation of the counterculture has been reared to accept the traditional American norms of consumption. Research on the attitudes and buying intentions of young people suggests that, for all the talk of "ecology" and "love," they are just as much concerned with acquiring material possessions as earlier generations were, and probably just as reluctant to give up what's here and now for the benefit of their unborn descendants.[4]

This apparent contradiction harks back to a central preoccupation of consumer psychology—the relationship of attitudes and actions. An individual may want something to happen and at the same time believe that his own contribution to making it happen is totally meaningless unless it is matched by an equivalent contribution from everyone else. He will not budge unless he knows that everyone else is moving, too. And yet, in the absence of coercion, how can he have this assurance?

PROMOTING VOLUNTARISM

Undoubtedly, there are innovators in the domain of social consumption just as there are in personal consumption. Like the people who want to be the first on their block to try a new product, there are probably some who will be first to give up personal benefit for a public cause. The evidence on this point is not overwhelming. There are, no doubt, many case histories of successful fund raising for philanthropic causes from among the general public, but effective fund raising generally combines mass media promotion with personal solicitation directed at elements of the public who have a direct link with the cause in question. (This was true, incidentally, even in the classic case history of mass media persuasion: the Kate Smith War Bond radio sales marathon, in which many of the volunteered pledges had been privately solicited in advance.)[5]

What actually has been the track record of promotional campaigns on behalf of the public interest? Over the years the advertising business has expended much time and talent and valuable media resources on behalf of worthy public causes. The Advertising Council has organized these admirable efforts with great efficiency. In its Annual Report for 1972-1973, the Council says:

> Even though we can't take complete credit for the results, we feel that the media's support of our current campaigns has helped in making the following contributions:
>
> • In 33 months the unemployment rate for Vietnam veterans dropped from a high of 11% to 3.6%.
> • The National Alliance of Businessmen found employment for 1,019,062 disadvantaged persons.

◆ $2.02 billion was donated to American colleges and universities last year by private sources.

◆ A Gallup Survey found that the concept of the large family as the 'ideal' was losing favor, and in the last two years the nation's birth rate has dropped steadily.

These are success stories of which an advertising agency's new business vice president would indeed be proud! No one can fault the Advertising Council for responding with the same vague and indefensible claims that are customarily used by any advertising department or agency in responding to management's unreasonable demands for "accountability." It is difficult enough to extricate the specific contribution of advertising to the success of a product under competitive market conditions. It is all the more difficult to assess the influence of advertising on the public temper in relation to great issues or to strongly rooted patterns of human behavior.

But the Advertising Council report is not the only basis on which to judge the accomplishment of public service campaigns. There are a number of other case histories, some backed by careful research.

An estimated investment of $51.5 million was contributed by the media between 1967 and 1969 on behalf of the National Safety Council's "fasten your seat belt" campaign. Before/after studies showed that this had no effect on seat belt use. It took an actual change in automotive design to make this an automatic habit for the motorist.

In a study made by the University of North Carolina, a television campaign on behalf of family planning was conducted in 1970–1971 in Columbus and Memphis at a level equivalent to a projected $20 million of national advertising, with no effect either on birthrates or contraceptive sales.[6]

Congressional hearings have revealed that in 1969, advertising worth—at the current media rates—somewhere between $12 and $20 million was donated for a fund raising campaign on behalf of Radio Free Europe. This resulted in total contributions of about $100,000.

The very extensive antidrug abuse campaigns prepared by a number of advertising agencies also received many millions of dollars of air time and space in publications. This advertising was reviewed in November 1972 by a conference of social scientists and experts in addiction, sponsored by the National Institutes of Health. The conclusion was that the advertising merely increased the visibility of drugs to potential users, and the campaign was dropped. Since then the incidence of drug usage appears to have leveled off, though I would hesitate to conclude that this is only because the advertising has stopped.

LIMITATIONS OF PUBLIC SERVICE ADVERTISING

It is impossible to assess these and many other campaigns, because they typically involve major social phenomena with respect to which attitudes and behavior might be transformed as a result of forces and trends quite apart from advertising. The incidence of forest fires inevitably reflects the rising mobility of the population, increased leisure and greater use of parks. Millions of dollars expended on behalf of fire prevention have certainly established Smokey the Bear within the bestiary of the American psyche. The number of man-caused fires per thousand forest visitors has been greatly reduced during the same period. Is it because of Smokey, or has greater use of the forests also increased the level of social surveillance? No one can really say. (The latest theory is that the reduction of fires upsets the natural ecological balance and is really harmful to bears and other living things!)

How successful was the antismoking campaign that followed the issuance of the Surgeon General's warning? The data on cigarette consumption before and after has to be untangled from the effects of price increases, the ban on TV commercials, the shifting age distribution of the population, and the changed position of women. There is certainly no clear-cut story here. (Americans smoked 90 billion more cigarettes in 1973 than they did in 1970, before the ban on broadcast advertising of cigarettes.) But is the problem of changing smoking habits inherently any more difficult than the problems of changing driving and eating habits?

The reduction in fuel consumption during the oil shortages of 1974 can hardly be attributed to oil company advertising that asked people to conserve energy. This advertising, along with all the other mass media coverage of the story, the editorials, presidential directives, as well as the real inconvenience of waiting on fuel lines, undoubtedly made some contribution to the general sense of crisis. What really reduced consumption was not advertising, but specific coercive measures—the lowering of the speed limit and, in many places, the rationing of gasoline. The 55-mph speed limit was generally accepted after the inevitable, initial grumbling. In fact, most social innovations are opposed at first and become acceptable after they have become institutionalized and familiar.

In many public service campaigns advertising has been expected to achieve targets that no one in product marketing would accept as reasonable. In product marketing it is taken for granted that to back up the advertising there will be a complete merchandising, sales, and distribution plan; that the product itself is widely available through the right kinds of outlets; that it is properly packaged and priced; and that it does its job.

In public service campaigns, the advertising is commonly expected to carry the whole load. Yet most such campaigns deal with serious matters on which we might expect the public's emotions to be more readily engaged than in facing the comparatively trivial decisions of brand choice. Yet somehow or other, it is generally taken for granted that advertising effects can be measured in the case of product movement and that they are generally insusceptible to measurement on broad public issues.

The promotion of causes in the public interest should be defined as a problem in marketing rather than as a subject of advertising. Advertising per se can contribute only minimally to changing strong and deep-seated habits of consumption in the direction of serving significant social needs that are not being satisfied through the operation of the open market. Advertising *can* help to create a climate in which a new or modified pattern of behavior acquires familiarity and acceptability, and it can undoubtedly help condition people to feel that what is required of them or exacted from them is useful, desirable and meaningful.

In confronting the economic crisis that beset his new administration in the fall of 1974, President Gerald Ford appeared before a nationwide television audience sporting a button with the acronym WIN for Whip Inflation Now. The cynics immediately turned the button upside down to spell NIM, for No Immediate Miracles. The predictable fiasco of the WIN campaign merely documents the limitations of sloganeering as a substitute for policy.

Major changes in people's habits demand sacrifices and, characteristically, they demand sacrifices among different sectors of the public and different interest groups. This inequitable distribution of the burden, in which someone always gets hurt, makes it almost impossible to achieve major changes in consumption on the basis of voluntary action. It requires coercion, in the form of regulation or taxation, to get people to change, and the use of governmental authority brings us out of the market and foursquare into the domain of politics.

THE FUTURE OF SOCIAL MARKETING

During World War II and for perhaps a decade afterwards, consumer researchers and other social scientists devoted considerable interest and effort to the subject of mass persuasion on behalf of lofty social aims. There was considerable optimism that the same techniques of investigation and promotion that worked well in the preparation of product advertising campaigns could also be applied effectively to solve social problems or advance public causes. This effort reflected a sense of participation by the research community in the objectives of government. But much of that identification disappeared with the disenchantment of the Vietnam War years and the disappointing record of research on the effectiveness of public information campaigns. The new interest in the marketing of public goods inexorably returns the marketer's attention to the challenging political problems of how to change established patterns of mass behavior.

It becomes increasingly difficult to separate people's wants as consumers from their other wants as citizens. We cannot understand consumption needs without regard to social needs. More and more collective needs and aspirations seem to call for satisfaction from the public sector and will not be satisfied in the open marketplace.

As it expands, the public sector should represent a significant market for marketing skills. These skills entail the disciplined use of teamwork among specialists (1) to identify consumers' needs through research, (2) to define the consumer benefit and strategy of making it visible, (3) to help design products and services in a form that fits those needs, (4) to package and present these in an attractive manner, (5) to help arrive at appropriate pricing to maximize demand, (6) to organize delivery systems that facilitate access and convenient use, and (7) to create through communication and promotion a receptive familiarity with the product that leads to trial and repeat use.

The field of public administration should be encouraged to make much greater use of marketing science and art, and it represents a promising area for innovative academic curriculum planning. Similarly, marketers should forge closer links with the accounting profession, since the concept of social accounting is meaningless without the application of consumer research techniques.

In the promotion of public goods, the challenges involve "remarketing" more often than "demarketing"—not so much reducing the level of consumption as redirecting it into new channels and helping to create the distribution system and organizational structure for this changed activity. The marketer of public goods must see the public as the client, rather than as the object of manipulation.

REFERENCES

1. See Philip Kotler and Sidney J. Levy, "Demarketing, Yes, Demarketing," *Harvard Business Review,* November/December 1971, pp. 74–80; and Philip Kotler, "Marketing During Periods of Shortage," *Journal of Marketing,* July 1974, pp. 20–29.

2. *Social Measurement* (New York: American Institute of Certified Public Accountants, 1972).
3. B. Bruce-Briggs, "Gasoline Prices and the Suburban Way of Life," *The Public Interest*, Fall 1974, pp. 131–136.
4. Leo Bogart, "Youth Market Isn't All That Different," *Advertising Age*, April 12, 1971; see also "The Young Homemakers," a study by the Newspaper Advertising Bureau, Inc., April 1974.
5. Robert K. Merton, *Mass Persuasion: The Social Psychology of a War Bond Drive* (New York: Harper & Row, 1946).
6. J. Richard Udry, Lydia T. Clark, Charles L. Chase, and Martin Levy, "Can Mass Media Advertising Increase Contraceptive Use?" *Family Planning Perspectives*, July 1972, pp. 37–44.

The business of Blood Bank

The Blood Business

Seymour Lusterman

Blood and blood products are obtained, processed, and distributed through thousands of independent entities that operate with a minimum of coordination, under widely disparate rules and principles, and without the control and discipline (except in terms of product quality) of either market mechanisms or government regulations.

It is this fragmentation and inconsistency, reformers believe, that account for the key problems of the system. Not only is there a weak organizational basis for recruitment of voluntary blood donors, for example, but the public is said to be confused and inhibited in its blood giving by the coexistence of voluntary and commercial banking, by charges for blood in some hospitals and not in others, by uncertainty over whether charges will be made for blood that has been freely given, by the availability of insurance coverage for blood as well as for processing costs, by appeals for donations from more than one bank in the community, and so on.[1]

Uncoordinated banking activities within metropolitan or other

Reprinted with permission of *Conference Board Record*, February 1974.

significant geographic areas also foster imbalances in supply and demand—leading to excessive inventories and outdating at some times and places, as banks hoard to ensure their own supply, and to shortages at others. In many areas or communities there is no organization clearly charged with educating either the medical profession or the public about their respective roles in the blood system.

A lesser (but no less real) problem in our highly mobile society is that blood credits are often valid only in the bank or community in which they have been established.[2] Also, blood banking fragmentation makes it impossible for national or regional businesses to develop company-wide programs. Each unit must work out its own arrangements with local banks.[3]

THE NEW NATIONAL POLICY

While all of these problems had been widely discussed in blood banking circles for some time, various factors in the fall of 1971 combined to bring about federal involvement—notably the development of unusually severe blood shortages and intense media attention to them and to the related hepatitis problem. At about the same time, there appeared a widely discussed book entitled *The Gift Relationship: From Human Blood to Social Policy,* by the English social planner Richard M. Titmuss,[4] which included an analysis and critique of the U.S. system.

The confluence of these events had several results. Elliot L. Richardson, then Secretary of the Department of Health, Education and Welfare, issued a directive to "move as rapidly as possible for the development of a new national blood policy." And, in 1972, Congress passed the National Heart, Blood Vessel, Lung and Blood Act, declaring blood and blood products to be "essential human resources."

The new policy, formulated after a year and a half of unprecedented study and data collection, has as its premise that the nation's blood supply, wherever collected, is the property of all the people, and represents a shared responsibility for a common supply. Its central aim is "to encourage, foster and support efforts designed to bring into being an all-voluntary blood donation system and to eliminate commercialism in the acquisition of whole blood and blood components for transfusion purposes."

A necessity for implementing the new policy, HEW officials believe, is the integration of blood banks into a regional system to achieve "greater resource-sharing and area-wide cooperation." The optimal number of regional banks has not been determined, although present HEW Secretary Weinberger has suggested it might be on the order of 100. But it is intended that the number reflect an accommodation of two goals: a region large enough for efficiency and self-sufficiency, but small enough to pose no logistical problems for intraregional shipment of perishable blood and blood components.

THE PRESENT BLOOD SERVICE COMPLEX

Blood banking functions intrinsically are strikingly analogous to industrial ones. They consist of (1) the procurement of supplies—that is, the recruitment and selection of donors; (2) various processing operations— blood collection, "characterization" (typing the blood and testing its quality), and the preparation of components and derivatives; (3) record keeping and inventory control; and (4) distribution.

These functions are now carried on by four types of organizations:

* *Hospital banks.* About 5,000 such banks[5] collect an estimated one-fifth of the total U.S. supply. A few obtain more blood than they need and are therefore suppliers to other hospitals.
* *Red Cross banks.* These comprise the largest segment of the system. Fifty-nine Red Cross banks in various parts of the country account for about two-fifths of the supply.
* *Other nonprofit community banks.* Like the Red Cross banks, these are independent of the hospitals. The 276 banks in this category account for something under one-third of the blood resource.
* *Commercial banks.* 63 of these augment the blood supply available from voluntary blood donors with blood that is bought from professionals and so-called walk-in mercenaries. They account for 10 to 15 percent of the total supply.

The relative portion of the blood supply that is produced by each of these sources varies widely from one community to the next. Many communities have been able, through effective donor recruitment campaigns, to satisfy all their needs with volunteers. The state of Connecticut, for example, is under a wholly voluntary system operated by the Red Cross. At the other pole are such large metropolitan areas as Memphis, Houston, and New Orleans in which a major portion of the blood supply comes from commercial banks.

The blood service complex includes pharmaceutical firms as well as voluntary and commercial blood banks. These firms are engaged in the manufacture and commercial marketing of various blood products—but primarily derivatives of plasma. Some of this plasma is obtained by separation from outdated blood and some from human placentas acquired from hospitals. By far the greatest portion, however, is collected from paid volunteers via a process known as plasmapharesis, in which the red cells are separated from drawn whole blood and returned to the donor and only the plasma retained. In 1971, 1.5 million liters of plasma was collected in this manner.⁶

THE BLOOD SUPPLY

Just as the discovery of means of storing blood, hardly more than a generation ago, has been the essential underpinning of modern surgery, so are such new procedures as open heart surgery and organ transplants further stimulating the need for blood. But voluntary and paid donations, even as extended through the use of fractionation and component therapy, and supplemented by importations from other countries, do not together produce enough blood today to meet U.S. needs, according to experts in the field.

While it is rare that life-saving blood is not available or cannot be quickly obtained for dramatic emergencies, shortages are somewhat subtler in character and consequence.

First, it is a common occurrence in many communities for surgery to be postponed because sufficient blood is not on hand for expected or possible need. Such surgery may not be of life-saving urgency, but its postponement is more often than not medically undesirable.

Second, there is not enough blood available for proper care of hemophiliacs. The incidence of moderate-to-severe hemophilia is estimated to be at least 26 per 100,000 population. Treatment is usually episodic and includes the introduction, intravenously, of various blood clotting factors. Appropriate preventive therapy could require, by some estimates, factors from the equivalent of up to 13 million units of whole blood.

Finally, even the system's ability to meet life-threatening emergencies is often achieved only through dramatic, emotional, crisis-directed appeals, rather than through an orderly and assured supply.

Voluntary Sources

Voluntary blood donations in this country are achieved under a multiplicity of arrangements. Monetary considerations are so prominent an aspect of them that donations are usually "voluntary" only in a special—and some feel inappropriate—sense of the word.[7] These include the following:

* *Credit agreements.* Members of a group are entitled to draw at no charge an amount of blood equal, or nearly equal, to that deposited by its members during the year, or to draw an unlimited amount if they meet a minimum participation requirement.
* *Insurance or assurance agreements.* Entitle individual donors and their families to receive blood during a stipulated period, usually a year, in exchange for a donation.
* *Replacement arrangements.* A portion of the hospital bill is refunded if recipients or their family or friends donate units of blood in an amount equal to or larger than the number of units that have been transfused.
* *Bank membership plans.* These assure blood to persons who pay an annual fee and agree to donate blood at the bank's request, typically with assurance that this will be less than once a year.

If it is unlikely that those who donate blood under these arrangements are prompted solely by motives of self-interest and financial protection, it is also true that many are spurred by additional tangible rewards. Noncommercial blood banks may themselves offer modest cash payments or such nonmonetary rewards as food, tickets, and personal gift items. Cooperating groups may provide their members with similar incentives, with such additional ones as time off from work—and even the remission of prison sentences—as well as with various forms of public recognition.

A portion of the blood supply is, of course, given under conditions in which there is no motive of personal gain or avoidance of penalty— although one would expect that "some sense of obligation, approval or interest, some awareness of the need for the gift, some expectation that a return gift may be needed and received at some future date must be present."[8] It is the hope of many reformers that ultimately an adequate blood supply will be derived on this basis—that group quotas, for example, will be perceived as analogous to community chest quotas rather than as a base for "credits."

Commercial Sources

Partial compensation with commercial blood for the insufficiency of the volunteered supply is achieved at considerable cost. Indications are that commercial blood is three to ten times more likely to be a source of infectious hepatitis than volunteered blood. It is drawn largely from people who, living under conditions of crowding, poverty and poor sanitation, are more likely to be in poor health. Commercial donors, furthermore, are far less apt than voluntary donors to answer truthfully the questions that enable blood banks to screen out those with doubtful health histories—and commercial banks may be less apt to press them. The nationwide incidence of post-transfusion hepatitis in overt form has been estimated as 3.1 cases per 1,000.[9] One-third to nearly one-half of all these cases of post-transfusion hepatitis are estimated to be transmitted by commercial blood. The consequence is nearly 1,000 deaths and 10,000 hospitalizations a year, a cost of over $85 million, and immeasurable suffering. Moreover, it is believed that for every case that presents overt symptoms of the disease there are about five subclinical ones. Its victims may become hepatitis carriers and may suffer such long-term adverse effects as cirrhosis of the liver.

For many people in and outside the medical world there are social and ethical as well as health-related objections to the buying and selling of human blood. "A society which cherishes the worth of the individual and fosters a high sense of social responsibility," observes a recent report for the government,[10] "cannot set a price on human organs and tissues." It has also been argued that giving blood is a means by which an increasingly depersonalized society can provide opportunity for altruism and foster a sense of human relatedness and community. From these perspectives the attainment of an all-voluntary blood system is desirable even if methods of screening blood for hepatitis, now about 25 or 30 percent effective, were to become wholly so.

WASTE OF THE BLOOD RESOURCE

In view of the limited resources, any wasting is plainly a problem. The most obvious wasting occurs through "outdating." About one-quarter of red cells, separated from, or in the form of, whole blood, were literally discarded in 1971 because they had been held by individual blood banks for longer than 21 days. Although a certain amount of outdating is inevitable, this ratio is generally agreed to be needlessly and excessively high.

The potential for extending the available supply of blood resources through fractionation and component therapy are also, authorities agree, greatly underutilized. About four out of five transfusions are of whole blood, but red cells alone are considered by experts to be therapeutically appropriate 70 to 80 percent of the time. Their wider use would free an additional supply of platelets, white cells, and plasma—and would reduce the need for plasmapharesis. Additionally, authorities believe that transfusions are often given when they are not needed, depleting supplies and introducing the risk of hepatitis.

INEQUITIES IN COST

It is doubtful that the price of any product or service in our economy is as often, or typically, unrelated to its cost as that of blood or blood products.

The economic cost of a blood transfusion is the sum of the costs of drawing, processing, and distributing the blood or blood product, and of cross-matching and administering it. In only a minority of transfusions is the blood itself an item of cost.

Nevertheless, a charge is often made for blood as well as for the services of the blood bank and the hospital. Hospitals often justify charges for blood they have gotten from voluntary donors, or charges that are in excess of their costs for commercial blood, as a device for replenishing the supply. (Patients' payments may, as noted earlier, be refunded if the blood is replaced.) Such "responsibility fees" or "replacement penalties" are varyingly productive in this respect, but place a heavy financial burden on those who cannot satisfy them—characteristically the elderly, the poor, those with unusually large and frequent requirements, and those who need rare and expensive blood and blood products.

Charges for blood transfusions range from $2 or so to over $100, and the total of charges for components may reach $200 or $300. Differences reflect not only varying hospital policies with regard to replacement penalties but also a lack of uniformity among blood banks in cost accounting practices (as well as, some assert, such neglect of accounting that processing costs are often not known). The price may also include nonprocessing costs like research, or represent the offsetting of other costs not associated with blood services.

LOOKING TO THE FUTURE

In attempting to sort out the blood system tangle, the government sees blood bank regulation as one of the activities falling within its own domain. Until recently, 70 percent of blood banks (accounting for about one-fifth of all whole blood drawn) were exempt from federal regulation and not covered by state laws. Early in 1972, intrastate as well as interstate blood banking activities were brought under the licensing and inspection authority of the Food and Drug Administration. Now HEW promises to make use of its "full regulatory authority" and to seek whatever new authority "may be necessary and appropriate for assuring uniform high blood and blood banking standards."

The emerging mechanisms for medical peer review—Professional Standards Peer Review Organizations (PSROs)—established by federal law in October 1972, will also be used by HEW to encourage the most efficient and effective practices in blood therapy. In addition, the Social Security Administration will be called upon to study the relationship between cost and charges for blood services. The government further promises to support vigorous research efforts involving "all scientific aspects" of the therapeutic and diagnostic aspects of blood and blood products.

It is generally agreed that of primary importance is the creation of a data collection and analysis system. Conceived as a joint undertaking of the federal government and the private sector, it will embrace the full spectrum of blood-related activities: the size, character, location, and utilization of the blood resource; cost and charges for blood therapy; the incidence of waste, disease transmission, incorrect blood matching, and so forth. Its realization will require not only a data collection and processing mechanism, but also the adoption of uniform nomenclature, record keeping, and cost accounting methods within the blood banks.[11]

Increases in federal costs for implementing the new policy are expected to be modest. They would stem in part from inclusion of a benefit under the Administration's national health insurance proposal to cover "the service aspects" of transfusing blood and blood products. Costs will also be incurred in maintenance of the information system, and in any expansion of research.

The private sector's response to the government's initiatives was characterized initially by agreement in principle but contention about means of implementation. Disagreement surfaced first over the question of whether a new national voluntary organization was needed, and if so what its structure and role should be.

The American National Red Cross and the Council of Community Blood Centers, for example, announced they were prepared to create a new organization, to be known as the American Blood Institute. They envisaged this as "an active operating body that can accept responsibility, be held accountable, offer continuity and provide a single interface with Federal authorities." The American Association of Blood Banks at the same time proposed a more informal structure to serve as a "forum" for those involved in blood banking and transfusion services and to promote cooperative efforts, but preserving "the autonomy of the individual organizations." But the head of still another group, representing the commercial blood banks, suggested that "the task of an all-volunteer blood donor program is so monumental that however desirable the goal, the effort to achieve it may be a needless diversion of resources."

The question of a national organization raises a host of other questions, among them: In what ways, if at all, must voluntary efforts be shaped and regulated by federal legislation? How rapidly should present credit and responsibility fee arrangements be replaced by a community donation concept? How can individual blood banks be persuaded to yield some of their autonomy and to institute uniform record-keeping and data collection methods? To what degree and how should the consumer interest be represented in blood service organizations? What criteria should dictate the size and boundaries of a blood service region? How can more medical expertise be brought into blood banking operations? What organizational forms are most likely to further the education of physicians in the use of component therapy?

Despite these acknowledged problems, agreement is reported close on the creation of an American Blood Commission and a plan for regional organization.

BUSINESS AND THE BLOOD SUPPLY

Places of employment have always been regarded as major and indispensable sources of volunteered blood. They can provide the blood banking system with access to large groups of people who are within the donation-eligible age range. Since this minimizes donor effort, inconvenience, and time, and offers favorable conditions for education and persuasion, it is particularly conducive to participation.

Information about the portion of the blood supply that is derived from employees of private industry as a result of management and/or labor programs is scant and impressionistic. In part this is because the results of some kinds of business support cannot readily be measured. Many companies, for example, publicize community blood drives and encourage employees to participate but do not make their own facilities available to local blood banks or otherwise participate formally in campaigns. Others call for volunteers on specific occasions when employees or their relatives need blood.

Actually, the total volume of donations made at places of

employment—or by employees at blood centers on released time—is not known because there is no nationwide data information system. The American National Red Cross has identified "plants and firms" as the source of at least 28 percent of the blood collected by its network of 59 regional centers in 1972, but believes that the true figure is higher. Several important Red Cross blood centers report that employee groups account for a substantial majority of their collections: Baltimore, for example, for 86 percent; Chicago for 64 percent.

The Community Blood Center of Greater New York estimates that employee groups provide two-thirds of its total—more, says an official of the bank, than these groups themselves call for during the year. In many communities, organized employee contributions are slight. Similarly, within individual firms that do take part in blood drives, the ratio of employees who volunteer ranges from under 5 percent to over 25 percent.

What accounts for such differences? Part of the answer lies, of course, in the orientation, programming, and effectiveness of the community blood banks themselves—the nature of the efforts they extend to enlist labor/management support, the facilities they devote to the effort, and their sensitivity to management interest in minimizing lost work time and production.

Blood bank officials seem to agree, however, that the most important single variable is the attitude and involvement of top management. "Where the president of a company," says one, "communicates his interest to employees—particularly where they are made aware that he's giving blood himself—and where the effort is well organized, we always get outstanding results. Where the organization and planning is good but we don't have that kind of real top management support, we'll get good-to-fair results. Where we have neither of these supports, we usually do poorly."

Another blood bank executive says: "Our main point of contact in a company is with the personnel manager. Whether he goes to top management, and what he asks for, often depends on what he's experienced at first hand with blood transfusions, and certainly on how sensitive he is to the need for volunteered blood. We then face the same kind of odds at the top, from where the critical support has to come."

Clearly, the response at the top reflects objective business circumstances as well as personal perspectives—profitability, union relations, the operations and the cost of released time, the number of employees at a location, company health insurance arrangements, and so on.

But where a company program is in effect, blood banking officials have found that employee participation can usually be increased through certain simple measures of planning and organization, typically:

1. A communication to employees from the chief executive inviting them to participate and, ideally, stating his own intention to do so.
2. Appointment of a campaign supervisor and a captain for every 25 employees.
3. A meeting of the supervisor with the captains to orient and educate them in their recruitment tasks.
4. Personal recruitment by each captain among the employees assigned to him or her; and distribution of literature.
5. Reminders and follow-up with those who have agreed to donate.
6. Careful planning by the supervisor with the blood bank and the captains of blood-drawing schedules.

WHY COMPANIES COOPERATE

Most company blood donation programs involve some cost to the company and are motivated primarily by consideration of employee relations and social responsibility. One 8,000-employee firm, for example, which gives donors three hours off, plus travel time for many who are at outlying locations, estimates its annual cost for released time at about $40,000, or $5 per employee. A spokesman explains:

> We happen to be insured by Blue Cross, which doesn't include blood in its policies. Our employees and dependents have been drawing about 1000 pints a year from the bank. Even if we were covered for blood there might be some net cost to us. But the dollars are not great either way. The fact is that you just don't go into a blood program to save money. You do it as a benefit for employees and because you have an obligation to the community.

Nevertheless, a number of offsets to blood program costs have been noted. Those firms that pay all or part of the premiums of indemnity policies covering blood will, if they are experience-rated, realize some saving in rates. (Whether the saving is greater or less than the cost of achieving it will be determined principally by the average hourly pay scale of the workforce, the amount of released time provided or required, and by employee needs for blood.)

Another compensation for costs: Insofar as company participation contributes to adequate supplies of volunteered blood in the community, there are likely, too, to be other health cost benefits—a lowered risk of absenteeism and hospitalization due to infectious hepatitis and to untoward consequences of delayed surgery.

Third, employee morale may be enhanced—not only by the availability of blood when needed, but by the opportunity to donate it as well.

And for many companies, particularly those which serve an important role in the social and economic life of a community, there are by-product benefits in improved public relations.

It is understandable, then, that spokesmen for the government and the volunteer blood banking sector say they now expect business to extend itself even further than in the past. They ask for executive involvement in the processes of regionalization, coordination, and management systems development, and in broadening the base and size of the volunteered blood supply. As a top HEW official puts it, "Employee groups are the most accessible and underdeveloped blood resource in the nation—and our greatest hope for moving quickly to an adequate, all-volunteer supply."

REFERENCES

1. Roughly half the U.S. population, or nearly 100 million people, are eligible to give blood, but only about 6 million do so.
2. To cope with this in some measure the American Association of Blood Banks (AABB), which represents hospital and certain nonprofit blood banks, has created a national clearinghouse whose functions parallel those of its financial counterparts—tracking credits and debts that result from transfusions made outside the geographic area in which recipients have established them, and arranging for physical transfer of blood units to balance accounts. In a less cumbersome arrangement, individual banks of the American National Red Cross honor credits established anywhere within its network without debit, credits, or transfers. The Red Cross also has a reciprocal arrangement with a group of nonprofit blood banks in other communities that are organized into the Community Council of Blood Centers (CCBB).
3. An exception, and insofar as it can be determined the only one, involves the Metropolitan Life Insurance Company. By agreement with the American National Red Cross and the Council of Community Blood Centers, blood is available to the company's employees (and their dependents) anywhere in the United States provided that 20 percent of them make donations each year—and even if in some communities the ratio is lower than 20 percent. This arrangement involves the Red Cross and CCBC with credit exchanges through the Clearing House so that employees outside the communities in which they have banking operations can be included in the program.
4. Richard M. Titmuss, *The Gift Relationship: From Human Blood to Social Policy* (New York, Pantheon Books, 1971).

5. There is no arrangement for collection and analysis of data relating to blood banking operations in the United States. However, an ambitious study resulting in a three-volume report was recently conducted by the Blood Resources Program of the National Heart and Lung Institute. It estimated the supply and use of the nation's blood resource as of 1971, examined its regulation, and studied the treatment of hemophilia. The three parts of the study are known collectively as NHLI's Blood Resources Study and are the source of much of the quantitative data in this article.

6. A liter contains the plasma from about five pints of whole blood.

7. In *The Gift Relationship: From Human Blood to Social Policy* (New York, Pantheon Books, 1971), Richard M. Titmuss contends that, including plasmapharesis, less than 10 percent of the blood resource of the U.S. comes from donations in which there is "the absence of tangible immediate reward in monetary or nonmonetary forms; the absence of penalties, financial or otherwise; and the knowledge among donors that the donations are for unnamed strangers without distinction of age, sex, medical condition, income, class religion or ethnic group."

8. Richard M. Titmuss, "Why Give to Strangers?" *Lancet,* January 16, 1971.

9. See *Post Transfusion Hepatitis: Cases, Death and Cost,* a mimeographed bulletin prepared for the September 1973 Conference on The National Blood Policy by the Office of the Assistant Secretary for Health, HEW.

10. *Report to the National Heart and Lung Institute of the Blood Resources Panel.* Volume IV, April 6, 1973.

11. Efficient management of blood banks has been impeded in general, some believe by the fact that many of their officials have been unavoidably preoccupied with the procurement function and, too, have relatively little training or experience in management techniques.

The Pleasures
of Nonprofitability

If Princeton New Jersey's Educational Testing Service were a public company and not a self-contained tax-exempt nonprofit organization, it would probably have long since emerged as one of the darlings of Wall Street. The knowledge industry has generally manifested more promise than performance, but ETS has demonstrated all the performance any promoter could wish. Over the past 30 years, it has easily racked up a record as one of the hottest little growth companies in U.S. business.

ETS' business is no longer limited to the well-known Scholastic Aptitude Tests required for admission to many private secondary schools, colleges and universities. ETS has helped devise programs to certify that you're qualified in gynecology, pharmacy, or auto mechanics, to license you as a barber, beautician, or real estate agent, and in some parts of the country to permit you to hold a job on the police force or the fire department, or as a social worker. Testing, in fact, has been taking on almost Orwellian proportions in recent years. Close to 6.5 million Americans took ETS' 17 educational placement tests last year. Another 260,000 took its 50-odd occupational certifying or licensing exams.

Reprinted with permission of *Forbes Magazine,* November 15, 1976.

ETS started out in 1947 with a mere $1.4 million in seed capital—much of that in plant and equipment—and a first-year sales volume of under $1 million. Nearly 30 years later, its sales were still doubling every six or seven years, and in fiscal 1976, ended last June, it boasted assets of $37.8 million, sales of $62.9 million, and a comfortable nonprofit of just under $1 million after deducting all its expenses. At the same time, without benefit of any additional infusion of capital, ETS' original $1.4-million stake has grown to nearly $25 million.

IN THE BEGINNING

The company (which is how its executives tend to refer to it) was created in 1947 as a repository for the testing operations of three big educational foundations: the Carnegie Foundation for the Advancement of Teaching, the American Council for Education, and the College Entrance Examination Board—this last a group of 2,500 colleges, universities, and secondary schools that use ETS scores in making admissions decisions.

ETS' president is William W. Turnbull, 56. He sees ETS' impressive growth as something of an accident of history. Like the canmakers who found they were really in packaging, ETS fairly soon discovered that its business was not really testing, but measurement—the measurement of everything from the effectiveness of *Sesame Street,* to the adaptability of programs by Britain's Open University, to the U.S. educational system.

As Bill Turnbull sees it, ETS simply happened to be on the spot in the late fifties when the postwar baby boom broke on U.S. colleges and universities like a torrent. "There was not enough space in colleges and universities to accommodate all the kids who wanted to go, and at the same time there was a tremendous need for help in making admissions decisions. As a result, more and more colleges required entrance examinations in the screening process." The various ETS testing programs—the SAT, the 15 subject achievement tests—afforded admissions officers quick, easy, objective assistance in making their choices.

Distributing, administering, collecting, and scoring millions of such tests obviously involved a mountain of paperwork, and ETS had to create a modern, efficient, technologically oriented management organization to handle the job. It had to automate and it did, funneling its cash flow into data processing and automatic test-scoring equipment on a large scale. (ETS' latest optical scanner now processes 18,000 answer sheets an hour.) "We had to automate or not do the job," says ETS' financial vice-president, David Brodsky, who came to the company in 1955 when the testing boom was just getting under way. "That's really where our capital has gone—into plant and data processing equipment."

Since then the collegiate demand has ebbed, but ETS' growth has nonetheless continued to be brisk. Between 1970 and 1976 the ETS' SAT volume dropped nearly 12 percent; ETS' total sales nonetheless shot up another 80 percent. If collegiate demand was off, the growth in the consumer movement had created a rising demand for accountability—in government, in business, in trade, in the professions. This opened up vast new markets for ETS, which had the testing instruments to measure performance.

ETS was ready for them. As far back as the 1950s, ETS had come up with a test for certifying medical specialists, and since then it has come up with a number of programs for licensing and certifying members of more than 50 other occupations—insurance agents, real estate brokers, actuaries, merchant marine officers, electrical contractors, moving men, city planners, nurses, opticians, Foreign Service officers, and architects.

Over the years ETS has grown so fast and so profitably that its competitors have sometimes complained that, thanks to its income tax exemption, ETS is well-nigh impossible to compete with. Even so, ETS has plenty of competitors. Though no other firm duplicates ETS' range of services, individual firms duplicate every one of them—universities, think tanks, consulting organizations, publishing houses. Even the SAT has its counterpart in the American College Testing Program's ACT tests, used largely in western states. Competitive awareness, says Turnbull, keeps ETS prices low, its quality high.

ETS controls its costs through the same sort of budgetary controls any profitmaking business uses. And, although it has no stockholders to reward, it needs profit for much the same reason any private business does—to finance its growth. Says financial vice-president Brodsky: "We have a rolling five-year projection of what our capital needs are, what we anticipate receiving from outside, and what level of activity we have to support. If it turns out we are making more than we feel we need for capital needs, we reduce our prices."

INVESTMENT AND REWARDS

In the late fifties and early sixties, when rising volume and automation were broadening ETS' testing margins considerably, ETS cut its rates again and again, and even then was able to generate capital aplenty to feed its expansion. ETS' SAT fees today are in fact only 30 percent higher than they were 30 years ago, a period during which the consumer price index just about tripled.

Which is not to say that ETS and its executives do not enjoy the same privileges and emoluments as do those of other successful corporations. ETS operates out of a spacious 380-acre estate in the country near Princeton, N.J. It maintains a conference center with accommodations for 200, a data processing center, a complex of modern offices, complete with recreational facilities. And it pays its employees well. Divide ETS' total labor costs by the number of its permanent employees, and you get a $17,000-a-year average, which is not bad, considering the range includes everyone from maintenance people to executives.

ETS is inherently a labor-intensive business, and so is especially exposed to the pressures of wage inflation. As ETS' growth rate has slackened and the benefits of volume and automation leveled off, the cost pressures have inevitably increased. So far, ETS has kept its labor costs down by shifting the burden from its temporary to its permanent staff. Since 1970, says Brodsky, though ETS' work load has risen 20 percent to 25 percent, the permanent staff has risen only 5 percent, while the temporary staff has declined 31 percent. But there are limits to how far this can go.

Just as it watches its labor costs, so does ETS look for growth opportunities. "We look around," says Brodsky, "and come to the conclusion that there is a need for a certain kind of service, so we develop that and see what kind of interest there may be." In the fifties and sixties, for example, ETS developed the College Level Examination Program to ease the transfer of students from two- to four-year colleges and to award academic credit for off-campus educational experiences. The program met strong resistance from both two- and four-year colleges, but the need existed, and ETS succeeded. Last year ETS administered 94,000 CLEP tests.

ETS has also been supplementing the research and development contracts it has undertaken for outside foundations and governments with projects financed out of its own funds. It specializes in areas like infant behavior, personality, creativity, and cognitive learning. "I think our physical growth is largely behind us," Brodsky says. "So the balance will shift toward research and development and away from the equipment needed to drive the machine." ETS' research contracts now make up 10 percent of revenues.

There's no denying the education markets look especially uncertain these days. A college education is becoming so costly that the colleges and universities could conceivably price themselves and ETS out of a portion of the market. At the same time, higher education is no longer as highly valued as it once was. "We're in a mature growth phase," Brodsky says. Therefore, ETS' trustees have been urging Brodsky to build up ETS' reserves against a rainy day. "We have a small invested reserve—about $3 million," he says, "and as a contingency fund, that's not much. The market abolished buggy whips, and it could abolish us. But if we no longer serve a useful social purpose, why not go out of business? Realistically, there's an instinct in the organization to perpetuation and even growth."

"My own feeling," says president Turnbull, "is that we've gone with measurement of traditional verbal and mathematical skills. The main impetus to growth now is likely to come from the emphasis on competent performance in a lot of different nonacademic fields. Our main contribution in the next ten years or so may be in attempting to put in the hands of college people more information about the noncognitive characteristics of young people—a better statement of their interests and desires. If we succeed, I think the individual's life chances are going to be improved."

Brave New World? Maybe so, but in a society that believes in equality of opportunity, why should such things be left to sheer chance?

Part 3
MARKETING STRATEGY

**Market Target
and Marketing Mix**

MARKETING STRATEGY consists of two distinct and interrelated steps: (1) selection of market target—the particular groups of customers to whom the organization wishes to appeal, and (2) the development of a marketing mix—the choice of the elements which the organization intends to combine in order to satisfy this target group (the 4P's: product, place, promotion, and price considerations). This approach to the marketing process has been successfully applied in a variety of organizations and sectors. Today, in most industries, marketing strategy formulation and implementation is well known and, as can be seen from this selection of articles, is currently being applied in many nonprofit organizations.

	Government	Education	Health	Religious and Charitable	Associations and Others
Health Service Marketing A Suggested Model Gerald Zaltman and Ilan Vertinsky	X		X		
Marketing Your Hospital Richard D. O'Hallaron, Jeffrey Staples, and Paul Chiampa			X		
Using Marketing Strategies to Put Hospitals on Target Richard C. Ireland			X		
Effective Marketing of a Cancer Screening Service Evelyn Gutman			X		
New York City: A Portrait in Marketing Mania William L. Shanklin	X				
Marketing the University: Opportunity in an Era of Crisis Leonard L. Berry and William R. George		X			
A Management Approach to the Buyer's Market William Ihlanfeldt		X			
Marketing's Application to Fund Raising William A. Mindak and H. Malcolm Bybee	X			X	X
King Cotton Fights to Regain His Throne J. Dukes Wooters					X

Health Service Marketing: A Suggested Model

Gerald Zaltman
Alan Vertinsky

Although marketing has traditionally been preoccupied with profitmaking organizations, recent developments suggest that it has important contributions to make to other social sectors, such as health care.[1] The authors contend that it is in the commercial interest of most profit-oriented firms in health-related industries to promote proper health practices. In doing so, firms engage in "social marketing." Social marketing has been defined by Kotler and Zaltman as the "design, implementation, and control of programs calculated to influence the acceptability of social ideas and involving considerations of product planning, pricing, communication, distribution, and marketing research."[2] It is also argued that nonprofit health agencies at the federal, state, and local levels would be more effective if they utilized marketing concepts more carefully and explicitly. Thus, the social marketing concept extends in two directions: to marketing organizations and to social problem-oriented agencies.

Reprinted with permission from *Journal of Marketing,* July 1971.

The health market is rapidly becoming one of the most significant markets in the economies of developed and less developed countries. It is, therefore, increasingly important that attempts be made to gain further insights into human behavior in health situations. This article discusses social marketing in a health context. It is concerned with developing a psychosocial model of health-related behavior with emphasis on less developed countries. Each component of the model is identified and defined, and some of the interactions among its components are noted. While the state of the art suggests that a complete model is almost an impossibility, the authors feel that the model presented here forms a modest but important step in integrating existing knowledge. A mosaic of variables and processes are assembled which are particularly relevant to the health care sector of social life. These variables will help to form a basis for the development and analysis of health marketing strategies. Since the authors' experience in the past two years has focused on nutrition and the improvement of general health practices in Latin America, the model draws heavily on examples in this area.

The presentation of the model and a treatment of its major components and their interaction is followed by a general discussion. The discussion focuses on selected elements of the model and illustrates the actual manifestation of these elements in the marketplace. The article concludes with the model's potential usage by agencies marketing proper health practice and products.

THE MODEL

The model in Figure 1 presents the basic variables and processes believed to be relevant to health care in less developed countries. It is these variables and processes that marketers involved in these nations should be most sensitive to in developing a marketing mix. In addition, most of these variables are probably equally relevant to the health sector of developed countries, although in many cases they will be manifested in different ways. Besides sensitizing the marketer or health agency to key health factors, the model permits an evaluation of the consequences of a chosen marketing strategy which may serve as a basis for either a computer or a manual simulation. Feedback loops provide the ability to trace the consequences of a strategy over time, indicating the existence of marketing facilitators or inhibitors.

The left-hand column in the model shows the exogenous psychosocial variables that have been isolated by health experts in less developed countries.[3] The central section represents the major processes and phenomena in the overall health decision-making process. The right-hand column contains factors frequently found to be operative in a health context, but not as consistent or powerful as the exogenous psychosocial variables.

The Stimulus

The model begins with a stimulus, such as a health education message. The stimulus may originate with disinterested peers or with a public or private change agent. The message or stimulus could also be physiological or it could be the result of some immediately preceding act. For example, the decision not to engage in sick-role behavior, that is, not to make any significant effort to cure an illness, can result in a deterioration of an individual's physical state. The decision in this case was a failure. This deterioration in turn, when it passes a certain threshold, serves as a message stimulating renewed health-related decision-making processes. When the message is a marketing decision variable and represents an intervention strategy by a change agent, care must be exercised in the selection of the message vehicle, the message form, and the message content. This is particularly important for two reasons: (1) Occasionally there is an interaction effect among the three message considerations; and (2) the nature of this interaction is partially culture-bound; that is, the nature of the interaction can vary among cultures so that the interaction effects must be reconsidered in each new cultural context.

Processes of Selection

The message is subject to the processes of selective exposure, selective perception, and selective retention. The intensity and distribution of messages will contribute both to the probability of exposure and retention. The form of the message includes its complexity, structure, and language, and will affect perception as well as retention. For example, the use of professional medical language might limit comprehension and retention of the message.

Three major exogenous variables appear to condition the selective processes: (1) level of formal education attained; (2) shared perception of health between the marketer and the change target; and (3) community social structure and information-flow patterns. In addition to these three major variables, the target market's perceived susceptibility to a given

Figure 1. Strategy evaluation model.

Compart-ment		Possible Selected Variables
Marketing Strategy		Media type (TV, radio, printed) Form (language) Content (specific, general, fear arousal) Intensity and distribution
Processes of Selection		Attitudes toward media (image) Cosmopolitanism Literacy Learning patterns Perceived susceptibility Perceived seriousness Subjective health information consists of: Perceived probability of contracting a disease Consequences Inventory of actions and benefits

Psychosocial Variables (Exogenous)

1 Message characteristics

2 Processes of selection (exposure, perception, retention)

3 Prior subjective health information

4 Change of subjective health information

6

5

14, 15

11 Community information flow

12 Education level

13 Learned perception of health

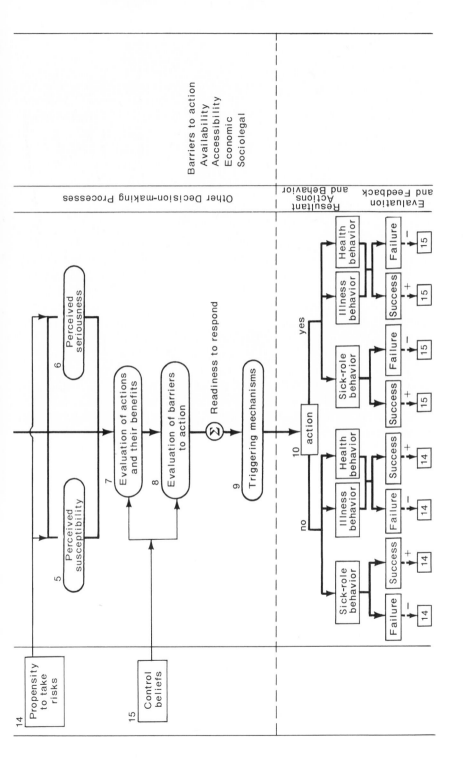

health condition and its perceived seriousness also appear to play an important role in influencing the perception and retention of health messages. For example, an increase in susceptibility to a medical condition may increase attention and stimulate search behavior. It has also been demonstrated that attitudes toward various media, cosmopoliteness, and degree of literacy are important inputs regulating the operation of the selective processes.[4] Finally, learning patterns, which vary among cultures, influence the way in which selective processes function.

Other Decision Processes

The message is thus transformed through a decoding process into subjective health information. This transformed health information modified existing information through a Bayesian process. The objective (transmitted) and subjective (transformed) health information vectors are composed of three subvectors: (1) perceived probabilities of contracting a disease; (2) the consequences of the disease; and (3) an inventory of specific actions and benefits. These data are fed into boxes 5, 6, and 7 as inputs to form perceptions concerning susceptibility, seriousness, and perception of possible actions and their benefits. Numerous studies and the authors' own experiences suggest that these subvectors are the major determinants of health behavior when barriers to a given action are removed.[5] There is also evidence that the total impact of perceived susceptibility and seriousness on behavior is additive. These two variables are discussed at length in a following section.

Perception of susceptibility and seriousness are conditioned by the propensity of the target individual to assume risks. The propensity to assume risk may be affected directly by the retained emotional content of the original message, past experience, and certain attitudinal states such as fatalism.

If the net psychological impact of perceived seriousness and susceptibility is sufficiently strong, there will be an assessment of alternative actions available to the individual. Both benefits and barriers related to alternative responses are weighed. A very important factor mediating perceived benefits and perceived barriers is control beliefs. Control beliefs refer to general feelings of being able to influence aspects of the environment which act upon oneself. In rural areas of less developed countries, control beliefs are generally very strong in a negative direction. Thus, the perceived benefits of taking preventive or curative health actions are discounted, and the salience of real and imaginary barriers to such actions is increased.

The net results of the evaluation of alternative paths of action plus perceived seriousness and susceptibility create a readiness to respond to an opportunity for medical care by either self-treatment or treatment by medical and paramedical personnel. It is assumed that a perceived path of action exists, although this assumption is not always tenable. A major task is to make the population in less developed countries aware of available action paths. While this consideration is not evident in the model, a high readiness to respond may be produced by perceived susceptibility and seriousness, but the individual is unaware of any available outlet to which his motivation may be channeled.

Trigger mechanisms are the stimuli that foster action. They may be physiological and beyond intervention by the marketer, or they may be health education campaigns prepared by the marketer. Frequently, controllable and uncontrollable variables occur together.

Resultant Actions and Behavior

The output of the model is the probability of taking an action. Four types of behavior or paths of action can be outlined, which may be useful for market segmentation.[6] The first is "health behavior," which refers to any activity by a person who feels healthy but undertakes preventive action. The annual physical examination is an example of this type of behavior. However, despite generally favorable attitudes toward such a checkup, few people behave in this manner.

Most immunization services or activities depend on health behavior. Yet, even when no cost is involved and physical distance is minor, it is still difficult, except under epidemic conditions, to mobilize people in less developed countries to take advantage of immunization services on a voluntary basis. Those displaying health behavior tend to be better educated, have higher incomes, and are more integrated into their community's informal communication network than those who do not exhibit this type of behavior. Information obtained from the mass media and from personal sources appears to be equally important in stimulating health behavior, although each performs a different function and is used in a different way. Local disseminators have been effective in persuading people to use a service just prior to the time it becomes available.[7] The mass media function earlier in the decision-making process and act as a source of awareness. This is consistent with communication behavior in other contexts.[8] According to the model, it is reasonable to assume that people who display health behavior must exhibit high-perceived susceptibility and/or high-perceived seriousness. In addition, they must possess sufficient knowledge (regardless of its scientific base) to perceive a condition as being serious and easily contracted. Given these perceptions, the next important consideration is the individual's perception of the state of technology. If he believes the technology is capable of dealing with the medical problem, then he will be in a high state of readiness to respond since there are clear benefits to taking action. The preferred path of action, the outlet for the social product or practice, could be a private physician or a community health clinic. The trigger mechanism would be some phenomenon (for example, an epidemic or health education program) which increases the salience of a serious and easily contracted condition.

A second type of behavior, illness behavior, is "any activity undertaken by a person who feels ill for the purpose of defining the state of his health and of discovering suitable remedy."[9] To define his state of health and search for a suitable remedy, the individual may employ his own health knowledge and/or that of friends, relatives, and professional medical personnel. The individual is likely to use nonprofessional medical personnel if (1) there is little perceived risk of complication; (2) the probable illness is not considered serious; and (3) there are readily available nonethical drugs to treat the illness or its symptoms. The greater the perceived seriousness of the illness, the more likely professional sources will be used.

Perceived susceptibility is not necessarily relevant in this case. In one sense the person has already contracted the illness, and the matter of susceptibility to it becomes irrelevant. Some illnesses, however, can lead to other complications. The synergistic effect of malnutrition and infectious disease is an illustration.[10] In this instance, perceived susceptibility to other illnesses does become relevant.

The third type of behavior, sick-role behavior, is "the activity undertaken by those who consider themselves ill for the purpose of getting well."[11] Sick-role behavior is closely related to illness behavior. People visit physicians to obtain cures as well as to define their state of health. However, sick-role behavior is curative-oriented, whereas illness behavior is diagnosis-oriented.

The ready availability of ethical and nonethical drugs and the knowledge and beliefs about their effectiveness will be a prime factor in the decision to visit a physician or a health service. The mass media have been shown to have an important impact on beliefs about the effectiveness of drugs.[12] This is especially important in less developed countries where ethical drugs are openly sold without prescriptions. Indirectly, endorsements by professional societies may increase the therapeutic credibility of ethical and nonethical medication.

ELABORATION OF SELECTED VARIABLES

This section of the article focuses on the experiences of the authors and others in assisting various private and public agencies in Latin America to market proper health practices. In general, these marketing efforts are directed at members of the lower socioeconomic classes and persons living in rural areas. In most of these countries, this market segment represents the majority of the national population. Given the size of the market, the seriousness of the problems, and the nature of the obstacles involved, the marketing of proper health practices in less developed countries is a formidable task. What follows is not a case study in the sense of analyzing one single health marketing effort, but rather a compendium of relevant marketing episodes and empirical findings. The authors feel that taken collectively these episodes and findings represent an accurate picture of the obstacles and opportunities for health marketing in Latin America. It is not possible, of course, within the scope of one paper to cover each component of the model in Figure 1. The following discussion only highlights some of the more important components and some of their elements.

Psychosocial Variables

Research has shown that there is a wide array of psychosocial variables which have a logical and intuitive relationship to health. Among those empirically shown to be relevant are reference group aspirations, stage of life cycle, family relationships and dynamics, education, race, cultural background and patterns, control beliefs, attitude and peer group pressures, cosmopoliteness, and income.[13]

Psychosocial variables are important for a number of reasons. First, they set parameters for many other variables and processes of relevance to social marketing strategy. For example, if fatalism or feelings of lack of control over occurrences affecting oneself is sufficiently high, then subjective barriers to taking action are likely to develop. In addition, people may become indifferent to the question of susceptibility to a given condition, and little may be gained from campaigns concerned with increasing perceived susceptibility. Similarly, if an individual or a group's ability to empathize is high, the client may have a strong identification with the change agent, thus creating a high readiness to respond.[14]

Psychosocial variables also suggest which appeals to use in health education or promotion campaigns. In a nutrition education campaign being conducted in Nicaragua, El Salvador, Costa Rica, and Panama, the authors are attempting to overcome some of the resistance to change which stem from fatalism found among rural mothers. A series of posters and billboard messages have been developed stressing the fact that a mother does have some control over the child's health. One poster, for example, depicts an infant who is obviously suffering from a severe case of malnutrition. The caption on the bottom simply but firmly states: *"You can prevent this."* This effort alone will not produce substantial or even modest changes in fatalistic attitudes. However, in conjunction with similar efforts by other programs and agencies, slow but definite changes will come about.

With regard to psychosocial variables, it must suffice to say that (1) many other variables have a strong intuitive link with health behavior but have not yet been researched; (2) many of the variables cited above have been inadequately explored and must be studied further; (3) there have been few attempts, if any, to group variables according to the type(s) of health situations for which they are most relevant; and (4) researchers must make a serious effort to study the influence of a given variable in different contexts.

Perceived Susceptibility

Among the most important factors affecting health behavior is the individual's perceived susceptibility to a particular illness.[15] This factor is measured by the subjective probability the individual assigns to contracting an illness. Perceived susceptibility is determined, in part, by selective exposure, perception, retention, and other psychosocial variables such as health knowledge, social class, and ethnic norms. Perceived susceptibility, however, helps activate and determine the character of the selective processes by directing attention to relevant environmental stimuli. An individual who knows little about an illness may think it unlikely that he will contract that disease. For example, people in lower socioeconomic groups perceive themselves to be less susceptible to mental illness than do people in higher-status positions.[16] This is due, in part, to the lack of knowledge among the lower-status groups which would allow them to identify a problem as a mental illness.

The authors' efforts to explore perceived susceptibility in Central America have produced mixed findings. In Panama, many individuals in a pilot study claimed that most children in their community were not properly nourished. However, they did not believe that their own children were malnourished, even though they indicated that their children were about as well fed as other children in the town. What may have occurred is a reluctance to admit, at least to the interviewer, that they are not providing a properly nourishing diet for their children. Another possible explanation is the psychological tendency to deny the existence of a threatening problem which is believed to be uncontrollable. In this case, the denial of existence is handled by lowering the perceived susceptibility. Perceived susceptibility is also a partial function of the nature of the problem. Some illnesses can only be contracted once, others are largely confined to certain geographical areas, and still others are likely to be contracted only during a particular age range. Also, if the illness is hereditary, relatives of a sick person may have a high perceived susceptibility to it. Similarly, if a sickness is communicable, those having contact with a sick person will have a relatively high perceived susceptibility if they are not already immune.

In addition to being susceptible to illness itself, there is the question of susceptibility to the means of contracting illness. Someone who does not understand or accept the germ theory of disease cannot be expected to believe he can become ill by drinking untreated water. Surprisingly, many persons in the United States and elsewhere believe themselves to be susceptible to malnutrition only if they do not eat a sufficient amount of food. Little or no attention is given to the composition of their diets.

Perceived Seriousness

Perceived seriousness is measured by the net financial, physical, and social cost involved in contracting an illness. Whether an illness is considered to be very serious depends on the level of public knowledge about that illness. For example, malnutrition is not always perceived as serious even in its advanced stages, especially, but not exclusively, in the developing countries. The problem here is that some consequences of malnutrition are irreversible at certain ages. If the consequences of an illness are believed to be reversible, then the illness is not likely to be considered very serious. The complexity of an illness is another consideration. If a patient perceives an illness to be highly complex, he will probably believe it is quite serious. Also, the greater the number of symptoms experienced, the greater the perceived seriousness.

In Latin America, and probably in other developing areas, symptoms of illness must be acute before the illness is considered serious. This may be partly due to a lack of medical knowledge which would prohibit early detection. It may also result from different cultural norms. For example, in a medically advanced society there are social sanctions against having a sick child. This appears to be particularly true with regard to nutrition.

The impact of these sanctions is to increase sensitivity to any symptoms of illness and to seek medical advice. This, of course, is facilitated by the relatively greater availability of medical attention. In medically deprived societies where considerable sickness is prevalent, a general norm or sanction against illness is untenable.

The combined effect of perceived seriousness and perceived susceptibility constitutes an important force which can either retard or promote health behavior. These two variables are key determinants of consumer behavior in a health context. If there is little perceived seriousness and/or perceived susceptibility to a real problem, it becomes the task of the change agent, for example, the marketing group, to increase the salience of these factors among the target audience. The modest use of fear techniques can often prove as effective as straightforward educational programs. An increase in either perceived seriousness or perceived susceptibility should produce a corresponding increase in the individual's readiness to respond to such cues or triggering mechanisms as the broadcast media delivering health messages or the arrival of an immunization team for the mass vaccination of a village.

There are many unanswered questions concerning these variables. For instance, what is the relationship between perceived susceptibility and perceived seriousness? Is there an interaction effect? It is quite possible that perceived seriousness affects perceived susceptibility. Knowledge about the seriousness of a condition produces anxiety which, in turn, leads to the belief that one is more likely to contract the particular condition. While this idea has not been empirically validated for any market segment it does suggest that marketers should be somewhat more concerned with perceived seriousness than perceived susceptibility. Additional research is required to determine if the relative importance of the two factors varies under different conditions and for different market segments. It is also necessary to discover the levels of perceived seriousness and susceptibility that maximize the likelihood of a response.

Perceived Benefits

Another important variable is the perceived benefits of taking action. If no distinguishable benefit can be seen, a person is unlikely to use medicine or medical services. The benefits perceived, of course, can be real or imaginary. There is probably an optimal level of perceived benefits for most health items. An unrealistically high perceived benefit can lead to disappointment and a lower readiness to respond in the next time period, while unrealistically low perceived benefits lessen the readiness to respond which tends to preclude any treatment.

The benefits of taking action should be coupled with a proper understanding of the nature of the problem. In many developing countries there is an incomplete understanding of an illness coupled with excessive expectations of medical services. For example, many mothers are aware of only the more reversible visible effects of malnutrition, for example, distended stomach, but they are not aware of invisible and less reversible consequences such as retardation in brain growth. When the visible signs indicate malnutrition, a mother will bring the child to a clinic or hospital where he recovers quickly and is returned home. Because of the apparent effectiveness of the medical treatment, the mother does not pay attention to feeding the child. She can always return the child to the clinic. There are many instances in which the same child was admitted to a medical facility three or more times for the treatment of malnutrition. During all this time, except for the period of the visits, the child's intellectual capacity becomes increasingly retarded. Therefore, the marketing communications mix in developing countries should contain a significant educational component as well as persuasive and motivational components. The educational aspect provides the basis for persuasive and motivational messages. In effect, the educational messages define the need for health, illness, and sick-role behaviors.

Perceived Barriers to Taking Action

Some barriers to taking proper health action have already been mentioned. Barriers may be psychosocial, economic, physical, or a combination of these. In one survey in Central America, it was determined that persons avoided the hospital because it is a place where many people die. This is a case where the individual's attitudes toward a health service channel or outlet play an important role in the use of health facilities. In another campaign to market health services among the educationally and economically handicapped, it was found that the psychological distance between patient and physician may cause patients to ignore the treatment prescribed by the physician. This distance was created in part by the physician's tendency to use professional language not fully understood by the patients who were reluctant to ask for a clarification of the treatment procedure. This can be overcome by having a nurse review the treatment procedure with the patient. Thus, one barrier to the use of medical facilities was reduced by introducing an intermediary in the channel of distribution between the original source of a health service and its ulti-mate user. Thus, some barriers are marketing decision variables; that is, they fall within the control of the change agent.

An error committed in another health marketing campaign was the development of standard posters for all Central American countries. One poster intending to urge mothers not to withhold food from sick children (a common practice) showed a sick child and his mother, both of obvious Indian parentage. While this poster was appropriate for El Salvador and Guatemala, it was not appropriate for Costa Rica, which has virtually no Indians. Mothers in Costa Rica were less apt to empathize or identify with the situation in the posters. As expected, the posters were found to be less effective in Costa Rica than in countries with large Indian populations. Here, the change agent failed to consider audience segmentation on the basis of cultural factors.

Fatalism is another relevant variable particularly prevalent in less developed countries. Fatalism refers to the degree to which an individual recognizes an inability to control his future. The more fatalistic and ac-cepting an individual is, the less likely he is to see any benefits resulting from his own or an agency's efforts to improve his health status. Another important variable concerns the time span of the reward. In general, the more distant the reward the longer it takes to be cured, the lower the perceived benefits.

The authors' work in Colombia disclosed another barrier which re-sulted from an improper reward system. In one program, all members of families which had one or more cases of malnutrition were given food free of charge. After the signs of malnutrition disappeared, the food was dis-continued. When the program first began, cases of malnutrition started to decrease, but shortly thereafter they began to increase. It seemed that despite the provision of food, there was always one malnourished child in the family. After considerable probing it was found that the mothers were deliberately keeping the child in that state in order to continue receiving the free food. Thus, a situation was created in which the health of one child was jeopardized in order to provide adequate diets for others in the family.

There may also be physiological barriers to taking action. For exam-ple, feeding programs often ignore the physiological capacity of the chron-ically malnourished to digest rich foods. In some of these programs, the authors have observed side effects which led to the defeat of the program. Also, many treatments and drugs "which are relatively harmless to nor-mal patients, may be 'the straw that breaks the camel's back' in a starving individual."[17]

Readiness to Respond

Readiness to respond is a function of several factors. The key factors appear to be perceived susceptibility, perceived seriousness, and the net outcome of the perceived costs and benefits of taking actions. Little is known about the relative weightings of these variables in determining the state of readiness, although such weightings are important in formulating marketing strategy; for example, indicating whether to emphasize the seriousness of the problem or to stress the benefits of a given action.

Trigger Mechanism

Many trigger mechanisms can precipitate an action, including an epidemic, a change of seasons which is relevant for influenza immunizations, or a physiological change. The trigger mechanism can also be a marketing decision variable such as a health education campaign. Focusing on marketing strategy, the basic research question is, how do communication processes function in the health sector?

Mass media alone generally will not induce attitudinal or behavioral change unless other environmental conditions are also oriented toward change.[18] In addition, it has been observed that conventional and relatively brief use of the mass media will produce little change.[19] At the same time, however, attitudinal and behavioral change is often impossible without the information input provided by the mass media. More important, the mass media often can be change agents because of the presence of certain environmental conditions or through novel uses of the media. One study demonstrated that radio and audiovisual media were both effective in creating participation in a health program.[20] This study also found that different media served different functions in terms of the type of action and effort they induced.

A study in Costa Rica found that the radio was perceived to be the most believable and reliable mass medium for family planning information, and that magazines were the least believable and reliable mass media.[21] Specialists (priests, teachers, and physicians) known personally were perceived as more creditable than unknown specialists. Relatives are the most reliable and believable nonspecialist personal sources of information. When all channels of communication are considered (personal and mass media), the five highest rated channels are school teachers, relatives, medical doctors, priests, and radio. However, despite the high rating of personal sources of information, they may be one of the most difficult and uncontrollable sources of information for the health agent to use. It is far easier to plan and sustain a health-improvement program using the mass media than it is to marshall the cooperation of hundreds or even thousands of priests, teachers, and physicians. It should be added, however, that the Central America Malaria Control Program is using a "voluntary collaborator" approach with some success. This approach involves training a village resident to identify and take blood samples from persons suspected of having malaria.

An educational campaign conducted through the mass media may effect health knowledge and, eventually, health practices. First, there is the positive experience of communications research in low-health areas of underdeveloped countries. Second, many conducive environmental conditions exist in less developed areas. Many people are exposed to at least one of the mass media. For example, 75 percent of a national rural sample taken in Costa Rica owned a radio, and only 15 percent of the sample had no regular exposure to radio, television, or newspapers.[22] Third, more creative use of the mass media, such as the use of radio forums or structuring broadcast programs to encourage a sense of common identity among an essentially atomistic or noninteractive audience, will help to develop some of the untapped potential of the mass media. The radio-forum technique has been particularly effective, even when individual predispositions and other environmental conditions were not initially oriented toward change.[23]

The information message is also an important consideration. One study of the relative impact of "informational" versus "testimonial" messages in stimulating inquiries about family planning techniques emphasizes the importance of this problem.[24] Another consideration concerns the level of abstraction of the message. For instance, is it best to promote the concept of adequate nutrition or to concentrate on specific nutrition practices, or is there an optimal blend of the two approaches? Current evidence suggests that the greatest need is for information on specific nutrition practices. The authors' data from Latin America, for example, indicate a strong need and desire on the part of the rural population for specific instructional messages. In one instance, the recognition of this need dictated the use of an extensive remedial advertising campaign geared to change selected child-feeding practices.

CONCLUSION

There are some advantages and limitations to using the model in a social marketing context. The model's main contribution at this stage of its development is in structuring and organizing diverse sources of knowledge and data. Many new relationships are suggested which were not previously considered in the literature. The relationship between risktaking and perceived susceptibility is an example. The model also furnishes a basis for simulating health processes which provides a testing ground for health policies before their actual implementation. Furthermore, the model's viewpoint is uniquely suited for developing social marketing strategies. Finally, the model promises to encompass health market behavior in different cultural settings.

However, additional steps are necessary for refining the model. First, the model only promises to be generalizable to contexts other than those used as illustrations. The model should be used carefully, systematically, and in an exploratory way. The model and its discussion do not address questions such as how perceived susceptibility or seriousness is altered by being in a high state of readiness to respond for an extended period of time without any triggering mechanism functioning. Still other problems concern perceived susceptibility and seriousness and readiness to respond. These variables and dispositions are deceptively simple, but, in fact, they are complex and multidimensional. Finally, the importance of the characteristics of the health item or the behavior about which a decision is being made needs to be considered and incorporated into the model in a better and more explicit way.

In closing, the authors would like to repeat a point made earlier. The health and allied industries are becoming an increasingly large factor in the economies of developed and developing nations. Marketing activities represent an important force for developing and tapping this important market and in making a significant contribution to human health welfare.

REFERENCES

1. See, for example, Julian L. Simon, "Some 'Marketing Correct' Recommendations for Family Planning Campaigns," *Demography,* Vol. V, 1968, pp. 504–507; John Zeigler, "Social Change Through Issue Advertising," *Sociological Enquiry,* April 1970, pp. 159–165; and Philip Kotler and Gerald Zaltman, "Social Marketing: An Approach to Planned Social Change," *Journal of Marketing,* July 1971, pp. 3–12.
2. Kotler and Zaltman, op. cit.
3. Nan Lin, Ralph Hingson, and Juan Allwood-Paredes, "Evaluation of Receptivity to a Mass Immunization Campaign in Central America," Department of Social Relations, The Johns Hopkins University, 1971 (mimeogr.).

4. Prodipto Roy, Frederick Waisanen, and Everett M. Rogers, *The Impact of Communication on Rural Development* (Hyderabad, India: National Institute of Community Development, 1968).

5. Irwin Rosenstock, "Why People Use Health Services," *Milbank Memorial Fund Quarterly,* Vol. 44, 1966; see also Godfrey M. Hochbaum, *Public Participation in Medical Screening Programs: A Socio-Psychological Study,* Public Health Service Publication No. 572.

6. Stanislov Kasl and Sidney Colb, *Health Behavior, Illness Behavior, and Sick Role Behavior,* unpublished review (Ann Arbor: The University of Michigan, Institute for Social Research, 1965).

7. Nan Lin and Ralph Hingson, "Communication Processes in a Mass Communication Campaign in Four Honduran Communities," Department of Social Relations, The Johns Hopkins University, 1969 (mimeogr.).

8. Everett M. Rogers with Floyd Shoemaker, *The Communication of Innovations: A Cross-Cultural Approach* (New York: The Free Press, 1971).

9. Rosenstock, op. cit.

10. N. S. Scrimshaw, "Synergism of Malnutrition and Infection," *Journal of the American Medical Association,* July 8, 1970.

11. Rosenstock, op. cit.

12. Lin and Hingson, op. cit.

13. See, for example, Audie L. Knudsen, *The Individual, Society, and Health Behavior* (New York: The Russell Sage Foundation, 1965); Thomas Davis et al., "Review of Studies of Vitamin and Mineral Nutrition in the U.S. (1950–1968)," *Journal of Nutrition Education,* Suppl. Fall 1969; Johanna Dwyer et al., "Adolescent Attitudes Toward Weight and Appearance," *Journal of Nutrition Education,* Fall 1969; and Edward A. Suchman, "Ethnic and Social Factors in Medical Care Orientation," *Milbank Memorial Fund Quarterly,* January 1969.

14. Everett M. Rogers and Dilip K. Bhowmik, "Homophily-Heterophily: Relational Concepts for Communication Research," *Public Opinion Quarterly,* Winter 1970–1971.

15. For other treatments of this variable and another perceived seriousness, see Don P. Haefner, "Preventive Actions in Dental Disease, Tuberculosis, and Cancer," *Public Health Reports,* May 1967; see also John P. Kirscht, "A National Study of Health Beliefs," *Journal of Health and Human Behavior,* Winter 1966.

16. Edna E. Raphael, "Community Structure and Acceptance of Psychiatric Aid," *American Journal of Sociology,* January 1964.

17. John Mayer, "Famine," *War on Hunger,* March 1971, USAID.

18. Melvin LeFleur, *Theories of Mass Communication,* 2nd ed. (New York: David McKay, 1970); see also Rogers, op. cit.

19. Roy, op. cit.

20. Philip Spector, S. Lichtenstein, and H. O. Preston, *Communication and Motivation in Community Developments:* An Experiment (Washington, D.C.: Department of State, Agency for International Development, 1964).

21. F. B. Waisanen and J. T. Durlok, *A Survey of Attitudes Related to Costa Rican Population Dynamics* (San Jose, Costa Rica: American International Association for Economic and Social Development, 1966).

22. Gerald Zaltman, Juan Allwood, and Graciola Camillo, "A Survey of Child Feeding Practices, Communication Behavior, and Education in Costa Rica," *Bulletin of the World Health Organization*, 1971.

23. Roy, op. cit.

24. Jean Hutchinson, "Using TV to Recruit Family Planning Patients," *Family Planning Perspectives*, March 1970.

Marketing Your Hospital

Richard D. O'Hallaron
Jeffrey Staples
Paul Chiampa

Over the past 10 years, dramatic changes in population, competition, and government regulations affecting the health community have created problems for many hospitals throughout the United States. Projections of a 20 percent drop in inpatient census following the full implementation of professional standards review organizations is enough to cause any board of directors to think twice about the hospital's future. The purpose of this paper is to recommend that nonprofit hospitals with adequate financial resources create the position of director of marketing in order to deal with the problems at hand, to develop new sources of business and revenue, and to better manage the long-term growth of nonprofit hospital systems.

In profit-oriented industry the marketing director's role has traditionally been to deal with problems similar to those now faced by hospitals, and there is no reason why marketing as a discipline cannot be applied to nonprofit institutions. To support the case for such a position in the typical nonprofit hospital, the article will explore the different areas in which the marketing director might operate in order to demonstrate the utility such a position could have. The analysis will cover health care marketing in general, with special emphasis on marketing organization, marketing information services, and marketing research for the private nonprofit hospital. Hospital marketing may seem a novel concept, but it is one that can work.

At the present time, nonprofit hospitals engage in a number of activities which can be classified as marketing. Certain hospital personnel are responsible for employee relations, public relations, and other communications efforts inside and outside the hospital; many hospital auxiliaries mount fund drives and run various community activities; and the administration, in general, is responsible for long-range planning. Many activities carried out by various hospital departments, such as x-ray, laboratory, nuclear medicine, and emergency service, constitute marketing behavior. There is no apparent direction or coordination among these groups in most situations, however, that could ultimately pay off in greater awareness and use of hospital facilities by people in the area served by the hospital.

While planning is one key to a hospital's steady growth, a concerted effort to market the hospital and its services should be employed in order to maintain the superior image of the institution, to keep the public and physicians aware of the services the hospital has to offer, to insure the hospital's financial health, and to acquire both large and small charitable donations and funding from the many available appropriate sources which include individuals, private industry, foundations, and government. The marketing director would try to maximize these funding flows and would serve key hospital administrators as they need marketing and public relations assistance in dealing with all their publics—patients, doctors, employees, and members of the local community.

Appointing a marketing director, improving the hospital's marketing information system, and directing more marketing effort toward other publics should benefit the hospital in several ways:

1. By increasing the flow of funds and volunteer interest in the hospital.
2. By improving the hospital's ability to meet the needs and wants of its patients, the community, and hospital visitors.
3. By attracting more and better physicians and other professionals to affiliate with the hospital.

4. By assisting in the development of long-range strategies and objectives.

5. By helping to answer questions related to allocation of resources and product pricing policies in order to ensure a reasonable rate of return on investments.

6. By developing and overseeing the hospital's overall communications effort.

7. By dealing in an organized manner with local, state, federal, and regional planning and regulatory agencies.

The marketing director for a private nonprofit hospital would focus attention on four broad marketing areas which represent the relevant publics of a hospital: patients, physicians, the community, and government.

PATIENT MARKETING

The hospital's first step in patient marketing is to define the patient population, since the nature of this market will influence the hospital's choices of services to offer, the doctors it will seek, and its potential sources of financial support. "With the patient market defined, a hospital has four broad options from which to select its own marketing orientation; that is, it can choose a community orientation, a special public orientation, a research orientation, or a mix of these options."[1] In the past, many hospitals have been oriented to the community surrounding their hospital. The marketing director should assume responsibility for collecting information on population shifts in the area and changes in hospital usage by this population, in order to determine how these changes will affect the hospital, and recommend appropriate reactions to any significant changes found.

The key phases of a patient's experience with any hospital are (1) knowledge of services offered; (2) confidence in services offered; (3) admission to either inpatient or outpatient services; (4) exit from inpatient or outpatient services, plus contact through follow-up billing and repeat services.

The marketing director could work with nursing and administration to determine the level of care and satisfaction that should be rendered to patients in all service areas. "Dissatisfied patients can lead to an exodus of physicians, diminished benefactor support, and government agency intervention."[2] Since hospitals usually do not compete in this area of service, it could constitute an excellent opportunity for a hospital to gain a competitive advantage or distinctive competence.

PHYSICIAN MARKETING

Because most hospitals rely heavily on the medical staff to bring patients to the hospital, physician marketing becomes a vital area of concern for all administrative personnel. "This reliance on physicians creates two related problems: (1) attracting doctors to the hospital staff, and (2) making sure the doctors actually use the hospital's facilities once they are on the staff."[3] It is common for a hospital to grant privileges to physicians who have similar rights in three or four other hospitals in the vicinity. The hospital then finds itself very much in competition with other hospitals for the favor of these physicians. Many hospitals today are attempting to solve this problem by developing an office building for physicians adjacent to the hospital. Providing special equipment, such as gamma cameras, cardiac diagnostic equipment, and CAT scanners, special radiology diagnostic services, nuclear medicine, ultrasound, radiation therapy, and special care facilities, is another means used to lure physicians to a particular institution. The marketing director could serve as consultant to both a medical director and an administrator in determining what new services should be offered both to attract doctors to the hospital and to increase the utilization of the hospital's personnel and facilities. Developing an environment in which "a doctor wants to practice" is a highly important goal which requires sensitivity and coordination to achieve.

COMMUNITY MARKETING

"The purpose of community marketing is to develop close relationships between the hospital and the main organizations in the community."[4] Employees, volunteers, physicians, and patients all have community ties which should be exploited in the most effective manner possible. The marketing director should also maintain close contact with representatives of local media to promote news coverage of the hospital's programs and activities. An individual in this position should be prepared to disseminate pertinent news and information about the hospital via annual reports, publications, and personal appearances, and in addition this person must organize the hospital's means for gathering information on community health needs and perceptions and for providing health education programs to the community. A strong marketing information system is seldom seen but sorely needed in all health/hospital situations today. The marketing director's function is not only to increase the hospital's frequency of contacts with outsiders but also to ensure that the hospital projects a consistently professional image to the people it wishes to attract.

GOVERNMENTAL AGENCY MARKETING

The full impact on the health care system of PL 93-641, The National Health Planning and Development Act, will probably encourage hospitals to set a high priority on the concept of a recognized marketing director for three reasons:

1. PL 93-641 has teeth—congressional guidelines which must be followed—and to a significant degree requires the "quasi" use of the rules of evidence in its hearings and review of various projects and programs. In other words, the decisions of the local health systems agency (HSA) boards and the state health coordinating council must be logical and based on the presentation of hard facts. An HSA that makes politically motivated decisions contrary to the facts presented to it will surely be challenged in the courts, and its decisions will not be upheld.

In the future, hospitals must know where they are, where they are going, and where their competition is if they are to obtain approval for their requests from local and state comprehensive health planning agencies and to succeed in developing new programs. A good marketing information system will help them accomplish these goals.

2. In the future, PL 93-641 will play a very important role in the evaluation of existing services in all hospitals throughout the country. A smart hospital executive, therefore, will want someone on the staff who is both interested in and able to monitor clinical service usage within the institution and community.

3. The health planning and development law has two major parts. One involves planning, coordination, and review of existing programs, and the second requires aggressive efforts to develop and organize new systems for the delivery of health care in each region. The marketing director could assist department heads, physicians, and administration to clearly conceptualize innovative ideas which are in their minds and hearts and also help them gain acceptance for these innovations. The hospital has the talent necessary to develop new ideas and new systems, but the

handling of day-to-day problems keeps administrators from sitting down and completely thinking through many of their ideas for improving the various types of care the hospital delivers. The marketing director could pull together these thoughts, translate them into coordinated programs throughout the community, and fulfill a very important role in regard to PL 93-641.

ORGANIZING FOR MARKETING

Marketing, as a concept, is basically foreign to the people who work for and in a hospital. It is probable that most of these people—staff, employees, and physicians—would be extremely skeptical and somewhat annoyed at the very idea of hospital marketing. To overcome these attitudes, an effective marketing effort will require a director competent in both marketing and interpersonal skills who can communicate to these groups what the job really is and, more importantly, what a marketing director can do for them.

It is extremely important that this person report directly to the chief executive officer (CEO) of the hospital. If this position is structured otherwise, or if it does not receive full commitment from the CEO, the marketing director runs a very good risk of being misunderstood and/or ignored. With the full commitment of the CEO, however, the marketing director would be in a position to supply administration and department heads with the latest facts about the environment and about the market—its size, composition, and trends. He would be able to participate in setting annual objectives and to help the departmental staff establish plans and obtain and allocate the resources required to achieve its objectives. He would serve as the marketing conscience of the organization, helping to overcome the tendency of administration to become so engrossed in its operations that it loses sight of the fundamental market forces and relationships. He would be responsible for coordinating and managing the various marketing services needed by others in the organization. For example, if the head of the x-ray department decided that his equipment and staff were being underutilized, he could consult with the marketing director; together they might discover a solution latent in the situation or, alternatively, search out ways to develop new business and better utilize the department's tremendous investment in personnel and equipment.

The marketing director, in addition to his other duties, should assume responsibility for the hospital's public relations effort, since public relations departments carry out numerous marketing activities in hospitals.

The public relations officer is responsible for managing the organization's routine communication with its regular publics, developing campaign strategies for special projects, filling requests for information, and in general putting the organization in a favorable light.

Public relations, however, does not handle all the marketing activities normally occurring in an organization. Public relations does not carry out marketing research into consumer needs, perceptions, and preferences. It does not take responsibility for developing and introducing new products or services, nor does it determine the characteristics of the basic products being offered to the market. Thus, the marketing director should assume responsibility for functions carried out in other areas of the hospital and for developing activities which are not currently being implemented.

The size of the hospital, its resources, opportunities for improving efficiency, and the need for some central source of marketing leadership are the factors that determine whether a hospital will establish a new marketing position and the scope of such a position if established. Hospitals of significant size should consider setting up a marketing department staffed by the marketing director, a research assistant, and a secretary. The anticipated out-of-pocket cost for the department, including data collection costs, would depend on the compensation set for the staff and the extent to which the department develops.

MARKETING INFORMATION SYSTEMS

Various managers within a hospital may have very specific marketing information requirements. In order to design an internal record system, the marketing director would query a cross section of manager-users about their informational needs. Of ultimate importance to an information system are questions related to the types of decisions these managers make and the information they think they need to make these decisions. When opinions have been gathered, the director can proceed to design an efficient internal record system that reflects (1) what managers think they need, (2) what managers really do need, and (3) what is economically feasible.

Such information might include a list of potential donors, data on the activities of rival hospitals, and a forecast of future economic conditions affecting the hospital. Hospital personnel should be given incentives to pay more attention to gathering and passing along information to the marketing director.

The research assistant is essential to the marketing director in carrying out this information service and in conducting the necessary marketing research studies. The research assistant should determine market characteristics and market potential, analyze market share and sales, study competitive products and new product acceptability and potential, engage in short-range forecasting, study hospital trends, and keep aware of governmental and health planning activities at multiple levels.

In summary, hospital administrators need timely, accurate, and easily retrievable marketing information if they are to make intelligent marketing decisions, and this information can be supplied by an active marketing department.

QUALIFICATIONS FOR POSITION

The type of person needed to fill the role of marketing director should be one who is a self-starter, has leadership ability, relates well with people, has a basic understanding of marketing and management, and has a facility with statistics. This individual must have some degree of sales orientation and a willingness to learn and work. It should not be difficult to find well-qualified people to develop the marketing programs described in this paper.

Such an individual is typical of many of the young people graduating from colleges and universities every year. An individual with a bachelor's degree in marketing or a master's degree in related subjects with an ability to write would be an excellent candidate. The level of students and the range of subjects they cover in the normal course of a university education in some of this country's higher quality schools are impressive. It takes a highly motivated person to handle all these subjects, and many such graduates would be willing to enter the hospital system at reasonable salaries. A person qualified as marketing director would be comparable in age, responsibility, training, and knowledge to many key managers presently in hospitals.

CONCLUSIONS

The typical nonprofit hospital faces many of the same problems which challenge larger, profit-oriented businesses and organizations in terms of a changing consumer, a more competitive environment, and increased governmental regulation. Unlike these organizations, however, most hospitals do not have an effective mechanism for dealing with such problems. Traditionally, demand for hospital facilities far exceeded the supply so that it was not important to think of such matters. As this supply-demand relationship begins to shift, marketing factors become all the more important and should be handled.

Marketing as a concept is novel to hospital administrators, although marketing behavior is not. Marketing activities carried on by a marketing director, rather than being antithetical to the goals of a nonprofit hospital, should be seen as a tool by which the hospital's administration can more effectively reach its goals of providing more and better care to the patient at a more affordable price.

REFERENCES

1. Philip Kotler, *Marketing for Non-Profit Organizations* (Englewood Cliffs, N.J.: Prentice-Hall, 1975), p. 308.
2. Ibid., p. 310.
3. Ibid., p. 312.
4. Ibid., p. 314.

Using Marketing Strategies to Put Hospitals on Target

Richard C. Ireland

Ask any administrator what the purpose of his hospital is, and the answer is likely to be, "We're in the business of serving the needs of our patients," or, "Our primary purpose is to provide high-quality health care to the community that we serve." Both are marketing statements. The first statement is somewhat too limited in scope; a hospital actually serves other people's needs as well, such as those of its employees, physicians, other health agencies, and the various constituents of its service community. The second statement, though a good one, is too broad to be completely meaningful. The words "quality," "community," and "serve" demand further definition.

Regardless of how they are phrased, such statements clearly imply a basic motive to serve patients. However, a comparison of philosophy with reality seems to point up a basic contradiction: complaints from health care consumers are increasing, as shown, for instance, by the rising

Reprinted, with permission, from *Hospitals, Journal of the American Hospital Association,* June 1977.

number of malpractice suits. All of which points to a basic fact of life: what is said philosophically, or even practically, does not always get translated into actuality.

The implication is not that hospitals are failing to serve their patients, but that they are making marketing statements without really practicing marketing. Moreover, many of the basic tools of marketing, such as publications, public relations, and even research, used for decades by hospitals, have not usually represented a coordinated effort—an effort that is part of an overall marketing program.

Marketing is as old as civilization and has evolved from simple bartering and selling into a professional discipline whose primary purpose is to orient the organization or enterprise toward the needs, wants, and desires of the markets it seeks to serve. For example, before developing many of its consumer goods, the General Electric Company carefully studied the habits of homemakers to determine their needs, how they liked their kitchens organized, and what their problems were in preparing meals. The result has been a plethora of small electrical appliances to meet virtually every need that a homemaker has in preparing meals. GE used an "outside-in" approach: rather than developing a product based on assumptions about what people need and then taking it to the market, the firm used a marketing approach, which demands that the market's needs, wants, and willingness to purchase be determined before the product is developed.

Today, hospitals, as well as many other not-for-profit organizations, are looking to the field of marketing in hopes of finding a fresh approach to solving the problems of maintaining a productive census level, attracting physicians and resources, building strong community commitment and awareness of their existence and capabilities, and the like. Marketing by itself, of course, cannot completely solve many of the problems faced by today's hospitals. In fact, given the extraordinary regulations that hospitals are subject to (far more than any business enterprise), the momentum toward a national health plan of some kind, and the involvement of third-party payers, a true market orientation, in an economic sense, is probably not possible.

The proper application of marketing principles and techniques can, however, to the extent that they are supported by top management, make a significant contribution. It is vital, after all, that hospital resources be used in the best way, and marketing is one management system, perhaps the only one, that can help a hospital make maximum use of all its resources in delivering the kind of health care patients need and want, while developing the kinds of programs and services that will attract and retain needed medical and supportive staff. Hospitals need, in fact, to gain a deeper knowledge and understanding of their markets—namely, physicians, patients, employees, donors, the community, and so forth—if they are to remain competitive, to optimize resources, and to provide the right services at the right place at the right price and at the right time.

IMPORTANT DIFFERENCES

To look to marketing, and specifically business marketing, is to look in the right direction. To compare marketing as it is practiced in business with how it might be applied in a hospital is a useful exercise. But there are some important differences to note.

For instance, a hospital marketing program is a management system that effectively links the hospital with all the elements of its service community and, in this regard, is far more complicated than business marketing. Hospitals deliver services primarily on the basis of referral. Physicians, agencies, and others refer patients to one another and ultimately to hospitals. While business marketing certainly operates on the basis of referral, or word of mouth, the primary emphasis is on selling.

Another important difference is that, in health care, service delivery involves more people, all of whom influence patient satisfaction. Admitting clerks, nurses, various technicians, physicians, and supportive personnel are all involved in delivering services directly to patients. In business, the salesman acts as sole agent.

WHERE TO START

All marketing programs, whether in investor-owned or not-for-profit organizations, begin with an analysis of where the organization has been, where it is now, and where it wants to go. Ideally, a hospital that is developing a marketing program should begin by conducting a series of research studies to gather information that will help define the characteristics, needs, and wants of its market and market segments, so that it can develop or revise its services and communications accordingly. Following are the types of studies that should be conducted:

1. An *historical audit of records* to determine the pattern of service utilization over the past three to five years. Such a study would include a tabulation of patients admitted by diagnosis, by date, and by patient days for the given diagnosis; average length of stay by diagnosis and by physi-

cian; patients admitted by physician; demographic variables of patients, such as age, sex, income, religion, occupation, and geographic location; services performed by patient diagnosis; and other pertinent information.

2. An *attitude and needs survey* of major market segments, such as current and discharged patients, physicians, hospital employees, and the community. Such studies are complicated and expensive. However, if a hospital wants an effective marketing program, an attitude and needs survey is a necessary expense. The results of such a survey will provide the basis for developing services and communications, estimating demand, and so on.

3. An *interview survey* of key individuals in the hospital to draw upon their intimate knowledge of operations and goals.

Obviously, the first and third surveys are the easiest to conduct. However, even if a hospital cannot afford to conduct an elaborate attitude and needs survey, there is much that can still be done. Every hospital, for example, has some type of patient evaluation or "we'd like to know" form to determine patient satisfaction and to solicit suggestions. Most, however, ask for simple "yes" or "no" responses, which are of limited value in determining real patient satisfaction. By redesigning the form to capture better data on patient satisfaction and by coding the form so that responses can be tabulated by computer, a hospital can develop an important survey instrument, one that can be used to continuously monitor patient needs and satisfaction.

At any given time, a hospital will be dealing simultaneously with several segments of its overall market. It may be attempting to recruit a specialist to the medical staff, trying to attract newly graduated nurses, appealing to the community and physicians to use a new diagnostic service, or just building goodwill and career awareness by hosting a health fair. In every case, each market segment and problem will require its own mix of marketing principles, techniques, and strategies.

The idea of the marketing mix is represented by the "four Ps": product, price, place, and promotion. It is the task of the marketer to relate these elements to the consumer.

Research, or trying to find out the who, what, when, where, and why of consumer behavior, and the management elements of planning, organizing, staffing, and controlling all fall within the context and relationships of the four Ps.

The marketing mix stresses the fact that the marketing process is total and provides a platform for developing and explaining the relationship of marketing to the rest of the organization. The key to success in applying and understanding the marketing mix lies in the concept of rightness—the right product in the right place at the right time with the right promotion.

A hospital develops a mix strategy for each of the four elements on the basis of what it knows about its markets and of the marketing objectives it must achieve. The emphasis is placed on developing a mix combination that will simultaneously serve the best interests of the target market and the hospital.

THE HOSPITAL "PRODUCT"

Hospitals do not normally view their services as products. But when a product is broadly defined as something that fulfills a need or want, the term fits comfortably in the hospital domain. If hospitals do not sell services, they do sell the benefits, or satisfactions, that their services provide. Diagnostic services, for instance, usually reduce anxiety, increase chances of recovery, and contribute to better health.

One of the first tasks of the hospital marketer is to develop an inventory of available services complete with costs, utilization, target market, demand, and benefits offered. Such an inventory will help in planning and in deciding what is needed and to what extent there is duplication with other health care facilities. Ideally, a hospital should also conduct a service inventory of all health care facilities within its service community. The service inventory should be part of the historical audit.

It should be noted that the development of services depends on a number of factors, not all of which are related to marketing. Capital to purchase equipment, technical problems involved in a service department, and state regulations are just a few such factors. A key responsibility of the hospital marketer, however, is to report to the management team on the demand for and utilization of services by physicians, support staff, patients, and the community.

THE ROLE OF PLACE

A group of concerned citizens recently approached the administration of a large urban hospital and demanded that certain services be provided in their community. A careful investigation disclosed that there was, in fact, a real need for these services, and a satellite outpatient clinic was set up. A service was thereby provided at the right place. However, while the hospital is to be complimented for its responsiveness, it should have uncovered the need and responded before the fact. That's marketing.

"Place" refers to the efficient distribution of goods and services through distribution channels, outlets, and sales territories, so that the products are, theoretically, convenient to the market. "Place" in business includes warehousing, inventory, wholesalers, transportation routes and fare structures, production facilities, and access to raw materials. In a hospital situation, place refers to the hours the admitting office is open, the surgical suite schedule, the by-appointment-only policy of the x-ray department, the 24-hour emergency department service, the distance from the hospital to a physician's office, the location of satellite units, the signage directing people to various departments, and the proximity of one department to another.

Therefore, in analyzing its service/product inventory, a hospital needs to ask such questions as the following in order to determine the "right" place: Is each service scheduled so that it is convenient for physicians and patients? To what extent should variations of the service, in the form of home-based nursing care, for example, be provided to the community? A well-formulated place strategy, based on solid market information, can greatly improve the ability of a hospital to deliver needed health care services.

Family practice clinics, patient support groups, home care, emergency ambulance services, school-based training programs, "dinner at your door" programs, the physicians' office building located next to the hospital, and volunteer programs are all examples of decisions to offer the right product in the right place.

THE RIGHT PRICE

Pricing decisions are complicated for both businesses and hospitals. However, within the limits of antitrust legislation, business organizations have far more control over pricing than hospitals do. A business can, if it chooses, charge what the market will bear, offer discounts and trade-in allowances, and adjust prices on a regional basis. Demand for a product is often stimulated through price strategy decisions. Furthermore, price decisions are more closely related to the marketing function in the business sector than they are in the hospital sector. Generally, prices in business are determined by costs plus a fixed margin or markup, as well as by the market. Such is not the case with health care.

Pricing is probably not in the domain of the hospital marketer. The right price, the one that the health care consumer is willing to pay, is not dictated by the hospital fee schedule but by the extent of the consumer's insurance coverage. In fact, demand for health services is related directly to the extent of coverage; the more coverage, particularly of first-dollar costs, the more the demand (A. A. Ehrbar, "A radial prescription for medical care," *Fortune,* February 1977). However, the relationship between hospital fee schedules and perceived quality of service and the effect of rising hospital costs and insurance costs on the health care consumer are interesting and legitimate problems for the hospital marketer.

Pricing strategy can become an important factor with regard to those services that are not covered by insurance, such as certain educational programs, some patient services, and so on. Price is an important consideration, too, in decisions to provide services to physicians and in-house staff.

THE RIGHT PROMOTION

Promotion refers to paid advertising, public relations, selling, premiums and incentives, trade shows, and atmosphere.

The most notable difference between the hospital and business sectors in promotion efforts is the use of selling. Selling assumes that the prospective customer will not buy unless first approached by a salesperson with a sales presentation. Although hospitals could lean a little more in this direction, it is doubtful that they will ever need to develop a sales force to call on prospective patients. Selling is probably not a useful tool for the hospital marketer.

However, hospitals need people—administrators, trustees, public relations staff—who are effective in maintaining liaison with influential people in their markets and in building key personnel relationships that will ultimately benefit the hospital. Working closely with reporters and media representatives is a good example of this "soft," or "missionary," form of selling.

The term "promotion" is used frequently in business, but the term "marketing communications" probably has more meaning for hospital marketers. Many hospitals send out appeals and messages to individual markets and publics without the benefit and organization of a marketing plan. As a result, they run the risk of creating a distorted, fragmented, and perhaps even contradictory image of what they are all about. Such an approach ends up being a waste of the public relations budget.

A new logo, well-designed publications, and a local advertising campaign can only be effective when each communications element is part of a total hospital marketing program. Failure to coordinate the promotion effort is a major weakness in many hospitals and one over which the hospital marketer has the most control.

In developing a framework for communications, it is a useful exercise to take the inventory of services that a hospital currently offers patients, physicians, employees, and the general community, and to analyze each service in terms of the satisfactions, or benefits, that it provides the consumer. Here's how to do it:

1. Develop a four-column list with these headings from left to right: service, feature, benefit/satisfaction, proof.
2. In the service column, list all hospital services. Leave plenty of space between items.
3. In the feature column, list, for each service, at least three distinctive aspects that will hold true regardless of whether or not the service is ever used. For example, a feature of the x-ray department could be the fact that all examinations are scheduled or that all personnel are highly qualified or prominent. These features would hold true whether or not anyone ever came in for an x-ray.
4. In the benefit/satisfaction column, list at least one benefit that will be derived from each feature if it is used. For example, a benefit of scheduled x-ray examinations is reduced waiting time; another benefit may be more effective medical diagnosis and prescribed treatment.
5. In the proof column, list evidence to substantiate the claim that are usually used as proof of a benefit claim. In some instances, proof can be implied.

A TEN-STEP APPROACH

A hospital marketing program should begin with a genuine commitment from the administration to invest a specific amount of money and staff resources. Hospital marketing should be viewed as an investment, rather than as an expense, that will help optimize the capacity and ability of the hospital to effectively respond to the needs of its market segments.

The following step-by-step approach should help guide the marketing effort:

First, set up a marketing task force under the leadership of someone who is thoroughly knowledgeable and experienced in marketing.

Second, conduct a situation analysis to answer the question, "Where are we now?" The analysis should include a definition of the nature of the hospital's purpose and organization, an analysis of the hospital's environment and competition, a market audit of the hospital's capabilities and possible opportunities, a historical audit of records to determine utilization and trends, and an interview survey of key individuals in the hospital. Third, prepare a preliminary report to management that includes recommendations on how to proceed.

Fourth, based on an analysis of exploratory work and management support, develop research priorities, certain benefits are derived from service features. The claim that scheduled x-ray exams reduce waiting time is probably so obviously true that it need only be printed as such in hospital brochures without any need for proof. Statistics, case histories, photos, and testimonials and objectives are evaluated to determine the nature of the organization's markets and image.

Fifth, conduct research studies as follows: an audit of patient load and physician staffing over the past three to five years; an attitude and needs survey of a sample of former patients, physicians, and staff; positioning studies to determine where the hospital stands in relation to existing medical/health care facilities and the health care needs of the community; consensus surveys on possible distinctive competencies of the organization; and an audit of other health care facilities in the community.

Sixth, analyze research results, outline market potentials, and draw up possible objectives that state where the organization should be heading.

Seventh, assign priorities to markets, and formulate a market mix test for one or two target markets.

Eighth, using results from the first step, develop a complete annual marketing plan with policies, objectives, strategies, marketing programs, priorities and schedules, organization and assignments, budgets and resource allocations, and feedback and review procedures.

Ninth, devise an implementation schedule, or calendar of who will do what.

And, finally, establish a report system and tie it into the hospital's management information system.

SUMMARY

Hospitals would do well to explore the techniques and strategies of marketing as they search for new, more effective, ways to attract patients, qualified personnel, and other resources, and to deliver services that are needed and wanted and that will be used. A coordinated, ongoing program of touching base with the hospital's markets and employing marketing strategies to ensure that the right resources, once determined, are obtained and that services, once developed, are used is a concept whose time may have come in the health care field. Marketing is, in short, nothing more than keeping a hospital on target.

Effective Marketing of a Cancer Screening Program

Evelyn Gutman

Effective marketing of selected health-care services can stimulate more active and conscientious participation by people in safeguarding against disease. The intrinsic importance and appeal of good health can facilitate a positive response to communications aimed at promoting health. Although cancer is a widely feared, devastating, and often fatal disease, but if detected early, its prognosis is markedly improved, costs are reduced, and cure is possible.[1,2] By discovering early cancers, screening services improve cancer care.[3] Instead of allowing fear-induced paralysis to predominate, appropriate marketing motivates people to help themselves. A well-marketed, high-quality screening service that brings the benefits of screening to people at significant risk for cancer will contribute to the optimal treatment of this disease. This chapter discusses the target groups for a cancer screening service, and suggests a marketing plan to reach these groups.

TARGET MARKET

The target market may be segmented into two groups: the health consumers and the supporting agents. The health consumer market includes the potential screenees and the general adult public. Potential screenees are the ultimate consumers, while the general adult public, which serves as a powerful influence group, comprises potential screenees and younger people not yet old enough to qualify for periodic screening tests. These groups are differentiated in terms of their roles. For example, potential screenees are asked to participate in the screening program, whereas the general adult public is encouraged to initiate and promote participation of friends and relatives who are eligible for screening.

Potential screenees include consumers who fit the risk profile for a particular disease. This population can be broadly identified according to age, sex, geographic location, socioeconomic level, race, and religion. Cancer screening programs are generally aimed at men and women over the age of 40, who live within the catchment area of the health facility. Forty is considered the appropriate starting point because this is the age at which screening for early detection is most effective in breast, colon, and uterine cervical cancers, which begin to appear in significant numbers.

The target population is further refined at the screening service to include people who require screening. A questionnaire is used to identify whether risk factors are present in the individual's profile. Consumers at significant risk are encouraged to return periodically for a routine checkup.

The target group of the general adult public comprises people who can be expected to stimulate participation by potential screenees. Men and women 30 years of age and over are generally chosen because their opinions are most likely to be respected by potential screenees, who are their peers. The general adult public can initiate and promote participation of friends and relatives because they have a strong impact on decisions concerning proper health care. As an added bonus, by distributing information to younger people, and helping them to become attuned to the value of good health care well before they actually become eligible for screening themselves, they will be prepared to participate when they come of age.

The market of supporting agents includes external and internal groups that provide credibility, approval, and the support needed by a screening service. Of the possible sites for screening, consider the example of a hospital-based service. Here, external groups may include the media, potential donors, social and civic organizations, the local community, purveyors and reimbursement agencies, health regulatory agencies, local community physicians and medical societies, regional medical societies, hospitals and other health providers, health-related industry representatives, government health agencies, and government-elected officials and governing bodies. Internal groups may include organizational governing committees and administration, medical staff and employees, the Board of Trustees, the Development Office, the Health Education Department, Training Programs, the Nurse Education Department, the Volunteer Department, and the Women's Auxiliary Group.

Two segments of the supporting agent market have special importance: the physicians throughout the region, who serve as a critical link to a substantial portion of the consumer market; and the health-related industrialists, labor leaders, and politicians, who represent a large financial and potent political force within a given region.

Physician groups include local community physicians and medical societies, regional medical societies, such as the American Cancer Society and the Oncology Society, and organizational committees and medical staff. The physicians that comprise these groups set the rules for practicing medicine within the region. Their support will improve the image and acceptability of the service markedly. Many physicians are members of several medical groups, thereby expediting information transfer among them.

The lay person is most familiar with two types of physician: the primary care physician and the specialist. When seeking advice about health care and checkups, consumers often look toward their primary care physician—the internist or general practitioner who delivers general medical care. Certain specialists also serve a primary care function. For example, many gynecologists perform preliminary breast examinations, and general surgeons will carry out examinations of the uterine cervix.

All physicians who play a primary care role communicate directly with the potential screenees and, therefore, should be informed about the benefits of the health service so that patients at significant risk for a particular disease can be screened. The specialist—particularly the cancer-related specialist—should be educated about the effectiveness of screening so that when consumers and other physicians ask for advice, he or she can provide an answer based on up-to-date, thoroughly evaluated information. General physicians who are busy and may not have the time to evaluate all specialized information themselves will look toward these experts for the final word on screening.

Health-related representatives in industry—both in management and labor—can give valuable support to the service. Medical directors, labor leaders, and top management have an interest in maintaining worker

health to ensure high productivity. Many of the major industrial companies have set up occupational health and medical facilities to meet
industry health needs recognized by both management and labor unions.
Exxon, DuPont, Johns Manville, and others have well-equipped medical
facilities for employees. Politicians can also take a supportive stance for
screening programs to help services get started and, more importantly,
attract broad-based support. Since both groups wield strong political and
financial influence, it is wise to promote their support.

Although screening makes sense to most of the supporting groups,
and many are willing to approve a screening service, these groups still
need extensive background information and education in order to provide
the best assistance. Neither these groups nor the population at large fully
appreciates the value of screening or how it can be done effectively. A
deeper understanding of screening by key supporting agents—including a
knowledge of why some screening models fail while others succeed—will
promote solid proposals and strong support from these groups.

MARKETING OBJECTIVES

Marketing is targeted to facilitate acceptance, utilization, and support for
the screening service by the target groups. Short-term objectives are
aimed at increasing awareness, explaining the purpose of the new service,
bringing those who have positive or neutral attitudes into the service, and
maintaining continuing involvement of supporters. Long-term objectives
are geared toward maintaining awareness, changing attitudes for higher
utilization, promoting continued support, and obtaining the cooperation
of additional professionals and institutions to support screening.

Service Objectives. The service is designed to gain acceptance and
win approval of all target markets. If screenees find the service both
pleasant and worthwhile, they are apt to return for checkups as well as
personally endorse screening to friends and relatives. The standards and
techniques employed must be acceptable to the supporting agents for
their continued approval and support.

Place Objectives. The channel of distribution is chosen to be easily
accessible to users, physicians, and staff. An established, well-respected
facility improves the credibility of screening as a reliable and useful health
service.

Price Objectives. The price element is intended to gain acceptance
from potential screenees, encourage participation by people at significant
risk, and win approval from supporting agents, particularly third-party

payers, for incorporating screening as a reimbursable item in their policies. In order to connote the high quality and inherent value of the service, the program is offered at an appropriate charge.

Promotional Objectives. Designed to reach large portions of the target population, the promotional elements include public relations, personal selling, sales promotion, advertising, and packaging.

1. *Public relations.* Informs, increases awareness, and promotes support. Done properly, public relations provides high credibility and a positive image for the service as well as its institutional supporters.
2. *Personal selling.* During the introductory phase, triggers personal communications channels and builds confidence and support. By providing immediate feedback, it permits modification of the message based on receivers' needs. For the long term, personal selling can modify health-care attitudes and behavior.
3. *Sales promotion.* Encourages trial utilization and fosters goodwill for the service. It develops enthusiastic supporters and reinforces the public relations effort.
4. *Advertising.* Brings about widespread awareness, reminding the market about the service and its institutional supporters.
5. *Packaging.* Stimulates acceptance and utilization, fosters positive feelings about the service, and strengthens other promotional elements.

Recognition of these marketing objectives provides direction and measurable goals toward which the screening center staff may aim. Short-term objectives can be accomplished during the first or second year, while plans for long-term objectives should aim for completion in the third and fourth years of operation. Management by objectives of the service and its marketing plan leads to a high level of success in the service.

MARKETING ELEMENTS

The marketing plan combines all the marketing elements to maximize convenience for the user and effectiveness for detecting early cancers:

- ◆ *The service.* Modern and appealing.
- ◆ *Channel of distribution.* Credible and easily accessible.

◆ *The price.* Affordable yet connoting high quality.
◆ *Promotion.* Should influence large portions of each target market.

The Service

In order for the cancer screening service to keep pace with medical advances, an advisory board of experts should be available at certain stages to evaluate results and propose modifications. Maintaining high standards helps win continued approval and support of influential supporting agents.

The screening tests included in the service should be relatively inexpensive, quick, and painless. Since screening is designed for large numbers of people, costly tests are avoided. High-cost periodic exams are unacceptable for most health consumers. More important, expensive tests for large populations would be undesirable to the regulatory and reimbursement agencies that might pay large portions of the screening bill in the future. Whenever diagnostic efficacy can be preserved, painful tests should be avoided in order to promote consumer acceptance.

The service should provide a worthwhile experience for the screenee, if the desired levels of utilization and repeat visits are to be achieved. Emphasizing consumer education throughout the screening process creates an informative environment. The general approach in the communications message is to accurately represent the cancer problem and its possible consequences, coupled with direction for constructive action to avoid advanced disease.

People tend to be more receptive to information regarding health matters while participating in a health checkup than they are during their normal daily routines. A health education program can transform waiting time into a constructive learning session. Educational programs may include oral and poster presentations, take-home written materials, well-produced films, and well-trained, warm, responsive attendants to answer individual questions. This results in a service which improves public understanding of cancer—particularly the factors within the individual's control. Furthermore, since the screenee becomes better educated, the relevant ideas and suggestions will tend to be communicated by word of mouth to friends and relatives.

Positioning[4] the service with reputable health-care agencies fosters a quality image and credibility. Since screening is relatively new, publicizing the support of recognized agencies improves credibility. Such agencies might include well-respected local health providers, Blue Cross, the American Cancer Society, and the Department of Health.

Channel of Distribution

There are several alternate channels for delivering a cancer screening service. It can be offered directly through the outpatient facility of a modern community hospital, as a part of the primary care function of physicians in their daily medical practice, at medical facilities located in industrial plants where annual examinations are already being performed, by traveling screening teams offered to special groups who cannot readily reach a screening facility, at local board of health facilities, or at private health facilities that specialize in screening and health maintenance. One or several of these alternatives is possible.

Modern, clean, attractive hospitals can be ideal screening sites. Many hospitals are equipped to train and provide the primary, ancillary, and backup services required for screening. Community hospitals are often respected and established within the market area, and many target market members look toward them for their health care needs. Community hospitals are usually easily accessible for most members of the target market.

Since the physician is the gatekeeper for a large portion of the potential screenee market, ultimately, the best and most efficient site for performing screening may be in the physician's office. For this reason, a service center should consider adding a professional training program that teaches the physician screening techniques not learned in medical school, which enables the physician to offer modern screening services in his or her own office. Professional training is also a valuable means for recruiting physician support.

Providing screening services at industry medical facilities is often appealing to large companies. Groups of people can be screened through these facilities. Here, screening has two major advantages: The screenees are sent to the service during the course of a normal work day, and the cost is covered by the company. Since the employees are readily available, efforts can be concentrated on delivering a high-quality service including pertinent health education. Another advantage is that the worker's health history is available, thus permitting assessment of the worker population's screening needs. Here, screening services can be planned in advance.

Traveling teams of screeners are a special type of alternative. The American Cancer Society and the Guttman Institute for Breast Cancer Detection have used this approach to introduce screening to the general public. However, traveling teams have been very costly. While they may be useful in promoting a special trial offer, this approach seems impractical and unnecessary as a channel of distribution for the long term, except for special disadvantaged groups, which have difficulty reaching an established center.

Finally, local Board of Health facilities and private health facilities can help institute screening. The roles of these groups vary according to the nature and scope of their ongoing activities.

The Price

The price is designed to be affordable, yet imply the high quality of the screening service. A charge should be attached to screening, as to most medical services, because people tend to have more confidence in a service that requires a fee. Although consumers say they prefer a free service, many believe that a good service cannot be offered gratis. Therefore, a fee should be charged to all except the medically indigent (defined as those people with a family income of less than $7,000).

On the other hand, since charging a fee directly to the patient tends to reduce consumer participation in screening, the best alternative is for third-party payers to include cancer screening as a reimbursable fee. Coverage by third-party payers would also improve the service image and credibility, as well as help gain acceptance for the service. Third-party support underwrites the quality of the service and avoids the barrier of direct payment by individual screenees. Many medical services are provided on this basis—that is, the physician or medical facility will perform a reimbursable service more readily because there is no direct extra charge to the patient, while nonreimbursable services are avoided.

Promotion

Of the promotional elements, public relations and personal selling communicate best with the target groups. Initially, public relations and sales promotion deserve emphasis. Subsequently, personal selling, advertising, and packaging play a major role.

Public relations helps establish the credibility of the screening service. Particularly, support from experts and subsequent coverage in editorial sections of the media have more credibility than advertising sponsored by the health facility. Because cancer is a "hot" issue, local newspaper and radio support can often be recruited, and sometimes the media will adopt a health issue as a worthy cause. Public relations is critical because an expensive promotional campaign could be attacked as a misappropriation of health resources.

Personal selling is another major element of implementing a successful screening service. It is directed toward key members of each target group in order to maximize impact. The sales force is not the traditional type of personal selling group. It differs in that members of the service and other health personnel will handle the selling function in addition to their specific capacities in the hospital. Training them to respond effectively to cues and feedback permits modification of the message according to the receiver's needs. Personal contact adds a persuasive human element to communications designed for influencing health-care behavior. For some target groups it is primary, whereas for other groups different promotional elements warrant greater emphasis. It reaches the people in the media, who in turn influence health care behavior through articles, reports, newspaper items, and TV spots. Personal contact adds a human element, which reinforces earlier public relations and advertising messages to potential screenees and to the general adult public. Personal selling by knowledgeable professionals is a key to promoting a screening service among physicians.

The initial function of sales promotion is to get media support and, later, to engender the goodwill of selected target groups. For example, an opening event may be planned to publicize the service and get media support. Also, incentives may be offered to encourage publicity by local shopkeepers.

Advertising stimulates primary demand, promotes participation, and associates screening with its institutional supporters. Advertising works well with people who have either positive attitudes about screening or who have not yet formed attitudes. People harboring generally negative attitudes are not influenced by advertising. During the introductory phase, advertising introduces screening and increases awareness of the service. As the service continues, other promotional elements predominate, while advertising continues to remind people about the screening program and keeps the service and its supporters' names in the minds of the members of the target market.

Packaging creates an appealing, convenient service facility. It gains acceptance from physicians, gets approvals from regulatory agencies and financial assistance groups, and ensures easy access and utilization by the consumer. Packaging elements include ambience at the service, hours offered, attitude of the staff, types of services offered, type of equipment used, fee charged, effective messages and presentations, and an appealing logo. Effective packaging builds confidence and creates a tranquil, non-threatening image for the screening service.

GENERAL MARKETING STRATEGY

In order to achieve the first-year marketing objectives, the general marketing campaign incorporates the following strategies:

- Introduce educational approach to bring the cancer problem into perspective.
- Emphasize personal advantages to stimulate the interest of the particular target group.
- Characterize the service in terms of familiar personalities or other people who have benefited from screening.
- Turn the disadvantage of risk for cancer into an advantage of being able to seek a cure.
- Emphasize multi-institutional supporters to promote credibility.
- Provide informational approach that directs target groups to action.

Educational Approach

The publicity received by the cancer issue has hindered a proper educational approach to the problem. The many different types of specialists involved with cancer express a plethora of conflicting viewpoints. This results in information that is patchy and frequently misleading. For instance, one widely held misconception that must be discouraged is that cancer strikes suddenly—like catching the flu. In reality, most cancers develop over a lag period of approximately 20 years. Explaining this incubation phase opens the door for understanding that prevention can help preclude certain cancers altogether, and how screening can detect developing cancers and render cure possible. Further explanation of how the service fits into the total picture of solving the cancer problem helps the target audience position prevention and screening in their minds. Thus, introduction of a proper educational approach—obtainable only through the assistance of a unified group of cancer experts from different fields—is the first strategy of the marketing campaign.

Messages vary according to the information needs of each target market. Messages to the medical profession can be more detailed, while broad concepts should be explained to lay people. But with all the confusion surrounding the cancer problem, both professional and lay people need to have screening and the cancer problem put into proper perspective.

Personal Advantage

The personal advantages of screening may be emphasized to convince market members why they should support or participate in screening. Advantages vary from one target group to another according to their particular needs. For example, to potential screenees, screening is one way to protect against the consequences of advanced cancer. The general adult public's desire to help their family and friends can find expression through promoting screening and prevention—in particular, mothers and fathers can be reminded of their responsibility as family health agents and as family providers. Explanations to physicians can demonstrate how this service helps promote screening for their private practice and results in curing more patients in their community. Emphasizing the personal advantages that screening and prevention offer to the individual stimulates interest and gives the audience both a reason to be attentive to the message and a reason to act.

Familiar Personalities

Characterization of the service in terms of well-known personalities who have benefited from early detection helps promote acceptance of the service. Either someone famous who has been cured of cancer, or an appealing "everyday" person who has a cancer success story is enormously encouraging news to people paralyzed with fear of the disease. When such famous personalities as Mrs. Ford and Mrs. Rockefeller publicized their successful battles against cancer, the result was a striking increase in consumer demand for early detection, particularly at breast cancer detection clinics.[5] Personalities for the marketing campaign should be chosen with care and must be bona fide cancer victims.

Disadvantage vs. Advantage

The strategy of turning a disadvantage into an advantage can be used to change the risk for cancer into a selling point. The potential screenees, who are at risk for cancer, are given the chance to fight at a time when the insidious disease is silent. In contrast to the usual announcements that frighten people and offer no solution, the audience can be reminded that although they may be at risk for cancer, they can defend against it if they act now, while they are still asymptomatic. Creating a sense of immediacy encourages people to act, not merely think about the issue. Explaining why screening works and providing numbers that people can understand helps people work toward a positive conclusion about the screening service. Namely, the screening service offers the opportunity to discover cancer while it is silent, which gives it the best chance to be cured. This strategy motivates potential screenees to satisfy their needs for survival and security by participating in the screening program.

Institutions and Credibility

Support of the sponsoring institutions should be emphasized in the marketing campaign. Several major cancer-related agencies sponsoring a service that offers comprehensive, high-quality screening, showing a unified approach, with broad-based support, creates a positive image that is not self-serving, and gives the program the credibility it needs to gain acceptance. This strategy of emphasizing the institutional advantage is incorporated into the campaign by identifying each supporter on the logo for the service. Logos are displayed in all newspaper advertisements and direct-mail pieces, as well as on stationary and other promotional tools. In addition, a brief account of the multi-institutional sponsorship can be printed in the literature of the service.

Information to Direct Action

Finally, people need direction toward immediate concrete action to help prevent delay by target market members. Potential screenees can be urged to participate in the screening service; and specifics, such as hours offered and where, can be explained. The general adult public can be urged to support the service, take responsibility for promoting it to their family and friends, and demand that screening services be more widely available.

Special influence groups can be urged to initiate or promote specific programs that will improve cancer care. More screening programs are needed, as is more preventive action. For example, smoking lounges in schools can be closed, nitrosamine carcinogens can be removed from school lunches (nitrites in frankfurters, bacon, and other preserved meats are converted to nitrosamines), and carcinogenic candy can be eliminated from school candy dispensers (red licorice has milligram quantities of coal tar-derived red dye). Specific information about what action should be taken must be explained if the audience is expected to support the service and improve cancer care at this time.

The underlying campaign theme should emphasize the benefits of screening. First, and most appealing to the consumer, is that he or she is not defenseless. Screening is a pathway for fighting certain cancers successfully. Reminding men and women of their roles as family health agents and their responsibilities to protect and provide for their families broadens the screening effort from a self-directed act into a recognized societal obligation.

The second benefit of screening is that the detection of cancer in its early stages reduces hospital and treatment expenses. For the consumer, the high cost of late cancers exceeds the coverage offered by most types of health insurance. For hospitals and third-party payers, early treatment of cancers reserves available resources for advanced cases which cannot be detected early. Finally, through his support of screening, the physician demonstrates leadership in reducing costs while at the same time promoting high quality health care. This expression of leadership helps counter outside criticisms that doctors practice medicine without sufficient attention to its costs.

EVALUATION SYSTEM

An evaluation system is required to measure the effectiveness of the marketing plan. Indicators that may be used include:

- ◆ Response rates according to yearly objectives
- ◆ Surveys of screenees and potential screenees
- ◆ Qualitative determinations of physician support
- ◆ Level of follow-up rates achieved

The overall evaluation is based on the marketing plan's ability to impart the desired impression and information, and to motivate target groups to action.

Response rates from relevant target groups to each of the marketing elements serves as one measure of effectiveness. The level of utilization is a good indicator for the impact of the total marketing plan. Other evaluation points may include response rates from social and civic organizations following marketing presentations; number of requests for information from potential screenees and the general adult public; geographic origin of requests to determine which areas are responsive and which need more attention; level of support provided by key members of relevant target groups (community approvals of the screening service activities and amount of media coverage); amount of time and financial assistance provided by volunteers and donors; and levels of approval by such groups as the health regulatory agencies, community physicians, and other local health centers.

Special surveys measure efficacy of various components of the marketing mix. Each screenee can be asked about what stimulated him or her to participate and how he or she heard about the service. Monthly tabulations of such data monitor the impact of each marketing element and indicate how the marketing mix can be strengthened to increase utilization. Questionnaires administered periodically to screenees at the service can determine level of satisfaction with various service components. Telephone surveys can measure the level of awareness, general impressions about the service and its attributes (convenience, hours offered, price), and intention to participate among potential screenees.

Small meetings with key members of the hospital's medical staff and community physicians are useful to determine levels of satisfaction and identify any problems they perceive in the service or its operations. Since one goal is to increase the demand for screening, community physicians can be surveyed quarterly to determine how many of their office patients (1) inquire about the established screening service, and (2) request a screening examination from their doctor. This information can be collected at a central location where doctors congregate (for example, in a hospital medical record room which doctors visit every week to "sign out" patient charts).

The level of compliance for follow-up by physicians and screenees should be determined for all positive screening results. Any subsequent diagnostic workup or treatment recommended after screening should be done promptly for the screening program to be effective in detecting early cancers. A series of three follow-up letters, one to the doctor and two to the patient, can achieve a high level of compliance; however, in some cases, follow-up phone calls may be needed.

Careful evaluation of target group responses and intentions provides a monitor which can maximize the effectiveness of the marketing program. Molding the screening service to meet the needs of relevant target groups and to influence market behavior and participation is critical to the success of any screening program. Effective marketing of a high-quality screening service that brings the benefits of screening to the people at significant risk of cancer is a major step toward making cancer a curable disease.

CONCLUSION

Marketing efforts are directed toward making cancer screening desirable to the relevant target groups. Market acceptance and utilization of the service is necessary to reap the benefits screening offers for conquering certain types of cancer. Similarly, proper marketing of health-care practices, including prevention and health maintenance, can be expected to improve the individual's health and extend his life expectancy. For instance, proper marketing offers invaluable assistance to the following kinds of campaigns and programs: antismoking, avoidance of excess salt, reduction of dietary fat, weight reduction, and maintenance of physical fitness.

Marketing can hasten the introduction and adoption of more responsible health care. Through increased frequency and effectiveness of the health message, people can be persuaded to safeguard their health. People often take good health for granted and seek medical assistance only in the face of overt illness. This climate makes especially meaningful the marketing of products, services, and ideas that foster health preservation. Potentially, this enables marketing to improve the health standard of our society.

REFERENCES

1. U.S. National Cancer Institute, *Cancer Patient Survival*. Report No. 5 National Institute of Health, Publ. No. 77-992. Washington, D.C.: U.S. Government Printing Office, 1976, pp. 8–9, 78–117, 160–163, 168–170.
2. Scotto, Joseph and Leonard Chiazze, *Third National Cancer Survey: Hospitalizations and Payments to Hospitals*. National Institute of Health, Publ. No. 76-1094, National Cancer Institute, Bethesda, Maryland, March, 1976, pp. 65–89.
3. American Cancer Society, *1977 Cancer Facts and Figures*. New York, 1976.
4. Heskett, James L., *Marketing*. New York: Macmillan Publishing Co., 1976, pp. 52–53, 209–210.
5. Fink, Raymond, News Events and Response to a Breast Cancer Screening Program. *Public Health Reports,* May/June 1978.

New York City:
A Portrait
in Marketing Mania

William L. Shanklin

A substantial amount of contemporary marketing literature focuses on the utility of applying marketing thinking and techniques to the problems of nonbusiness organizations. Its genesis lies in the mentally stimulating works of Kotler and his collaborators.[1] Kotler and Levy's[2] thesis, that marketing is more than a business activity, has gained widespread acceptance since their often-cited 1969 article was published. Today, there is considerable agreement among marketing scholars that the conceptual framework of marketing can be applied effectively to fulfilling the needs of nonbusiness entities and their salient publics.[3]

One nonbusiness problem with overwhelming societal and economic ramifications is the plight of New York City (NYC). Events in the largest U.S. city frequently augur national urban trends. Moreover, the city's financial demise could cause detrimental reverberations throughout the nation's banking infrastructure. The portfolios of some of the country's leading banks are heavily invested in NYC securities.

A proposition concerning the NYC crisis is advanced in this article: namely, that the crisis can be explained succinctly within the structure of perhaps the most rudimentary thought in all of marketing—the marketing concept. The exposition is intended to show (1) that the NYC dilemma is in no small way attributable to years of mismarketing on the part of the city's elected officials; and (2) that competent marketing can aid in restoring the city to solvency and in preventing recurring crises.

The problems of NYC are not singular. The city's maladies are really not so different, except in degree, from those of numerous other financially plagued municipalities. The underlying causes tend to be the same. Thus, the ensuing discussion is also applicable to an assortment of local governments, even though the well-publicized NYC example is used as a familiar case in point.

CONSUMER ORIENTATION

The first postulate of the marketing concept holds that a business should fulfill consumer needs and wants in the target markets in which the firm chooses to operate. If a firm is to remain competitive, it must take its orders from the marketplace. The validity of this principle has been corroborated time and time again. Analogously, the goal of a city government should be to fulfill its constituents' municipal needs and wants. Consumer orientation in city government is achieved through the introduction and fine tuning of needed services at prices the public is willing to pay in the forms of taxes and selective remunerations such as bus and subway fares.

Local governments provide some services to all their citizens on an equal basis. In addition, a variety of specialized or tailored services are provided to groups of residents with disparate and unique needs. Consequently, it is sometimes a gross oversimplification to speak of services as though they were homogeneous and of publics as if they were singular. Whenever government renders diverse services to multifarious publics, for the quid pro quo of taxes or selective recompense, it is practicing market segmentation.

Table 1 casts major municipal services into a typology. The purpose of classifying services is to establish a frame of reference for discussing services throughout the remainder of this article. Services are first categorized as differentiated and undifferentiated. A city government engages in market segmentation with the former but not with the latter. Water, sewage, sanitation, parks, and street maintenance are undifferentiated services; the vast majority of the public benefits from them.

Table 1. A typology of municipal services.

	ESSENTIAL		NONESSENTIAL	
	COMPENSATORY	NON-COMPENSATORY	COMPENSATORY	NON-COMPENSATORY
Undiffer-entiated	Subways Buses Water Sewer Sanitation	Fire Police Courts	Zoo	Parks Libraries Radio/TV stations
Differ-entiated	Low-income housing	Welfare Medical care Primary schools Secondary schools	Museums Universities Swimming pools Skating rinks	

Welfare, low-income housing, primary and secondary schools, and museums are paradigms of differentiated services; they are utilized selectively. Middle-income publics normally do not qualify for welfare, businesses do not use low-income housing, retired citizens have no need for primary and secondary schools, and museums are selectively attractive to some social strata.

Second, services are dichotomized into classifications of essential and nonessential. The nomenclatures are meant literally. Without essential services (fire and police protection, garbage collection, and the like), a city could not long survive. Nonessential services (zoos, parks, libraries, and so on) inarguably are culturally, recreationally, and aesthetically desirable but, if absolutely necessary, a city could function without them.

Third, services are typically either compensatory or noncompensatory. Zoos, museums, and subways usually produce revenues sufficient to defray all or part of their costs of operation. Libraries, parks, and fire departments generate no revenues, only costs.

One fact is undeniable: NYC provides its citizens with a plethora of services of all descriptions. Yet this fact by itself is insufficient information upon which to base judgments about its degree of consumer orientation. Service orientation cannot be perfectly equated to consumer orientation—to augment services is not necessarily to become more responsive to consumer needs and wants. Fewer services, improved services, and lower taxes might be more congruent with the majority of the public's preferences.

CONSTRAINTS ON CONSUMER ORIENTATION

The marketing concept calls for a constraining influence on consumer orientation. In the absence of constraint, the idea of fulfilling consumer needs and wants can be carried to illogical extremes. Levitt[4] pejoratively terms unbridled, runaway consumer orientation "marketing mania." Marketing mania is descriptive of the organization that becomes obsessively responsive to fleeting consumer whims without adequate concern for cost and price considerations.

Profitability is the restraint imposed upon consumer orientation in business firms. The firm is expected to fulfill consumer desires, but only if doing so contributes to long-run profitability. This constraint is manifestly inappropriate for nonbusinesses since earnings are not their goal. Two alternative normative constraints are proffered. Normative here means that the constraints are ideals that an organization should continually strive to achieve.

For compensatory services, the constraint of revenue adequacy is suggested. The incremental revenues from these services should be adequate to cover their incremental costs. As Moyer[5] has stated, even though the nonbusiness shuns profits, it nevertheless must price its services to meet their costs. On balance, this criterion has been spurned in NYC. For instance, until the advent of the financial crunch of 1975, subway fares were kept at artificially low levels by subsidies.

The idea that compensatory services should sustain themselves is anathema to some individuals. For example, the chairman of NYC's Board of Education was outraged by what he called a "means test" for higher education. His indignation arose from a suggestion by New York State's Commissioner of Education that the tuition-free NYC university system charge the same student fees as the state universities. Paradoxically, raising the maximum fees to $800 per year would actually enable the poorest third of the students to save money through the state's aid programs. In reference to the board chairman's outrage, a leading newspaper commented that the habit of such preposterous cant is the city's root problem.[6]

The constraint of cost minimization is viable for noncompensatory city services. While few or no revenues can be expected from fire and police departments, primary and secondary schools, and welfare programs, costs nonetheless can be controlled. However, evidence is lacking that costs in NYC have been controlled, much less minimized. Compare the per capita spending for vital services in NYC with those in other municipalities: NYC spends $100 for police and fire protection, Atlanta $41; NYC spends $151 for health and hospitals, Chicago $30; NYC spends

$295 for education, Philadelphia $217; NYC spends $316 for public welfare, Detroit $26; NYC spends $88 for pension funds, Los Angeles $21.[7]

Inadequate revenues from compensatory services, coupled with the excessive costs of all services, have forced the price (taxes) of living in NYC to record levels. The burden of confiscatory taxation falls particularly hard on middle-income and business taxpayers who contribute the most dollars to the city's support. The denouement has been a gradual withdrawal from the city by these all-important segments of the population.[8] It is axiomatic that exchange is unlikely to occur when consumers believe the price of a proposed transaction to be too great for its perceived value. The erstwhile NYC resident has avoided forced exchange with the city by fleeing from it.

INTEGRATION AND COORDINATION

The marketing concept also holds that all marketing activities should be integrated under one line executive so that they can be effectively coordinated. The corollary, of course, is that all functional areas of the firm should be integrated to facilitate effective coordination within the entire organization. These requirements reflect systems thinking. The efficacious coordination of system components promotes the attainment of a synergism.

There is every indication that NYC officials have given short shrift to systems thinking and to the classical management functions of planning, organizing, directing, and controlling. For instance, services have proliferated. The quality of services, notably sanitation and welfare, has often left much to be desired. Incompetence in or inattention to the pricing and administering of services has driven prices (taxes) so high that many taxpayers have abandoned the city. Forecasting, budgeting, planning, and control have either been inadequately performed or ignored, as evidenced by the city's financial straits.

RECAPITULATION

A paradigm developed by Levitt,[9] called a marketing matrix, assists in clarifying the true meaning of the marketing concept. The matrix, with terminology slightly adapted to fit a government organization, is shown in Figure 1. The horizontal axis depicts the degree to which government's

Figure 1. The marketing matrix.

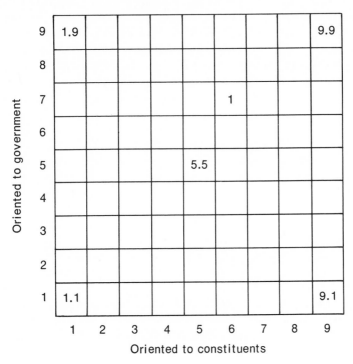

Adapted from Theodore Levitt, *The Marketing Mode: Pathways to Corporate Growth* (New York: McGraw-Hill, 1969), p. 220.

actions are oriented toward satisfying constituents' needs. The vertical axis shows the extent to which government's initiatives are in its own best interests. On both scales, 1 is the lowest and 9 is the highest rating.

Coordinate 1,1 represents the position farthest removed from correct implementation of the marketing concept. At this point, neither the welfare of the government nor the public is served. Illustrative is the government that provides few services, or ineffective services, to the public and wastes taxpayers' dollars in an inefficient, bloated bureaucracy. Location 1,9 is the position of a government that tends to its own internal needs but is remiss in serving the needs of the public. So much emphasis is placed on fiscal conservatism, rigid record keeping, and operating "by the book," that consumer needs and common courtesies are overlooked in the process. Position 9,1 indicates a situation where government is so bent on pleasing the public, catering to almost its every need, that it endangers its own financial survival. As services proliferate, the government's financial position deteriorates accordingly. Coordinate 9,9 is the ideal locus in terms of adopting the marketing concept. A proper balance is struck between the benefits government can provide to constituents and the costs of providing them.

The marketing matrix cogently captures the essence of NYC's problems. The city is assigned a rating of 1 on the vertical axis. The fact that the government is in its present financial condition is proof enough that its actions have not been compatible with survival. On the horizontal scale, the low-income market segment is given a scale value of 8 or 9. This segment has been treated well. It received a vast number of differentiated services, in addition to the undifferentiated services available to all citizens, and contributes much less in return. The market segments composed of middle- and upper-income citizens and businesses receive a rating of, say, 3 on the horizontal scale. The city has not been consumer-oriented toward these publics. They pay dearly for the services available to them and for the differentiated services intended primarily for low-income and indigent residents.

NYC has committed figurative suicide by intrepidly adhering to the misguided policy of "services to the people, exorbitant spending notwithstanding." The protracted indulgence of elected officials in a kind of euphoric binge in marketing mania can be attributed partly to the admirable motive of wanting to serve the public well, and partly to the reprehensible, but understandable, self-interest motive of currying public favor and thereby staying in office. Motives aside, the fact is that municipal policymakers who confuse providing a costly myriad of services with fulfilling consumer needs are certain to suffer a rude awakening eventually.

WHERE TO TURN?

The state of affairs in NYC is the culmination of years of mismanagement and thus will take time to remedy. Nothing short of bankruptcy or a federal or state bailout may be able to save the city from its present predicament. However, city administrators can militate against recurrences. Although it is not a panacea for curing the city's ills, the marketing concept can serve as a helpful guide to better times.

The first step toward recovery requires that the city fathers gain correct insights into their true mission: to provide services to fulfill relatively lasting (vis-a-vis temporal) citizen needs which legitimately lie within the purview of municipal government. Historically, they have instead mistakenly sought to redistribute income through an extensive welfare system, through low-cost education, through rent control, and so on ad infinitum. The goal of income redistribution cannot be accomplished in the long run because taxpayers who must assume the burden will leave. Raising taxes to compensate for the revenues lost in the exodus will only accelerate withdrawal. The job of income redistribution is that of the federal government, not NYC.[10]

Because the city government has pushed into spheres beyond its charge, it has ample opportunities to narrow its service offerings and, in so doing, to obtain a welcome respite from pyramiding debt. Urban experts approach a consensus in their belief that the city should work to free itself from endeavors that would redistribute income (welfare and public housing), those that require geographic scope (transportation), and those that are ordinarily state obligations (higher education, courts, prisons). The city should also consider divesting itself of services which are usually provided by the private sector—such as NYC-owned and run radio and television stations.[11]

In addition to paring services, increased attention must be devoted to putting compensatory services on a sounder financial basis. These offerings should be modified so as to eliminate, or at least significantly curb, their onerous financial effects. This might necessitate, for example, consolidating related existing services, seeking increased federal and state funding for mass transit, vigorously soliciting private donations for museums and the arts, and increasing prices to more realistic levels.

There is vast room for improvement in cost control of city services. The largest item in the municipal budget is the payroll, which amounts to half the total.[12] Although intransigent municipal unions have vehemently opposed personnel cuts and modest wage increases, there arrives a time when unfortunate choices like these cannot be averted. Certainly other U.S. cities have been successful (compared to NYC) in negotiating with unions. There is no defensible reason why NYC cannot emulate its sister municipalities. What is required is for elected officials to demonstrate the fortitude and courage—and possibly sacrifice their political features—to make the hard decisions needed to put the city on a solid financial foundation. Anthony Downs cut to the heart of the matter in a statement made at a *New York Times* symposium on the cause of the fiscal debacle: "The only thing Mayor Beame can do is to decide if he wants to solve the fiscal crisis and not run again. If he wants to run again, he can't solve it. . . ."[13]

The task of allocating finite dollars to city services is conceptually akin to the business firm's task of capital budgeting under conditions of funds rationing. In such circumstances, the firm initially selects the most profitable investment project available to it, then proceeds to choose the next most profitable, and so on until the rationed capital is depleted. Some profitable ventures are foregone for lack of the wherewithal to undertake them. Similarly, a city should order needs according to their perceived importance and subsequently allocate funds, first to fulfill the most important class of needs; second, the next most important category of needs; and so forth, until the available funds are exhausted. Of financial necessity, some worthy but low-priority needs will go begging.

The most crucial public needs are those fulfilled by essential, undifferentiated services. Rudimentary city services not only benefit all citizens but are essential to everyone's subsistence. Dealing with matters of water, sewage, and sanitation may not be interesting work, but such matters are the fundamental obligations of municipal officials. The second tier of needs is fulfilled by essential, differentiated services. Services that are basic to the physical well-being of mostly low-income residents, and that do not rightfully fall into the domain of federal or state bureaucracies, should be of high priority in the budgeting process. After a suitable job has been done of fulfilling all essential public needs, residual funds can then be appropriated to the less crucial areas of culture and recreation. Because of the nonessentiality of these needs, budget cuts should most affect them. Given the choice, for instance, between dangerously lowering the quality of police protection and not building a number of new city swimming pools, officials should opt for the latter alternative.

Consumer research is requisite to the establishment of a valid hierarchy of citizens' municipal needs. The mayor and city council, operating from the isolation of Gracie Mansion and council respectively, cannot know the degree to which needs are being met unless scientifically obtained feedback from the citizenry is at their disposal. Only empirical research can reveal how the public feels about the adequacy of police and fire protection. Only empirical research can divulge how residents feel about the need for and the price of existing services or proposed new services. Only empirical research can provide the demand, cost, and revenue forecasts which are essential to realistic budgeting.

NYC's problems also stem from its cumbersome bureaucracy. At first glance, all large bureaucracies appear to be unmanageable behemoths laboring ponderously along mostly on the sheer force of their own inertia. Yet, the appearance of unmanageability is often illusion. Using imaginative and innovative organizational designs, executives in giant firms in the private sector have succeeded in shepherding enterprises often spanning the globe.

The expertise that has enabled private sector organizations to maintain control of vast empires can surely be brought to bear on the situation in NYC. The city is ripe for a massive systems audit conducted by an independent, interdisciplinary task force drawn from virtually all the administrative sciences. The team's charge should be to work toward the development of a streamlined organization (and information system) appropriate to the needs of NYC now and in the coming years. The organization envisioned is one that would facilitate and promote the efficient and efficacious planning, integration, coordination, and control of the many arms of city government. The organization might take any form, possibly even a morphology rarely or never before used in the public sector, such as an adapted product or market manager model.

CONCLUSIONS

NYC is the all-time classic illustration of the dangers of the idea of consumer orientation in the hands of the uninitiated. It is a portrait in marketing mania. It is the polar opposite of the myopic organization that tepidly serves consumers. Like its myopic counterpart, it is the antithesis of the organization which has successfully operationalized the marketing concept.

A therapy to assist in returning the city to solvency, and keeping it so, has been suggested in this article. The therapy is deceptively simple. It requires proper interpretation of and close adherence to the principles embodied in the marketing concept. Services intended to fulfill the public's municipal needs should be initiated or maintained only after the magnitude and essentiality of the needs have been established through responsible empirical and secondary research. Even then, the public's willingness to pay for the services required to fulfill these needs must be ascertained. Compensatory services should be priced to sustain themselves and the costs of all services should be controlled to the fullest extent possible. A thorough and encompassing organizational analysis is needed to determine in what ways the massive government apparatus can be changed to facilitate integration and coordination within and among its departments.

It is improbable that NYC's mayor and city council have ever heard of the marketing concept. It is regrettable. If they had, they would have known that consumer orientation is but one tenet in a tripartite philosophy. They would have known that the pursuit of consumer orientation without restraint and integrated marketing is a blueprint for disaster.

REFERENCES

1. Philip Kotler and Sidney J. Levy, "Broadening the Concept of Marketing," *Journal of Marketing,* January 1969, pp. 10–15; Philip Kotler and Gerlad Zaltman, "Social Marketing: An Approach to Planned Social Change," *Journal of Marketing,* July 1971, pp. 3–12; Philip Kotler, "A Generic Concept of Marketing," *Journal of Marketing,* April 1972, pp. 46–54.

2. Kotler and Levy, pp. 10–15.

3. Burton Marcus, et al., *Modern Marketing* (New York: Random House, 1975), p. 703.

4. Theodore Levitt, "Retrospective Commentary on Marketing Myopia," *Harvard Business Review,* September/October 1975, p. 180.

5. Reed Moyer, *Macro Marketing* (New York: John Wiley & Sons, 1972), p. 9.

6. Editorial, *Wall Street Journal,* September 10, 1975, p. 18.

7. "New York's Last Gasp," *Newsweek,* August 4, 1975, p. 24.

8. Ibid., p. 19.

Marketing the University: Opportunity in an Era of Crisis

Leonard L. Berry
William R. George

Many colleges and universities in the mid-1970s find themselves caught in what might best be described as the "over and under dilemma"—overstaffed, overbuilt, overly scheduled with programs and courses, and underfinanced and underenrolled.[1] The extent to which the "university-in-crisis" trend has progressed was recently dramatized in the popular press when a large state university, faced with a declining enrollment, terminated tenured faculty. The current financial plight of private colleges and universities, some already out of business and many others struggling to stay alive, is even better known.

What is the college or university administrator to do? How is he/she supposed to react? The history faculty can't be just cut by a third, or can it? The dormitories are only two thirds full, but the bank expects to be paid. The faculty are already unruly, and they have yet to learn there are to be no raises next year.

Reprinted with permission from *Atlanta Economic Review*, July/August 1975.

Never before has the typical college or university administrator been so pressured to think in terms of such "business world" realities as productivity analysis and waste curtailment, cost centers and information systems, markets, and marketing. Yet many college administrators are not trained in business management, and most colleges do not have a tradition of being run like a business firm. Indeed, many administrators would argue that the university setting is different from the business one and, therefore, the techniques used in business by and large are not appropriate for the university.[2]

It is true, of course, that the university is different from the business firm. How different these types of institutions are, however, is a matter of debate. The university's tenure system sometimes protects incompetence or sloppy work, but then business unions sometimes, in effect, create the same result (and, in any event, a number of college and university faculties have unionized in the last several years). Business has a rich tradition of advertising, but the university, which does not have such a tradition, is beginning to develop one as administrators compare the cost per thousand circulation of *The New York Times* with that of the regional edition of *Time,* or consider a direct-mail campaign proposed by a consulting firm specializing in student recruiting. Business distributes its products in places like supermarkets and department stores, and its services in places like branch bank outlets and barber shops. But the university distributes its services on green, tree-lined campuses and/or in converted homes and offices in urban areas, in satellite campuses, even on television.

In short, there is much evidence to suggest that the differences between business and the university are not as severe as some would believe, and that some of the differences that do exist are there because only recently have universities had to hustle for students the way business has long hustled for customers.

The authors believe not only that many business management approaches and techniques are applicable to the management of the university, but also that they are acutely necessary today, given the "over and under dilemma" now facing or potentially facing colleges and universities throughout the country. This article considers one facet of the business management approach required—specifically, marketing management—from the viewpoint that there is much that can be done by the university to improve its marketing and, as a likely result, its market and financial position.

The reality that the effective practice of marketing has become a high-priority challenge for the university, as well as for other nonprofit institutions such as certain community orchestras and local mass transit systems, really should not be too surprising, since the practice of marketing is inherent in all organizations in society. Whether they be business or nonbusiness in character, all organizations in society offer some kind of product to some kind of consumer and more or less use marketing strategy to regulate demand.

The product may be a physical entity (a book from the library), a service (health care), a person (professional singer), or an idea (limiting family size), but it nevertheless is an offering designed to prompt some kind of exchange relationship with members of the market.

The consumer normally may be called a donor, patient, or student, but he/she nevertheless is a consumer of the offering.

Marketing strategy may involve the optimum way to distribute police services rather than cake mix, or the most powerful way to solicit March of Dimes donations rather than magazine subscriptions, but it nevertheless is marketing strategy.

In short, all organizations in society practice marketing; it is inherent. When March of Dimes made the decision to switch its emphasis from polio to birth defects following the advent of the Salk and Sabin vaccines, this organization made a marketing decision. When the Cleveland Orchestra implemented its ethnic night program several years ago to attract a new type of customer, it engaged in a marketing act.

MARKETING AND THE UNIVERSITY

Given that marketing is inherent in organizations, it follows that the appropriate question is not whether the organization will practice marketing or not, but whether it will practice it well or poorly.[3] Thus, although marketing itself is unavoidable to the organization, the effective practice of marketing requires special efforts.

The central challenge for marketing management in the organization can be thought of essentially as *providing the right product at the right place and time and at the right price to the right market segment and effectively communicating this offering to that market segment.* To the extent the organization simultaneously pursues a number of market targets with a number of marketing mixes (specific blendings of product, distribution, communications, and price strategies), the central challenge of marketing management repeats itself that many times.

This complex assignment for marketing management, undertaken in a constantly changing and competitive environment, reflects the need for conducting marketing research and systematically disseminating its results, formal marketing planning, and structural arrangements that pinpoint marketing management responsibility and authority and foster maximum coordination. There are certain key elements in the marketing management task for the university.

Marketing Research

In recent months it has become commonplace for individuals interested in the university crisis situation to point quickly to the fact that the population age-mix that favored the university so well in the 1960s is not now such a favorable mix. Perhaps more than any single factor, the reality that the babies from the baby boom years are now past college age influences the gloomy enrollment projections that many college and university administrators have been making recently for their institutions. Our shifting population from an age standpoint is a very real consideration in making student projections. Nevertheless, at least two additional considerations sometimes are given insufficient attention:

1. Even when the college-age population grows at a markedly decreasing rate, specific colleges and universities can (a) continue to grow solidly if they attract more than their share of the market or (b) more or less retain enrollment levels of prior years by preventing substantive erosion of market share.
2. In our knowledge-explosive world, the concept of college age is less and less an omnipotent one, and the potential of the over-25 market is more and more real.

Since increasing market share for one university necessarily means decreasing market share somewhere among the competition, it follows that a key to the futures of specific colleges and universities is the development of competitive advantage. In brief, the university must formally seek to better serve the needs of segments of the market than does the competition. Since the probability of better serving the needs of market segments is enhanced if those needs are first identified, the university, like industry, should do marketing research on a systematic and continuing basis. Some of the types of marketing research that colleges and universities should consider conducting are:

1. *Student attitudes.* Periodically, the university would survey a sample of its student body concerning attitudes toward the institution itself. What do the students like? What do they dislike? What are the differences in their responses based on such variables as grade-point average, academic major, and demographics? How can the university improve?

2. *Exit interviews.* In order to lower its percentage of valued students transferring out or otherwise leaving before they are supposed to leave, the university would determine, through a formalized exit interview procedure, the primary reasons these events take place.

3. *Ombudsman feedback.* In recent years some colleges and universities have installed ombudsmen to be available to students as problem solvers when normal channels are either unavailable or ineffective. Whereas the ombudsman's primary role tends to be one of making the bureaucracy more responsive in an immediate sense, an additional potential role is that of systematically feeding back to the administration tabulated summaries of the nature of requests and complaints received.

4. *Institutional image.* Periodically, the university would formally investigate its image as held by various nonstudent publics of interest—for example, alumni, local business community, high school and junior college students. For the university to change its image effectively, if deemed necessary, it first must establish what it is that needs changing. Moreover, periodic image investigations are needed to monitor progress and to locate emerging image patterns.

5. *Educational program focus groups.* To derive information helpful in formulating new or improved educational programs, the university would conduct focus group interviews pertaining to the "knowledge" interests and life-styles of existing and prospective market segments. This type of research involves small groups in dialogue "focusing" on some topic of interest. In the present context, the topic might be knowledge interests (What subject areas interest you?) and knowledge life-styles (How do you presently pursue these interests?). Nontraditional groups for the university—for example, middle-aged women—should be stressed at least as much as college-age individuals.

6. *Market analyses of new and existing educational programs.* Whether the university actually institutes a new program to serve certain needs it uncovers should depend in part on the results of a market analysis, a quantitative and qualitative investigation that answers such questions as these: Who are our prospects and how many are there? What are their demographics? What do they want in our proposed new program? Who comprises the competition, and what are their strengths and weaknesses?

Significantly, the market analysis is also a tool for analyzing existing programs. That is, not only is it important for the university to determine *what to do* in terms of new programs but, also, *what not to do* in terms of existing ones.

The university, like industry, does not totally satisfy its marketing research obligation by merely collecting and analyzing various kinds of data. To pursue optimum value per research dollar expended, the data also must be disseminated in a manageable form to the right personnel at the right time on a predetermined and regularized basis. In brief, the university stands to benefit from the development of a marketing information system which would provide internal data (for example, admissions data, student attitude data) and external data (for example, institutional image data) at predetermined times to predetermined administrative personnel.

Market Segmentation and Product Design

One result that an active marketing research effort will bring to the university is formal reaffirmation that the "education" market is far from homogeneous in terms of how people in it wish to satisfy their educational needs. It follows that competitive advantage tends to accrue to those institutions that tailor their marketing mixes to specific groups having more or less homogeneous needs within the broader and more heterogeneous total market. This process, market segmentation, involves the attempt by the organization to fill especially the needs of a particular group with a marketing mix designed just for them.

In the latter half of the 1970s more and more colleges and universities will use the segmentation approach in very imaginative ways, a trend already under way.[4] For example, should a university located in an urban area and interested in attracting more students institute a "Saturday MBA" program for full-time employed executives? Should the university extend its ambitions and start a "Weekend College"? What about a degree program for senior citizens or an MA in social science for housewives? Should the university consider a basic medical knowledge course for parents? Questions such as these are best handled on an empirical basis.

In offering a new educational program to the market, the university administrator will benefit from a good understanding of what a "product" is, since the new program is in effect a new product. In the most basic sense, a product provides potential benefits to members of a market who may be willing to make a transaction to receive these benefits. Product strategy involves product-related decisions within the organization designed to facilitate such a transaction with the market target sought.

Recognizing the product as a source of potential satisfactions, or problem solutions, is vital to the university's capacity for providing product offerings encompassing all the product-related attributes necessary for truly satisfying market needs. Much of IBM's success in marketing computers, for example, can be attributed to management's recognition that the product included installation, operator training, warranty protection, preventive maintenance, and other services, in addition to the physical entity called a computer.

In the same way, the competence and commitment of academic counselors, the extent to which needed classes are available, and the type of enrollees in a given program, among other things, are all part of the product the university offers to its market. All else equal, it follows that competitive advantage can be expected to accrue to the university whose products are strong in a total sense rather than to the university whose products are strong in only a partial sense.

Distribution

Distribution strategy concerns itself with the necessary actions to make the product available at the time and location desired by the market segment sought. The right product for a market segment provides reduced (or no) satisfaction to the extent that it is unavailable when and/or where that segment wants it. For example, *TV Guide* magazine's perceived value is significantly reduced to some of its customers if each week's issue is available only at retail stores or is available through the mails but often arrives several weeks late.

Traditionally, the university has distributed its product largely by asking the market to come to the institution instead of taking the institution to the market. This tradition is beginning to erode, as increasing numbers of institutions are recognizing the potential of branch campuses, extension centers, and courses televised in the home.[5]

The idea of taking the university to the customer is one that holds much potential in the seeking of competitive advantage. For example, a major chemical company located 45 miles from the nearest university might well be interested in strongly supporting that university's MBA program if portions of the curriculum could be handled by correspondence and televised lectures piped into the company's facility.

In brief, an organization's capacity for getting its product to consumers when and where they want it is typically a critical variable in influencing the level of success to be obtained by the organization. All other things being equal, a university located in an area like Denver, Colorado, probably has a better chance for pulling out-of-state students than does one located in Grand Forks, North Dakota. Similarly, urban universities commonly suffer from inadequate parking facilities, poor lighting, and the reputation for being an unsafe place to be after dark. Such distribution factors as these may lessen significantly the attractiveness of an otherwise strong product offering.

Promotion

Promotion strategy concerns itself with the communication of potential satisfactions available to market segments as a result of the organization's product, distribution, and price strategies. The provision of attention-getting, informative, and persuasive communications is a vital activity toward developing market awareness, understanding, and interest in what the university has to offer. That is, the building of potentially customer-satisfying attributes into the product, distribution, and/or price tends to be insufficient unless these benefits are clearly and impactfully communicated to prospects for the offering or to influencers of prospects, such as high school counselors. Among the major elements of promotion are personal selling, advertising, and marketer-inspired publicity.

Personal selling involves direct contact with the prospect or prospect influencer and, in the context of university marketing management, presents a number of possibilities for universities not already extensively engaged in such activities. Should the university, for example, consider formal sales training for its admissions staff and other pertinent personnel? Should the university more aggressively engage in the development of sales aids—for example, audiovisual presentations for specific schools or colleges within the institution for use in group presentations? Should the university establish formal programs of campus visitations for community college and high school counselors, student prospects, and the parents of student prospects?

Advertising is any paid form of nonpersonal presentation openly sponsored by the advertiser. The term "nonpersonal" means that the message is not presented person to person, but it does not mean that advertisers are restricted to impersonal messages. Advertising, too, raises possibilities for universities not already involved in such activity. Should the university, for example, develop sell-oriented materials to be used in an adjunctive sense with catalog materials that typically stress regulations, policies, costs, and program and course descriptions? For example, should an inquiring student receive, in addition to the appropriate catalog, one or more brochures or portfolios from the college and/or department of interest that present information on selected faculty and that highlight innovative courses?

Should the university sponsor media advertising—for instance, coupon-incorporating advertisements in selected magazines and/or newspapers? Should the university request each of its major colleges or schools to develop a periodic newsletter for distribution to relevant publics?

Publicity is a form of promotion in which the marketer uses such tools as press releases and press conferences to encourage favorable media coverage relative to the organization or its specific offerings. Not only can publicity aid the university in letting its pertinent publics know how the institution can be of service, but, in addition, publicity tends to be a particularly powerful form of communication because it is presented to the market by a third party (the media), not directly by the institution itself. The potential impact of a well-managed publicity program raises for at least some universities the question of whether more systematic efforts are needed to stimulate media coverage for significant faculty and student activities and accomplishments. At least some university administrators who have traditionally thought of the public relations function as a low-level, peripheral activity in the university are beginning to change their minds on this matter.[6]

Price

It has been stressed that the university's product represents the direct source of potential satisfaction to needs in the market. Making the product available at the right time and place (distribution) and communicating its need-satisfying properties (promotion) provide additional benefits to market members and, in the process, facilitate product acceptance.

Importantly, making the product available at an acceptable price also encourages product acceptance (just as an unacceptable price discourages such acceptance). Pricing strategy concerns price-related decisions designed to encourage the kind of product acceptance desired by the organization and to meet its economic objectives as well.

Private universities today face particularly sensitive pricing decisions as their tuition rates steadily climb to meet rising costs and as they face head-to-head competition from state institutions with tuition rates usually significantly lower. This is not to imply, however, that public colleges and universities face insignificant pricing decisions in the future. Indeed, in many instances in the years ahead, price may well be the decisive factor in determining which of several state institutions a prospective student selects.

It is likely that considerable imagination in pricing strategy will be shown by many universities in the future. For example, increasing mention is being made in the literature[7] of variable pricing, in which the attempt is made to align more closely the tuition charged for a specific program with the costs to the university for offering the program. Another illustration of innovative pricing is Fairleigh Dickinson's Comprehensive Family Plan, whereby members of a full-time student's family are charged reduced tuition if they themselves enroll.[8]

ORGANIZING UNIVERSITY MARKETING

From a marketing standpoint, one of the most dramatic developments in industry in the last 20 years or so has been the reorganization that has taken place in many firms toward placing specific marketing-related functions (like advertising, sales, and marketing research) under a single vice president or director of marketing. The rationale has been one of coordinating the various elements of marketing within the marketing program and with other organizational functions.

Given the growing complexity of the modern university, there would seem to be a parallel need for organizing marketing-type activities in such a way as to foster coordination. Moreover, since aggressive marketing still is more or less a new idea to the university, the kinds of activities considered in this article are not likely to be conducted on a sophisticated and broad-based level without organizational specification of marketing management responsibility and authority.

In light of these requirements, the authors would suggest consideration of placing certain marketing activities under a specific vice president who would be responsible for the planning/implementing/coordinating/controlling of such activities as marketing research, new product planning, advertising, public relations, and alumni and development activities. Considering the way academic institutions work, a new academic program in, say, public administration would not be designed by this vice president's office, but very possibly it could be initiated by this office. That is, the vice president might indicate to the dean of the business school that research data reveal the need for a master of public administration program and ask whether the business school would be interested in designing such a program. If such a program were designed, the vice president's office could supply liaison and coordinative services; appropriate research data; technical aid in drafting the program proposal; and, eventually, advertising, public relations, and other demand-facilitating services.

Importantly, for reasons of internal and external acceptance of the type of reorganization proposed, the university's marketing vice president would probably be called something other than that—for example, Director of Institutional Research and Planning. As vital as effective marketing management now is to the university, the notion of marketing the university remains a decidedly distasteful notion to some. Thus, a job title other than Vice President for Marketing might make a challenging job somewhat easier for the person who assumes such a position.

CONCLUSION

The practice of marketing is inherent in organizations of all kinds, including not-for-profit organizations. Hence, the relevant question is not whether the organization will or will not practice marketing, but whether it will practice it well or poorly. The university is now operating in circumstances many would label as being of crisis proportions: numerous private institutions struggling to survive financially, enrollment declines, half-filled dormitories, federal research grant cutbacks, rampaging inflation. In such circumstances as these, it would seem helpful to suggest the importance to the university of practicing marketing well instead of poorly.

Marketing is not the panacea for the university's problems, but its effective practice is instrumental to the development of competitive advantage; and, in an era in which overbuilt and overstaffed colleges and universities scramble for students, competitive advantage is important. A systematic marketing research effort, along with a systematic means for disseminating data once collected, provides a basis for seeking competitive advantage. Competitive advantage directly relates to a university's capacity for providing the right product at the right place and time and at the right price to the right market segment, and effectively communicating this offering to that segment. Coordinating the elements of marketing strategy is critical, and the university lacks a tradition for aggressive marketing. It thus is proposed that organizational shifts be made in order to pinpoint marketing management responsibility/authority and to facilitate coordination of various marketing activities.

Thus far, the rising interest of university administrators in marketing to a great degree has centered on promotional activity, especially in the context of recruiting students.[9] The result is that university marketing today is disproportionately concerned with selling, influencing, and persuading. Not surprisingly, these activities have been highly criticized in some academic circles.[10] Yet, when seen from the proper perspective, good marketing involves uncovering specific needs and developing marketing programs to satisfy those needs. When marketing is viewed in this context, a more valid basis becomes available on which to judge whether society is served or harmed through more elaborate university marketing programs. For example, is society harmed or served because Fairleigh Dickinson University offers a Comprehensive Family Plan allowing half-price tuition for family members of full-time students? Is society harmed or served because Cleveland Western Reserve University offers an Institute for Post-Retirement Studies for students 55 years and over? Is society harmed or served because the C. W. Post Center of Long Island University offers a Weekend College?

Promotion is part of marketing but is not the equivalent of marketing, and, properly seen, promotion follows rather than precedes an organization's drive to create products that will serve market needs.[11]

The university today, like other institutions in society, is being buffeted by environmental change of substantial magnitude. Much of this change (the energy crisis, changing population age-mix, inflation) cannot be prevented by the university. The realistic alternative, therefore, is for the university to initiate change within its control to adapt to environmental change beyond its control. In a marketing context, this means that the university cannot do anything about the birthrate in 1955, among other things; but it can do something about attracting more than its share of today's young people, and it can do something about attracting the not-so-young.

REFERENCES

1. Dennis L. Johnson, "Market Approach Starts With Product Evaluation," *College and University Business,* February 1972, p. 48.
2. See, for example, James R. Surface, "Universities Aren't Corporations," *Business Horizons,* June 1971, pp. 75–80.
3. Philip Kotler and Sidney J. Levy, "Broadening the Concept of Marketing," *Journal of Marketing,* January 1969, p. 15.
4. See, for example, Victor P. Meskill, "How Shopping Center Technics Work for a Weekend College," *College and University Business,* April 1973, pp. 48–49; Potpourri of People Pleasing Programs." *College and University Business,* April 1973, pp. 52–55; John A. Valentine, "Higher Education: Has It Found a Better Idea?" *Conference Board Record,* February 1973, pp. 61–64.
5. See, for example, "Potpourri of People Pleasing Programs," op. cit.
6. See, for example, Annette L. Bacon and Cletis Pride, "Trends in Campus Advancement," *College and University Journal,* March 1971, pp. 9–12; Herbert A.

Wolson and Rudolf B. Schmerl, "Communications and the University: Getting the Inside Out and the Outside In." *College and University Journal,* May 1973, pp. 9–13.

7. See, for example, Manuel Arula, "Peak Load Pricing in Higher Education," *Journal of Experimental Education,* Spring 1972, pp. 6–11; A. R. Krachenberg, "Bringing the Concept of Marketing to Higher Education," *Journal of Higher Education,* May 1972, p. 376; Myron H. Ross, "How to Save $1 Million: Vary the Price of Tuition," *College and University Business,* February 1973, pp. 47–48.

8. "Fairleigh Dickinson 'Family Plan' Offers Half Price to Relatives," *The Chronicle of Higher Education,* February 25, 1974, p. 2.

9. See, for example, John D. Chapple, "If Admissions Are Lagging Don't Overlook This Help," *College Management,* December 1972, pp. 27, 34; Stanford Erickson, "Marketing Is Only a Part of Admissions," *College and University Business,* February 1972, pp. 56–57; David S. Sutton, "Marketing Tactics Put System Into Recruiting," *College and University Business,* February 1972, pp. 52–53.

10. See, for example, David R. Treadwell, Jr., "Kandy-Kolored Katalogues Don't Fill Empty Classrooms," *The Chronicle of Higher Education,* December 24, 1973, p. 16; and replies, *The Chronicle of Higher Education,* January 14, 1974, p. 13.

11. Kotler and Levy, op. cit.

A Management Approach to the Buyer's Market

William Ihlanfeldt

Until recently the application of marketing principles to higher education has been of little interest to most college administrators and alien to many faculty who elect to refuse to recognize that the industry of higher education is in the initial stages of a prolonged recession. The core of the recession is the increasing excess physical capacity caused by unrealized enrollments. There are simply too many places in graduate and undergraduate education for the diminishing number of students. This is particularly true among the age cohort 18 to 24 which we historically have perceived to be the potential market. This lack of demand as measured by excess capacity has made higher education less of a budgetary priority among state governments and philanthropic organizations.

To offset this lack of support, to honor commitments once supported by federal dollars, and to keep pace with rampant inflation, colleges and universities increasingly are forced to look toward tuition as the primary source of income. With more of the financial burden being shifted to

Reprinted from *Liberal Education*, May 1975 with permission from the Association of American Colleges.

students and their families through increases in tuition, sustaining and, among some schools, increasing enrollments has become the "primary hope" component of the budgetary process. Many college presidents have arbitrarily increased their enrollment on paper in order to project enough income to satisfy next year's budget requirements. This state of affairs has created an intense marketing effort, with institutions opting for merit scholarships as a form of consumer inducement, commercial advertising, and recruiting on other college campuses; in desperation, some have even gone so far as to offer more attractive financial benefits to their admission staffs in the form of commissions.

On the other hand, few institutions have looked into the mirror and asked themselves the tough questions related to what makes them what they are. Are they any different from hundreds of other institutions? What faculty are they prepared to force into early retirement? What departments are they prepared to eliminate in order to make other departments stronger and more attractive? Does their institution even deserve to exist? Unfortunately, too often presidents and boards of trustees have opted for across-the-board cuts as the first response to the budget crunch. Such decision making cultivates overall decline rather than selective improvement.

The readjustments in institutional priorities brought about by this recession have been perceived by some colleges as an opportunity in the sense that limited professional mobility among faculty and decreasing enrollments have stimulated greater institutional involvement on the part of faculty and a greater concern for undergraduate teaching. As one reflects upon the past, it should be remembered that prior to the late 1950s and early 1960s higher education was a depressed industry.

Salaries of professional talent were not comparable to those of other industries and there had always been plenty of places for students to go to college, for "going to college" was more a function of social class than a function of ability. Not until after World War II did the G.I. Bill provide the incentive to encourage large numbers of first generation college students to enter higher education. They were followed by more veterans after the Korean War, and as enrollments peaked in the early 1950s and began to decline, the Russians provided an additional thrust with the launching of Sputnik. Congress responded with the passing of the National Defense Education Act in 1958. This Act, coupled with the earlier creation of the National Science Foundation and the emergence of state scholarship programs and state planning commissions, set the stage for the expansion of higher education, an expansion based on the assumption that the demand for higher education would continue to increase. However, even during the mid-1960s, no more than ten percent of the schools were in a seller's market. Most institutions eventually filled their classes, but seldom did demand exceed supply to the point at which a student who really wanted to go to college could not.

Demand did not exceed supply because of the rapid growth of public higher education systems stimulated by federal and state funding during the early 1960s and because of little or no statewide coordination. One result is that we now find community colleges in Illinois in competition with state colleges for the same student. The effect is excess capacity. As this excess capacity increases—and it will increase—state legislatures and governing boards will be confronted with the decision to either close state universities, thus frustrating local economies, or continue to operate such institutions for economic but not educational reasons. The choice is indeed a difficult one, for to elect the latter means that the more viable public institutions will not get their fair share of the state's higher education budget. The taxpayer, too, will find it difficult to understand why he must help sustain public higher education for political and economic reasons as excess capacity continues to increase.

State colleges and universities which will find themselves in such a dilemma are those that have traditionally attracted large numbers of students with marginal academic credentials. In all likelihood, they will be located in semirural or small town communities. Students who used to attend such institutions are no longer interested in higher education, at least on a full-time basis, for their primary reasons for going to college have been eliminated, e.g. the draft, peer group pressure, promises of a better job, etc. On the other hand, private institutions are facing less demand because their missions have either been undifferentiated from many public institutions or their presidents have been ineffective in communicating what they are about. Often the private institutions have overlooked their primary markets and special interest groups and in addition have been poorly managed. More generally, higher education—public and private—made the mistake of assuming that the public was demanding more of the same. We failed to recognize that we were not meeting the needs of many of our students. In fact, much of the literature on higher education indicates quite clearly that the diversity among students is far greater than the diversity among institutions. The decline in the 18- to 24-year-old market will continue; for many institutions, the only hope is to improve the effectiveness of their recruitment effort and to revamp programs which will appeal to the older student. Some institutions are able to respond; others are trying but most schools simply do not know how. However, colleges which are able to respond are changing their programs to accommodate students on weekends and evenings as well as reorganizing the calendar year to make the summer more an integral part of their regular curriculum.

In order to better respond to declining, depressed, or hoped-for new markets, increasing numbers of colleges have begun to elevate the position of their admission offices within their organizational structure. More college presidents are concerned about the functional aspects of admission, and various consulting agencies that historically have been involved only in development work are now increasing their services to include advice on student recruitment—ill informed as they are. The admission office budgets have become a priority on many campuses and represent at least one departmental budget that is increasing more rapidly than the rate of inflation. Some schools are now spending well over $1,000 to matriculate one student.

Increasing costs and less consumer demand require that each of us ask how effectively we are communicating what our institutions are all about, and how systematically have we been approaching the whole concept of student recruitment. The term "marketing" has been applied frequently and often without definition, and the use of the term often causes a certain amount of indigestion among presidents and faculty when mentioned in their presence. However, I do not believe that improving the marketing techniques in the admission operation is the answer to the problem of declining enrollments if a high rate of attrition shows that the school is not meeting the needs of its current students. The appropriate response is to make an effort to improve the undergraduate student environment by upgrading program quality and by providing better student services.

APPROACHING THE MARKET

There are three basic concepts that should be a part of our thinking as we approach our various markets: service, involvement, and openness. Higher education is a service industry; in fact, it is probably the largest service industry in the world. Regrettably, few faculty and few administrators perceive that they are performing a service. I challenge them to define it as anything but. As we perform this service, we have an obligation to meet the expectations of prospective students and their parents. Our failure to recognize this has been the primary reason for the declining credibility of our industry.

With regard to the concept of involvement, admission operations at many institutions have either systematically excluded faculty, alumni, and undergraduate students from being a part of the recruitment effort or they have lacked the know-how to get people involved. Too often professional staff members of the admission offices have been threatened by queries from members of the community with regard to procedures of the admission operation. This attitude has created suspicion and has diminished the effectiveness of the admission staff. It is primary to a successful marketing program to have as many faculty, alumni, and undergraduate students involved in the student recruitment effort as wish to be. Whether we like it or not, we are all in the business of selling our institutions. Every time we say "hello" and shake a new hand, we are communicating what we do. This applies to all members of the university.

The third concept—openness—is paramount to the concept of involvement. If a lot of people are going to be involved in the admission operation, then the admission staff must be held responsible for providing these people with direct, concise, and accurate information—information which will better permit them to understand their tasks and how they might have an impact of a positive nature on the institution. An admission office with a philosophy that emphasizes openness and involvement increases its impact externally and internally: externally in the sense that its field force has been geometrically expanded, and internally in the sense that admission staff recommendations with regard to student needs will be better received.

As a service industry trying to serve a declining market or a changing market, there must be a tolerance for such terms as program modification, program development, and consumerism. We are all in the business of attempting to accommodate the needs of various student constituencies and at times this requires program modifications as well as new program development. We are not unlike a profitmaking corporation that is constantly reviewing the demand for present products and investigating possible new products. The admission or marketing officer has the responsibility of assessing consumer needs and translating those needs back to the community for consideration. This does not imply that an institution must respond to every demand or fad that exists in the marketplace. To the contrary, only by staying abreast of the capricious nature of the marketplace can the institution make decisions of a noncapricious nature.

IDENTIFYING THE MARKETS

There are basically three markets: the primary, the secondary, and the test market. The primary market includes those candidates who, if admitted, are likely to enroll. They are considered primary because past candidates with similar profiles considered the school their first choice. The secondary market represents those candidates who are likely to be accepted but who are more likely to attend another institution. The test market includes those candidates who have been encouraged to apply by either alumni or by the institution itself but who represent a profile that had not considered the school as a primary or secondary choice in the past.

The enrollment of a freshmen class of a specific size is generated through various time-related stages through several pools of students. These pools, which become successively smaller, are: prospects, candidates, applicants, accepted applicants, and matriculants. For each pool there is a required critical number and a certain degree of elasticity related to that number. For example, each school has a critical number that must be in the prospect pool in order to generate a certain number of students in the freshman class. The critical number required is based upon the school's desirability quotient. A freshman class of one thousand at one school may require a critical number between 18,000 and 20,000 prospects. At another school, the critical number may be between 10,000 and 14,000. The range represents the degree of elasticity related to the critical number and the number of potential students in the pool from the primary market.

Each school must be able to assess at any given time the number in its prospect file to determine whether a critical mass exists. Should the number be below the critical range, additional contacts should be made to increase the number in the prospect file. The same concept can be applied to the candidate file which is differentiated from the prospect file in the sense that the candidates have expressed an interest in the institution by initiating contact or replying to information sent to them at an earlier date. The same thinking must be applied to the applicant pool. The critical number based upon the school's desirability quotient is determined by studying the yields of each pool over a period of time. A fair assumption is that the prospect file should be at least 15 times larger than the number desired in the freshman class. However, this number must be further analyzed with regard to the numbers that fall within either the primary market, a high-yield market, or within the secondary market, a low-yield market. The more prospects that fall within the primary market, the lower the critical number required.

Each school has several months to create its prospect file and to sustain it at a given number. At any time, the admission office should be able to ask itself how near it is to achieving the critical number in its prospect file so that its desired freshman enrollment can be achieved the following fall. The critical number and its degree of elasticity depend upon the overall effectiveness of the marketing effort and the desirability quotient of the school. As long as a college is able to generate a large enough critical mass in the candidate file from the primary market early enough in the processing year, it can feel reasonably comfortable that the enrollment objectives for the next year's freshman class can be realized. Sensitivity to the critical numbers in the prospect and candidate pools can point the way to the courses of action with regard to the improvement of recruitment efforts as well as better budget planning. The admission officer ought to be able to advise his president a year in advance whether the candidate pool is large enough to generate a freshman class of the desired size. If it is not, the president should be realistic enough to adjust the projected budget accordingly. Such coordination should permit better long-range planning and fewer budget deficits.

Many colleges have very small primary markets because of a lack of systematic cultivation. Such schools will find it extremely difficult to predict the critical numbers required for their prospect and candidate pools. The principal advantage of applying the above model to the admission enterprise is that it permits the admission office to upgrade its recruitment effort in a systematic manner. Such planning has long-range consequences and cannot be changed from year to year on the basis of intuitive judgments. As a part of this planning, each office must have a backup plan which includes the capacity to respond quickly if the prospect or candidate pools need to be increased.

The prospect, candidate, and applicant pools can be inflated by beginning the recruitment process earlier and through the acquisition of names made available through various organizations such as the Student Search Service of the College Entrance Examination Board and the Educational Opportunity Service Program of the American College Testing Corporation. However, if these pools are inflated, the yields will change and thus the critical numbers must be increased. We have deliberately inflated the numbers in the prospect and candidate files at Northwestern. We have consciously elected to add a promotional component to the objective of meeting our present enrollment goals. This additional component is our effort to communicate to a large number of people what Northwestern is about, and what its accomplishments and overall direction are. We believe it is crucial to begin to cultivate the parents of tomorrow with regard to the future of Northwestern. Our time schedule is, then, twofold—one related to the next academic year, and the other to another generation. We have elected to inflate our numbers by 40,000 to 50,000 names in our prospect file. Clearly there is an additional cost, but it is a cheap price to pay if it either stabilizes enrollment or is considered a substitute for the investment in other forms of commercial promotion in the future. When the prospect file has been inflated by the promotional component, direct cost-benefit ratios cannot be derived. The promotional effort should be chalked up as good will.

As one analyzes the current admission scene, it is not an infrequent occurrence to find small colleges which have confused their primary and secondary and, for that matter, their test markets. A school located in the midwest that enrolls the greatest percentage of its students from the East Coast is depending upon a secondary market for its freshman class. In such a situation, matriculant yields are difficult to predict and the viability of the institution is threatened whenever it does not have a strong primary market in its general geographical area. Such a college also is likely to suffer from a high attrition rate regardless of the quality of the program. For example, an institution which is located in the Midwest but which is extremely dependent upon students from the East Coast subjects itself to the vagaries of the economic and political climate of another segment of the country without the possibility of exercising much influence. As a general rule, the primary market does not exceed a radius of 200 to 500 miles from the institution. It is easier to increase the numbers of students from the primary market than it is from a secondary market, simply because the rate of return in the primary market is considerably higher related to the cost and effort involved.

MARKETING COMPONENTS OF THE ADMISSION OPERATION

There are three basic components to the concept of marketing higher education: research, strategy, and communications. The *research* component determines why potential candidates and other people like your particular institution or, for that matter, why they do not like it. The research effort also should provide information with regard to primary, secondary, and test markets and how candidates interested in a particular institution go about making the college choice. The decision-making process may be quantified by location, ability, race, socioeconomic background, and so forth.

Once the research has been completed and the data has been analyzed, the *strategy* can be developed as to how you can best approach the marketing effort. The traditional or historical strategy, if one wishes to call it that, has been for an admission staff to identify various areas in the country where they have been reasonably successful in attracting students and then to proceed to visit high schools throughout a given area. This creates a third party dependency in the recruitment effort which makes the overall marketing effort more complex and less predictable. Under the high school visitation model, the admission staff becomes extremely dependent on third parties, such as high school counselors, to assist them in creating the class. Regrettably, some colleges view the high school counselor as a referral agent. Although this kind of assistance is helpful, it has been for too long the principal method of operation for most colleges. With an extensive dependency on third parties, the image that high school counselors and teachers have of the institution may be the determining factor in meeting the objectives of the marketing plan. The image may be accurate or inaccurate or the counselors and teachers may not even have an image of your institution other than that it is good or bad. Logically, it is impractical to expect any third party to formulate an image of each of 2,600 different colleges. The more successful long-range strategy is one which eliminates third party dependencies and places the institution in direct contact with the potential market. The primary question related to any recruitment model that is developed should be, "How can we contact the largest number of potential applicants in the most efficient and personal manner?"

The strategy also takes into consideration various support functions that are necessary to the *communication process*. These include other departments, computers, alumni, undergraduate students, faculty, friends, parents, and current undergraduates. The communication responsibility can be divided into an internal and an external process. The internal function is to communicate effectively and persuasively the needs of the marketplace. The external function is to communicate effectively to the consumer what the institution has to offer. It is imperative to recognize that effective communication requires various forms of contact with different audiences, and a determination must be made as to the form of communication to be utilized for a specific market at a specific time. It is quite likely that a telephone call, an interview, a publication, or a letter may affect one mind-set but not another. This can easily be determined by studying various market cohorts over time. Markets can be analyzed with regard to the various kinds of communication received and the eventual college choice controlling for ethnic background, socioeconomic background, race, religion, academic ability, age, geography, high school attended, and so forth.

THE RECRUITMENT MOLECULE

We at Northwestern have taken the position that after one develops a plan and defines strategy, it is important to utilize all available resources to support the marketing effort in as complete a manner as possible. Currently, about 400 alumni are actively involved in the admission process, along with 150 faculty and 300 undergraduates. Involved parties are much more likely to be informed and are therefore more helpful than uninvolved parties. The admission office is constantly in the business of developing institutional credibility through the involvement of various audiences. The overall effect is that a strong marketing force can be developed and educated. The marketing staff is viewed as 800 strong. To visualize the communication support system, we have created the recruitment molecule, as diagrammed in Figure 1.

We refer to the system as a molecule because various parts as represented by undergraduate students, faculty, other departments, alumni, etc. must be fluid. Each group in the task force is strategically located in the molecule and best relates to the adjacent subgroup as indicated by the direction of the arrow.

The faculty's primary responsibility is to provide a quality undergraduate educational experience. If the undergraduate finds that his educational experience is a rewarding one, he becomes the university's best salesman and this affects whether or not other students from his high school will consider the institution. Candidates who spend time on the campus and have various other contacts with the university formulate an impression, either positive or negative, and communicate that to high school counselors, friends, etc. Alumni are most effective working with

Figure 1. The recruitment molecule.

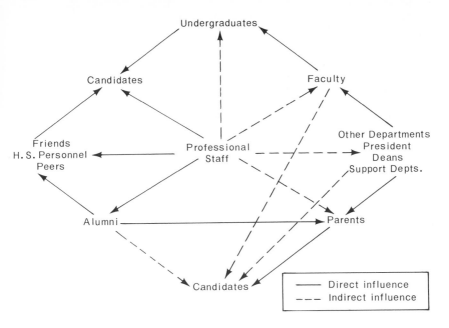

high school personnel, parents, and other friends who may be potentially helpful. They are less effective working directly with candidates. Members of other departments of the university establish a tone for the admissions office and can best be utilized in the communication process by writing to parents and speaking at special events. These responsibilities fall within the realm of the president and the various academic deans on the campus. This is not to imply that the faculty, alumni, and academic deans do not have direct contact with candidates, but we do not perceive this as their primary responsibility in assisting in the creation of a class. If each subpart of the molecule meets its responsibilities, a cohesive marketing network is formed.

In addition to the question of primary contact, time becomes a factor as to when the contact is made. Although the professional staff may initiate a contact, an undergraduate student making contact with the candidate can have a considerable influence. However, if the contact comes too late in the recruitment process, the candidate has already made up his mind and any communication from an undergraduate student will have little impact. Once the prospect pool has been defined, the faculty play a significant role in assisting the professional staff in conducting special on-campus and off-campus programs. The most effective on-campus programs appear to be those of the supermarket variety where candidates and their parents are able to visit with faculty representing various disciplines in a concentrated period of time, such as a Sunday afternoon. The alumni on the other hand, have a most important role in the home community in creating a sense of continuity to the communication process as well as providing a sense of local identity with the institution. Alumni are opinion leaders, as are friends of the college, and it is crucial to the development of a desirable image that the opinion leaders of any community think well of your college or university, especially within your primary market. I have often thought that to have one opinion leader speaking favorably of Northwestern at just one out of every ten cocktail parties that are hosted each weekend in this country would eliminate the need for a national marketing force.

The construction, then, of the recruitment molecule simply permits us to visualize how each part of the recruitment task force relates to the total plan and to achieving the objectives of that plan. However, there is no need to think of the admission enterprise in these terms unless the professional staff of the admission operation has the capacity to provide the kinds of informational support that each subpart of the task force will require. It goes without saying that this is the most crucial part of involving hundreds of people in helping your college meet its enrollment objectives. To solicit involvement and then not to be prepared to provide the required information is destructive.

THE NORTHWESTERN UNIVERSITY MARKETING PROGRAM

For the last four years, all accepted applicants have been sent a questionnaire related to the college decision-making process. Information has been gathered with regard to the education of the parents, career plans, numbers and names of institutions to which candidates applied, size and quality of media exposure such as radio programs, magazines read, and what and who were influential in their college choice as well as the amount of financial aid received if a student applied for financial aid. Because of this rather extensive data base, we have been able to determine those features of the University which are the most appealing and those marketing techniques related to the college admission process which are the most effective.

We have found that the more ability a student has, the more likely he is to be interested in acquiring information on academic programs related to his interest than he is in the emotional reasons for selecting a given college. However, a college which attracts students for emotional or nonacademic reasons must be willing to appeal to such interests. Further, we have found that the inclusion of the parents in the consumer cultivation process is of primary importance. Thus, our marketing information program includes the parents in all our efforts from the very beginning. We have found that anything which personalizes the admission process is most conducive to responsive consumer behavior. The two key components of persuasive communication are specific information and exposure.

To force the development of new and more comprehensive marketing approaches, we asked ourselves this question several years ago: "If high school visits were eliminated, how could we best attract a class?" As we assessed the cost-benefits of the high school visit, we found that we had spent an inordinate amount of time traveling from one secondary school to another, waiting for high school personnel, and being disappointed when students had to leave an information session or could not attend because of a class conflict. We came to the conclusion, however, that there were some high schools that we definitely should visit. These fall into such categories as principally preparatory, private, parochial, or schools serving students from minority backgrounds. Often at these high schools, we either found the secondary school college counselor or placement director very influential with regard to college choice because he was perceived to be an opinion leader in his community, or that the high school visit was the only way to make contact because direct mail was not read. Subsequently, the number of high school visits has been reduced from 700 to approximately 100.

As implied, the marketing plan is based upon the axiom of exposing Northwestern as completely as possible to the largest number of prospective applicants and their families in the most effective and efficient manner. This has been achieved by offering information sessions in major towns throughout the nation at a point of central location. These are generally conducted on an evening for a period of two and one-half hours. Candidates and their parents are asked to attend by personal invitation. At such gatherings, we will have members of our Alumni Admission program and, at times, secondary school counselors and teachers will attend. But the latter is an infrequent happening. The advantages of such programs are the existence of a captive audience including the parents.

To complement information sessions in the field, personal interviews are offered throughout the nation, for we strongly believe that the interview is a vital part of the admission program. It provides the personal touch which most institutions overlook or justify not offering on the basis that the interview has very little influence in the admission decision process. However, we see it as a part of our overall promotional effort and one which may identify a few students whom we clearly want to make every effort to attract, as well as eliminate a few whom we think, regardless of ability, ought to attend another institution. For the great majority that are interviewed, it is a service to help them identify more with the admission process and the institution and to provide some sense of humanization to the process. Also, we have found that high school students and their parents during the summer months prior to their senior year are quite interested in discussing college opportunities. As a result, we not only have moved to an extensive program of information sessions during the summer months, but we have expanded the summer campus visits and added a vacation flavor. We are able to offer overnight accommodations as candidates and their families travel through the Chicago metropolitan area.

Fall is devoted to more on-campus visits. These are organized around weekends beginning on a Sunday afternoon through a Monday evening and the numbers are restricted to 200. A student arrives on a Sunday and is assigned a roommate who is currently an undergraduate and studying in the candidate's expressed interest area. After an evening buffet, the student has the opportunity to attend a number of information sessions conducted by faculty members in almost every discipline. The next day the student attends classes with his roommate and at his convenience returns to his home late on Monday afternoon. Parents also are invited and are offered the opportunity to participate in the same programs with some special additions directed to parent interests. We have not concerned ourselves with student ability but we invite only those students from a specific geographical area who are a part of our candidate file.

Campus visits are not restricted to these weekends but also are offered on an *ad hoc* basis. Weekends and overnight accommodations are provided by the undergraduate students who are an integral part of the admission process. The key to the entire effort is the development of our prospect file which is computer supported and which over a period of time may include up to 75,000 different names for an eventual class of 1,800 freshmen from an anticipated 7,000 applications.

Until 1972, Northwestern, like most colleges and universities, initiated contact with prospective candidates through high school visits, inquiries, and test score reports forwarded to the University by the testing agency at the request of the student. Additional lists of names of prospective students have been acquired through the National Merit Scholarship Corporation and other agencies. However, most of these lists are not available until the student's senior year, and by then there is very little time to cultivate an interest in a particular institution. In other words, most students are focusing on one or two institutions by the time they enter their senior year.

In 1972, the College Entrance Examination Board began to offer a program called the Student Search Service. Through this program, colleges and universities could request the names of high school juniors who fell within certain parameters based upon ability, race, geography, and interest area. Although the names can be requested after a number of different test dates, we have elected to request names of students who have taken the Preliminary Scholastic Aptitude Test in October of their junior year. For the recruitment cycle for the entering class in Fall 1975, we have received 50,000 names selected through seven different sorts based upon our knowledge of our primary and secondary markets and institutional needs. This kind of direct mail approach initiated by a college to large numbers of students is the most significant recent innovation in college recruiting, and has the potential of completely changing the way prospective students and colleges relate to one another. One by-product is that a college is less dependent upon the high school visit and third parties to meet its enrollment objectives.

In soliciting the interest of a candidate, first contact is of extreme importance. The quality of the mail contact, phone contact, or the alumni contact can be the determining factor in whether a particular candidate ever considers the college seriously. At Northwestern, we have used a mail piece as our first contact. It is not a letter, for these students are being inundated with letters encouraging their interest. It is a mailer which is succinct and to the point, identifies some of the institution's strengths, encourages students' interest by asking them to return the perforated section of the mailer providing their names and requesting additional information. We have observed a response rate from 10 to 25 percent from the various markets. Upon receiving a response, a student is moved from a general prospect file to a candidate file. Students in this active file are likely to be personally contacted by undergraduate students and alumni during the summer months prior to their senior year in high school, and invited to various kinds of special programs, either in their own city or on the campus.

Our research indicates that the interview, the campus visit, the parents, and contact with either a family friend knowledgeable about Northwestern or a current undergraduate attending Northwestern are extremely important in the college decision-making process. Every effort is made to accommodate this interest. By the middle of the fall, approximately 20,000 students have had a personal contact with the University through one of the above activities of alumni, undergraduate students, or admission staff. Alumni and undergraduate reports must be filed by the contact person. We also require alumni as well as undergraduate students to attend workshops on a periodic basis to keep them abreast of admission activity. In turn, the admission office sends them newsletters on the activities of the professional staff.

At whatever time we consider appropriate, we put faculty directly in contact with the prospective student and his family. This may occur in the form of a letter, an information session, or a direct on-campus interview. The more faculty that are involved under the proper circumstances, the more students gain a better understanding of the kind of experience they are likely to have. I must emphasize that the admission office does not create the product; that the product must stand on its own as developed by the faculty. The admission office, as a marketing arm, is responsible only for effectively utilizing community resources in communicating the strengths of the product to the student consumer and his family.

Marketing's Application to Fund Raising

William A. Mindak
H. Malcolm Bybee

In a recent issue of the *Journal of Marketing*, Professors Kotler and Levy maintained that marketing is a societal activity which goes considerably beyond the selling of toothpaste, soap, and steel.[1] They suggested that the basic concepts of product development, pricing, distribution, and communication also apply to nonbusiness organizations interested in services, persons, and ideas. Furthermore, they challenged marketing people to expand their thinking and to apply their skills to an increasing range of social activity rather than to a narrowly defined business activity.

This paper is in part a response to that challenge. It discusses a specific case study which applied marketing concepts to a March of Dimes fund raising campaign. The concepts utilized in the study include many of those suggested by Kotler and Levy, plus some additional systematic factors (which are often peculiar to the marketing of ideas and causes). In addition, this paper provides some specific examples of communication factors.

Reprinted with permission from *Journal of Marketing,* July 1971.

187

THE CASE STUDY

This particular case concerns a March of Dimes fund raising drive held in Travis County, Texas, in January 1970. Despite limited funds and facilities, or perhaps *because* of these limits, the authors had an opportunity to experiment with marketing concepts in an area not traditionally considered a business enterprise.

Anyone who has worked with charitable or volunteer organizations probably is well aware that very few of these organizations have a formally established plan. If they do have a "handbook," it is usually filled with anecdotes, success stories, or invocations to positive thinking. This was not the case for the March of Dimes Foundation, which has pioneered many solicitation techniques that are widely copied by other associations and agencies. However, the perspective of the handbook seemed curiously dated, as if one were inspecting the organizational chart of a sales-oriented company back in the 1950s rather than a marketing-oriented company of the 1970s. Despite these difficulties, the authors attempted to translate the Foundation's handbook into a meaningful marketing plan, utilizing recent contributions from systems analyses as well as flow diagrams.

MARKETING ANALYSIS

The first handicap the authors encountered in conducting the marketing analysis was the lack of primary research data about the "heavy giver," his demographic characteristics, the location and size of this particular market, and his basic motivations for giving or not giving. In view of the fact that since its inception in 1934 through 1960 the National Foundation had raised $618.5 million, and that in 1967 it was the fourth largest public health agency in terms of contributions (some $22 million), one would expect a wealth of primary marketing data. However, the policy of the National Foundation of the March of Dimes has been to spend money on medical research rather than on consumer or marketing research. A review of past Chapter records data, in addition to exploratory investigations in the local community, did indicate the following problems:

1. *An apathetic and uninformed public who still considered the major aim of the organization to be the prevention of polio.*
   With the advent of the Salk (1955) and later the Sabin (1962) vaccine, an effective prevention for polio was achieved. Although

the National Foundation had announced interests in other related diseases, particularly birth defects, as early as 1958, relatively few people had changed their "image" of the March of Dimes.

A preliminary telephone survey conducted in Travis County indicated that only 17.5 percent of the respondents volunteered birth defects for the March of Dimes on the unaided recall basis. When aided, only another 13.4 percent made the association. Thus, 30.9 percent of those surveyed realized that the March of Dimes was becoming concerned with birth defects.

Therefore, although the product had been redefined, the Travis County public was not aware of this "redefinition."

2. *Decreasing interest in the organization and a subsequent decline in involvement by volunteers.*

This was attributed to a general deemphasis in the importance of birth and child-rearing by women, with subsequent lessened interest in the birth process, and increasing competition from other "causes" needing volunteers.

3. *Declining returns from each campaign in Travis County.*

4. *Lack of primary marketing research data on the composition of donors and the location of prime market segments for the current year or for the previous year.*

5. *Evidence that nationally prepared campaign materials did not apply to the local situation.*

There was a feeling that the national campaign was too organization-centered and not benefit-centered. The use of such themes as "250,000 defective babies are born each year with birth defects" was not personally involving, and the shock effect of a single poster child with missing and disfigured limbs seemed too negative and too removed to be effective.

In addition to the problems, a market analysis indicated several potential opportunities:

1. *A long public association of the March of Dimes Organization with the area of public health.*

A nationwide opinion survey conducted by the American Institute of Public Opinion found that 83 percent of the population in the United States could identify the March of Dimes.

2. *Recent breakthroughs in the area of birth-defect prevention and detection coupled with a high number of people exposed to the problem.*

3. *The organization and structure of the March of Dimes, with a nucleus of dedicated individuals.*
4. *Receptivity at the local level to experiment with new marketing and communication techniques.*

APPLICATION OF MARKETING TECHNIQUES

Once a marketing plan had been instituted and the problems and opportunities analyzed, various marketing techniques were applied using Kotler and Levy's classification.

Target Group Definition—Market Segmentation

In general, the National Foundation's fund raising strategy was to view its potential market as basically undifferentiated. Although the standard March of Dimes fund drive had attempted to contact business and industry, had conducted a mother's march, and had instituted teenage and school programs, the concept of locating the "heavy donor" or "user" was not used nationally or locally. Thus, very little market segmentation information was available.

However, in the marketing of consumer products, the "heavy-user" concept has been widely accepted as a truism. Several authors have indicated disproportionate consumption skews for several product lines. For instance, fewer than 4 percent of the male population make 90 percent of the car rentals; 8 percent take 98 percent of the air trips in a year; and 26 percent of the population uses 81 percent of the instant coffee.[2] What about fund raising? Common sense would indicate that the market for the March of Dimes and birth defects is also segmented, and this was validated by research conducted during the study. The prime market for the March of Dimes was felt to consist of parents. Past research had ascertained that 48.5 percent of the population could be placed into this category.[3] More realistically, however, it was estimated that only 31.4 percent (young married, no children; young married, youngest child under age six; and young married, youngest child six and over) would comprise the prime target for the campaign.

Another indication that the market could be segmented was provided by an analysis of contributions from the direct-mail campaign. It indicated that five of the 24 census tracts in the Travis County area (containing 19.8 percent of the population) had made 41.3 percent of the contributions.

Therefore, the key to a successful March of Dimes campaign appeared to be isolating the "heavy user" rather than marketing to an undifferentiated population.

The Search for a Differential Advantage

Despite more than ten years of promotion efforts, the "top-of-mind awareness" to the March of Dimes and birth defects was relatively low, as shown by the initial telephone survey. It was felt that a thematic perception test would aid in determining which type of appeal would best differentiate the March of Dimes' "new" birth defects' image from both the established image of polio as well as from the other charitable causes. This strategy utilized many current and past March of Dimes' slogans and a number of newly created themes. A trivariant analysis[4] test was then conducted on the various thematic appeals.

Twenty-four themes in three specific categories were rated on the three factors of *distinctiveness* (or exclusiveness), *interest* (rather than desirability), and *believability*. The first category of themes included the ones used by the March of Dimes during the last five years:

* Keep our future bright by fighting birth defects today.
* Give for a brighter tomorrow.
* Help make a child whole again.
* Shut the door on birth defects.
* Fight the great destroyer, birth defects.
* Give to the March of Dimes.
* Join the fight against birth defects.
* Where there's help, there's hope.
* Prevent birth defects.

The second category contained locally created themes that were largely centered around the emotional fear technique:

* Your next baby could be born with a birth defect.
* 500,000 unborn babies die each year from birth defects.
* Dying children can be helped.
* Birth-defect babies can't be sent back to the factory.
* Help tomorrow's birth-defect child live.
* Protect your family's health.
* God made you whole. Give to help those He didn't.

The third category also contained locally created themes, but their appeals were more rational:

+ 700 children are born each day with a birth defect.
+ A birth-defect baby is born every other minute in the United States.
+ Birth defects are cleft palate, club foot, open spine—curable.
+ The March of Dimes has given you: Polio Vaccine, German Measles Vaccine, 110 birth-defects' counseling centers.
+ Your gift to the March of Dimes is like money in the bank.
+ You owe it to your children to contribute to the March of Dimes.
+ Ensure your family's health by giving to the March of Dimes.

In trivariant analysis a representative sample rates various themes randomly on three factors. The mean scores for the themes are calculated on each of the factors, and are then plotted on a two-dimensional chart (the mean of the theme on the third factor, believability, is shown in parentheses). Figure 1 charts the results achieved by each of the March of Dimes' themes on the interest and distinctiveness factors, with the believability mean in parentheses. It is conceded that although the test is an efficient means of testing probable effectiveness of factual claims, it seems less applicable to advertising approaches that depend heavily on emotion or on graphics. Despite these limitations, Figure 1 provides some interesting insights (see pages 194–195):

1. The majority of the March of Dimes' themes did not score in Quadrant I, where the most interesting and most distinctive themes are found.
2. Themes dealing with *positive, active* aspects of giving, the *results of giving,* or a description of what March of Dimes had done with contributions in the past did well in creating interest, in being distinctive, and in being believable.
3. Some of the emotional appeals showed potential in being interesting, but they would need to be altered in order to achieve higher levels of distinctiveness and believability.

In any event, data were available and used to create strategies for finding a differential advantage.

Multiple Marketing Tools

One of the keys to the success of the March of Dimes' campaign was the "mothers' march," a day set aside for personal solicitations in the prospects' homes. Informal interviews with teams of marchers indicated a basic insecurity on the part of the soliciting mother concerning her behavior when confronting a potential donor at the door. Since these women were the key "salesmen," informational and motivational meetings were held. In addition, a detailed fact sheet was designed to explain the method of requesting funds and the use of prepared materials. Also, a brochure was designed to leave at the door in case the prospect was not at home.

Localized publicity materials which related to the other aspects of the promotional mix were prepared for both the print media, with its characteristic of permanence and exposure, and the broadcast news media, with its potential broad impact and visualization. The latter media had not been used with much effectiveness in the past.

Marketing Audit—Continuous Marketing Feedback

Some of the research or feedback techniques used during the campaign such as "top-of-mind awareness" of March of Dimes, pretesting of appeals, and analysis of returns have already been described. The most critical tests concerned the evaluation of the overall impact of the campaign in meeting its objectives.

One of the objectives of the advertising campaign was to increase the association of birth defects with the March of Dimes. A precampaign audit yielded a 30.9 percent combined aided and unaided recall for the March of Dimes and birth defects. A second audit conducted a week after the direct-mail campaign showed that the figure had risen to 45.3 percent (a 50 percent increase). A third audit, conducted a week after the mothers' march, yielded a recall figure of 61.2 percent (a 100 percent increase from the pretest). DAGMAR criteria would indicate that the advertising had been effective in achieving penetration.

With respect to "sales," total income realized for the 1970 campaign increased by 33 percent over the previous year, but the increased expenses of "tailor-making" a direct-mail program, of preparing radio and TV announcements, and of providing handouts for mothers increased expenses by 14 percent over the previous year. Nevertheless, it was the first time in 12 years that contributions *had* increased.

Based on these results, the major recommendation for next year's campaign was to move even more strongly toward the "heavy-user concept" in direct-mail advertising. The mass campaign suggested by the National Foundation consisting of impersonal "occupant-addressed" pieces did not take advantage of what marketers know about family life cycles and market segments. As many as half the census tracts in the

Figure 1. Trivariant analysis of possible themes.

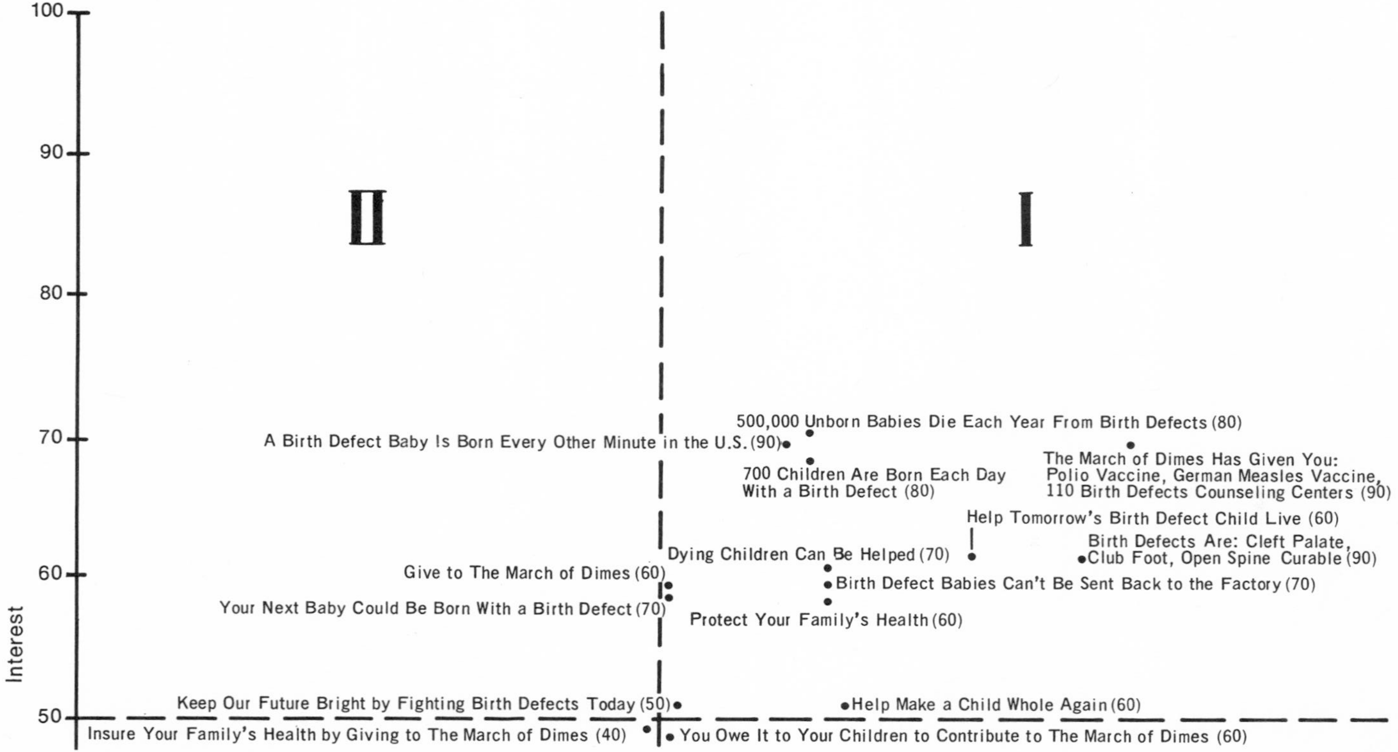

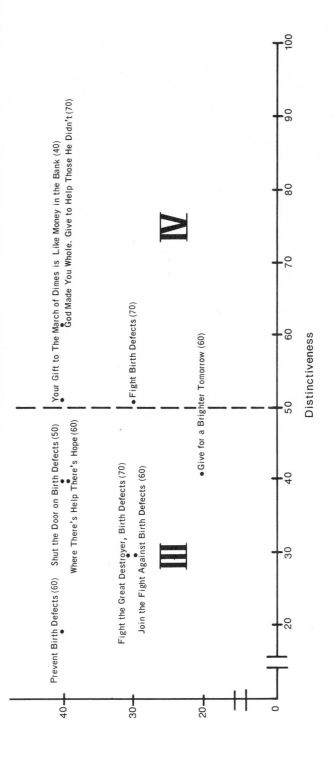

Distinctiveness

Travis County area could have been eliminated without substantially reducing net returns.

The same concentration could apply to the business and industry mailing. Although the number of direct-mail pieces sent to this sector was tripled, response actually decreased. This was attributed to the fact that a mass of letters was sent, rather than consecutive, selective mailings with personalized follow-up.

Much doubt was cast on the efficacy of publicity in motivating and stimulating response in the form of donations. The National Organization's primary emphasis in its communication program is to prepare news-release material containing appeals designed to elicit cash donations to the March of Dimes. It appears that this approach does not generate adequate donations and, in fact, may jeopardize the placement of other communications into the media dealing with the need for volunteers, meetings, and so forth.

CONCLUSIONS AND IMPLICATIONS

The results of the Travis County "test market" clearly suggest that marketing techniques and philosophy can be applied to ideas and social causes. It also seems clear that they could have national application for a foundation such as the March of Dimes.

Associations and their causes, like products, experience a life cycle. Patton suggests that a product will go through graduated intervals of development, beginning with an introduction stage which is followed by stages of growth, maturity, and decline.

> As volume rises and the market becomes increasingly saturated, marketing steps to the center of the stage. Generally speaking, at this point all competitive products are reliable, and there is less and less to choose between them. Improvements in the product tend to be small, with selling features or style changes dominant.[5]

The charity "market" has become increasingly competitive. Individual fund raising campaigns, exclusive of the United Fund campaign, are again on the upsurge across the country. Health organizations, which at first attempted to integrate with the United Fund approach, are now conducting their own campaigns. Furthermore, some members of the United

Fund are even conducting individual campaigns to supplement their United Fund receipts.

The increasing competition plus the problems already mentioned indicate that the National Foundation of the March of Dimes can be placed in the late stages of the "charity" life cycle, characterized by declining growth and campaign receipts. Even its advantage of being a pioneer in solicitation techniques seems to be dissipated by the competition for the volunteers needed in other organizations.

The question, therefore, is how long can basic market research be viewed as an unnecessary, unwanted expense by an organization such as the March of Dimes.

Research information could be translated into selective promotion, in contrast to the "mass" techniques used in the past. Computer data from the Internal Revenue Service are already available containing information on incomes, number of dependents, and taxes paid for each of the 35,000 postal Zip Code areas. These data, plus a regression and correlation analysis of March of Dimes' data from individual chapter records, could identify the means to efficiently reach the "heavy giver."

The need to apply other marketing management concepts is equally obvious. These concepts include redefining the "product" in a meaningful way, developing new marketing tools for the volunteer, and arranging national test markets to test different types and levels of promotional appeals.

Perhaps readers who have been exposed to the frequently high-pressure techniques of charity organizations and professional fund-raisers with their "disease-of-the-month-club" solicitations might be "appalled" by the prospect of these organizations becoming marketing-minded. At the same time, the dedicated professionals and volunteers associated with these organizations might be "appalled" by the prospect of applying business and marketing techniques to a nonbusiness area.

Both groups might profit from reviewing Kotler and Levy's definition of what marketing really means: sensitively serving and satisfying human needs.[6] Such a definition of marketing challenges organizations which specialize in the marketing of causes and ideas to ask themselves if they are truly consumer-centered and not simply self-serving. It challenges their understanding of the principle that selling follows rather than precedes the organization's drive to collect funds. It also challenges the marketing man himself to understand that he will have to fit his concepts and techniques to the special goals and objectives of the individual organizations. It is hoped that this case study helps in contributing to the satisfactory acceptance of these challenges.

REFERENCES

1. Philip Kotler and Sidney Levy, "Broadening the Concept of Marketing," *Journal of Marketing*, January 1969.

2. Carl H. Sandage and Vernon Fryburger, *Advertising Theory and Practice* (Englewood Cliffs, N.J.: Richard D. Irwin, 1967), p. 199; Philip Kotler, *Marketing Management* (New York: Prentice-Hall, 1967), p. 51; Daniel Yankelovich, "New Criteria for Market Segmentation," in *Marketing Management and Administrative Action*, edited by Steuart H. Britt and Harper W. Boyd, Jr. (New York: McGraw-Hill Book Co., 1968), p. 189.

3. John B. Lansing and Leslie Kish, "Family Life Cycle as an Independent Variable," in *Marketing Management and Administrative Action*, edited by Steuart H. Britt and Harper W. Boyd, Jr. (New York: McGraw-Hill Book Co., 1968), p. 213.

4. Dik Warren Twedt, "New 3-Way Measure of Ad Effectiveness," *Printer's Ink*, September 6, 1957, pp. 22–23; see also Dik Warren Twedt, "How to Plan New Products, Improve Old Ones, and Create Better Advertising," *Journal of Marketing*, January 1969, pp. 53–57.

5. Arch Patton, "Top Management's Stake in the Product Life Cycle," in *Marketing Management and Administrative Action*, edited by Steuart H. Britt and Harper W. Boyd, Jr. (New York: McGraw-Hill Book Co., 1968), p. 324.

6. Kotler and Levy, op. cit.

King Cotton Fights
to Regain His Throne

J. Dukes Wooters

Agribusiness is becoming the universal *nom de guerre* for what had been called farming. Increased interest among investors and speculators in pork bellies and soy bean futures is only part of the cause. The principal reason for the change that turned farmer into agribusinessman is the adoption of modern business management techniques, not the least important being aggressive marketing.

In the past seven years we have seen the New Zealand Meat Board carve out an ever-growing market for that country's surplus lamb at the same time that U.S. consumption of lamb dropped by one-third. The New Zealanders did it with an aggressive marketing program conducted by a company established in the United States solely for the purpose of competing in the U.S. marketplace. From 700,000 carcasses in 1971, imports from New Zealand grew more than 150 percent to 1.8 million carcasses in 1976. U.S. lamb producers, meanwhile, were selling 183 million pounds less of lamb than they did in 1971.

From *Management Review*, February 1978. Copyright © AMACOM, a division of American Management Associations.

We are witnessing a struggle within the beef cattle industry to organize the producers to create an organization that will promote beef sales aggressively. Last summer, the latest attempt to organize the industry failed. The proposed organization, financed by a $40 million per year checkoff on beef sales, would have conducted advertising, public relations, and sales promotion programs plus market research and new product development programs.

Why should beef producers be concerned? Beef consumption continues to rise. It is such a staple in most of our diets. How can anything threaten its domination of the meat market?

There are astute, clear-sighted people in the beef industry. They see faster growth of pork consumption. There is considerable antibeef comment in the media from the point of view of health—the cholesterol problem—and cost. Interest is growing in meat substitutes and extenders such as soy beans and fish meal. These far seeing people in the beef industry realize that if they don't prepare themselves with market research, new product development, and marketing programs, they may find themselves in a crisis a few years from now.

Like the railroads.

The railroads were once so mighty their owners felt invincible. As a matter of fact, no one did a better job of running a railroad than the owners. But look at what the airlines and truck companies have done to the railroads in the transportation business.

Myopic marketing is the title given this problem by Theodore Levitt in a recent article in the *Harvard Business Review*. It refers to an industry that feels so secure in its markets that it fails to identify potential competitors who will suddenly appear within their own private preserves holding the lion's share of the market.

COTTON: A CLASSIC EXAMPLE

In 1920, the fiber market was dominated by cotton—it had an 88 percent market share. In 1951, that market share dropped to 66 percent, and in 1973 it hit 29 percent. In 1951, synthetic fibers held only 4.6 percent of the market. A quarter century later the polyesters, acrylics, nylons, and other synthetics had a 68 percent market share.

What happened to King Cotton? Has it fallen to progress and a better fiber? To determine this, a number of studies have been conducted.

A Cotton Incorporated study, for example, showed that 79 percent of the people surveyed felt that fabrics made entirely or mostly of cotton were comfortable, while only 53 percent felt that way about fabrics made entirely or mostly of synthetics. A study by Opinion Research Corporation of Princeton showed that 86 percent of the people consider comfort the most important factor when they buy apparel; that 86 percent figure held up when the respondents to the survey were analyzed by age and sex.

WHAT HAPPENED

If cotton is still the fabric of preference, why did it lose favor in the marketplace?

It wasn't the excellence of polyester that made the difference. It was the fact that the cotton industry, king for so long, forgot to pay attention to what was happening in the world around it. For centuries, the cotton producer was a farmer who worried only about growing enough cotton to meet the needs of the people who always came down from the cities to buy. There was no competitive marketplace in which the cotton farmer could hone his selling skills, his competitive wits. The cotton farmer of the past was one-dimensional.

And then fewer people came to buy, and they bought less and less.

The synthetic fibers, of course, were developed by the big chemical companies—DuPont, Celanese, Monsanto, and Eastman. These companies were used to fighting each other in the chemical marketplace, and they all had finely tuned marketing organizations conducting market research, advertising, public relations, and sales promotion. The farmer was caught unprepared for the blitzkreig that followed. The cotton farmer's bank account got smaller and smaller right along with cotton's share of the textile market.

That cotton farmer who lost out to the big chemical companies was the model for the familiar stereotype: straw hat and overalls.

FIGHTING BACK

But times have changed, and a new cotton farmer is emerging. One example of the grower's changing outlook and maturing sophistication is his organization of Cotton Incorporated as a company to help him compete in this new marketplace.

We were formed in 1971 as a company that would have as its product a variety of ideas to tackle the "fall and rise" of cotton on many fronts: alter the farmer's psychology, research consumer preferences, advance cotton technology from the fields through the mills and at the manufacturers, but above all, sell cotton, aggressively and creatively.

I've been to talk with the cotton growers in the fields in such places as the San Joaquin Valley and the Coastal Bend area of Texas, and I asked them, "What kind of business are you in?" They answered, "Cotton farming." To which I said, "No, you're not, you're in the fashion business; you're selling comfort."

Armed with this new philosophy and the same skills as giant corporations, we're coming from behind, and here's how we're doing it.

To start, it must be recognized that the mills would rather use polyester fiber to make fabric—it's easier for them to work with and in recent years it's even been cheaper. If we can't get a mill to make cotton fabric, there's none to sell to a manufacturer, and if the manufacturer has nothing to sell to a retailer, the customer can't buy cotton goods. Throughout this distribution channel a lot of people are making decisions, and we must influence them all in order to increase the consumption of cotton. We call that "push" marketing.

We have to make an impact on all these people. Consumers must be made aware that comfort is hostage to modern industrial and advanced marketing techniques before they will go back to retailers and demand cotton goods.

GETTING THE RIGHT "BLEND"

Retailers have to be shown that if they sell cotton goods, even at a slightly higher price than synthetics, there will be buyers and profits. Manufacturers have to be persuaded that a large market for cotton goods exists. And the mills have to be shown how to make cotton and mostly cotton fabrics as easily and as profitably as synthetics. That's called "pull" marketing.

"Creative marketing" is the keynote of the Cotton Incorporated effort. We realized that to compete in this new textile marketplace, we had to take advantage of the constantly changing world of fashion, create excitement with new products, and develop new concepts in merchandising. From one end of the distribution channel to the other, we had to create an impact.

The most visible and one of the biggest markets for cotton is in men's shirts. Blends of 65 percent or more polyester, even 100 percent polyester, have become dominant. Shirts had to be a first and most important marketing target. Cotton Incorporated took its first step by commissioning a study to explore the advantages and disadvantages of different blends, ranging from 100 percent cotton to 100 percent polyester. A panel of men was asked to test the shirts under a variety of conditions. The findings showed consistently that the more cotton in the shirt, the greater the comfort.

This provided us with the statistical support needed to launch our program in the men's shirt market. Our research efforts to develop new fabrics had already produced a high cotton blend fabric suitable for use in areas in which durable press had become a way of life for the consumer. We call this fabric—60 percent cotton—NATURAL BLEND,™ and it has taken the shirt manufacturing industry by storm. Manhattan, Van Heusen, Arrow, and nine other manufacturers are producing men's and boys' shirts made of the NATURAL BLEND fabric. These woven shirts have been accepted readily by the consumer because of their superior qualities of comfort, absorbency, softness, freedom from static, snagging, and pulling, washability, and permanent press. Seven major mills are producing the fabric, and retailers from Sears and Wards to local haberdasheries are featuring the new shirts.

In the two years since Manhattan introduced the first NATURAL BLEND shirt, cotton consumption in men's shirts jumped from 48 to 50 percent of the market share, reversing the steady downward trend it had been experiencing over the past 30 years.

The immediate and solid success of NATURAL BLEND in men's shirts is having a ripple effect. Manufacturers are using the fabric in men's underwear and pajamas and, even more significantly, in women's apparel.

Double-knit sportswear scored an initial success in promoting NATURAL BLEND fabrics to women. Catalina began using the new fabric in 1976 and Jantzen joined in 1977. As a result, cotton's share of the women's and girls' market has increased 10 percent, from 20.9 to 22.6 percent.

After apparel, the most important lost market for cotton is in bed sheets, and NATURAL BLEND fabric is beginning to make an impact here also. A year ago we asked 454 women in nine market areas to compare the typical bed sheet, with its 50-50 cotton-polyester ratio, with a sheet made of NATURAL BLEND fabric. Sixty-nine percent of the women said they preferred the NATURAL BLEND fabric and would buy that sheet if they had a choice.

To get the full significance of this, consider that 90 percent of all sheets sold in 1976 were of the 50-50 blend, a figure that represents $580 million. If 69 percent of Americans buying sheets in the next few years would buy NATURAL BLEND sheets instead of 50-50 sheets, a lot more money would feed back down the cotton product distribution system, and that's what impresses the people who make decisions at the mills, the manufacturing plants, and the retail shops.

New product development based on down-to-earth market research is continuing in quite a few areas, and it is among the most important work we do at Cotton Incorporated. But it's not all.

The concept of "creative marketing" can be stretched to include "creative merchandising." This involves coming up with new ideas in merchandising products to the consumer that will aid the manufacturer and the retailer.

For example, when we were doing our homework on bed sheets, we developed an idea that should help sell more sheets and increase retailers' margins. Historically, sheets have been sold one at a time. Each mill markets a line with many different colors and patterns, and they all feature designer names. As a result, the retailer has to gamble on quantities of colors and patterns. The customer comes in and cherry-picks the retailer to death. He winds up having to take big markdowns on "white sales" to move the odds and ends he has left over.

Our answer to this was to persuade manufacturers and retailers to put three sheets in a package—a print bottom sheet, a matching print top sheet, and a coordinated solid top sheet. The result: bigger sales, a consumer educated on how to mix and match and create new effects at home, fewer sheets marked down, and higher margins.

We don't stop there. In creative marketing, you've got to keep one step ahead of the competition, continuously developing ideas that will attract the consumer and increase profit margins for everyone down the line. While we were thinking of sheets, we asked ourselves: what else do sheet manufacturers sell? They sell towels. So we put a coupon in the package of sheets enabling the customer to write directly to the mill and ask the manufacturer to send him or her a bath mitt made of terry cloth. The customer is thus introduced to the mill's towel brand, and you're well on the way to building customer brand loyalty as well as loyalty to cotton products.

MORE THAN CONSUMERS

The ideas that we develop at Cotton Incorporated aren't always directed at the consumer. We have to impact on all levels of the distribution channel. One reason the mills liked the synthetics in the first place was that the chemical companies showed them how easy and inexpensive it is to work with synthetics. If we're going to swing the mills back to cotton in a significant way, we have to improve the methods of working with cotton. Therefore, Cotton Incorporated has embarked on a number of research projects involving the processing of cotton and cotton fabrics.

For example, working with a group of processors and machinery manufacturers, we have emerged with a new system for dyeing cotton and NATURAL BLEND knit fabrics that is less expensive and more efficient than existing methods. This new system will enable NATURAL BLEND to be dyed for less than half the direct annual costs of processing polyester with existing technology. Initial capital costs are also significantly lower.

Creative marketing shouldn't be merely a reactive force, responding to challenges from the competition. It should anticipate areas that may become highly competitive in the future. This means quick identification of any change in the pulse of the market. For example, a major battle between cotton and synthetics has emerged over one of the clothing staples of our time: jeans made of 100 percent cotton indigo denim.

Denim fabric consumes 9 percent of U.S. cotton production. Denim has grown threefold over the last ten years, so that in 1976, an estimated 820 million square yards were produced, practically all in 100 percent cotton. As a single fabric, denim has been more successful during this period than any other individual fabric.

However, a trend to dress-up denims has been growing. Some denim users would like to have a neater look and garments with little or no shrinkage. Polyester-blend imitation denim has the potential to wrest this market away from cotton, but we recognized this challenge early and are meeting the chemical companies head on.

Cluett-Peabody, in conjunction with a Norwegian textile firm, developed a new process called "Sanfor-Set," a process that reduces wrinkling and puckering after home laundering and limits shrinkage to less than 2 percent. Cotton Incorporated recognized the virtues of this new product. One hundred percent cotton jeans with the Sanfor-Set finish first appeared on retail counters in 1975, manufactured by the Sedgefield Division of Bluebell. Next, Lady Wrangler Sportswear adopted 100 percent cotton Sanfor-Set denim.

In 1977, the entire Wrangler manufacturing operation—men's, women's, and children's—the H. D. Lee Company, and Sears Roebuck boys' and girls' division jumped on the bandwagon. To date, leading retailers have expressed satisfaction with the new neat-look Sanfor-Set finish.

The effect of neater 100 percent denim on the jeans market has been stunning. In 1973 and 1974, 100 percent cotton jeans saw their market share erode from 76 percent to 72 percent. In 1975, with the introduction of Sanfor-Set jeans, 100 percent cotton jeans regained their 76 percent market share. Last year cotton jumped to 79 percent. A market share of more than 80 percent was expected for 1977.

Any creative marketing program isn't complete unless you include sales promotion, advertising, and public relations. And we're doing some exciting things here also.

We have a "Cotton Seal" that goes on all our new products and many of the old ones that are 100 percent cotton. The idea, of course, is to call the consumers' attention to the cotton content in the product; it also provides a link between the product and our promotional messages.

Recognition and awareness of the Cotton Seal were tested in 1973 and received an 18 percent awareness rating. Last year that awareness was up to 46 percent. It's not just the Cotton Seal and the advertising that are responsible for this rapid growth in awareness; it's having the right product at the right time, supported by marketing, merchandising, promotion, and advertising—the combination of all these factors—that is creating the impact on our markets.

To recapitulate: We have a classic story of an old established industry that became too set in its ways. Overly content and complacent, it was suddenly caught naked by a marketing powerhouse from a competing industry. As a result, it lost three-fourths of its traditional market. But the industry reappraised itself, formed a new company to market its basic product along modern, aggressive lines, and took the fight directly to the opposition. What have the results been so far? What is the bottom line? Is Cotton Incorporated for real or are we just a paper tiger?

The most telling data come from retail stores where consumers are buying more cotton, not only in apparel, but in home furnishings as well. Figures released by the Market Research Corporation of America in July 1977 show a continuing trend for more cotton in women's, men's, girls', and boys' clothing. All categories are up 2 percent or more from lows reached in 1974.

I firmly believe that this is the beginning of a trend and not just a wrinkle in the statistics. With NATURAL BLEND fabrics catching on, with a more aggressive and creative marketing posture being taken by the entire cotton industry—particularly the grower, through Cotton Incorporated— we feel that the pendulum has swung over to us.

Part 4

MARKETING PLANNING, OPERATIONS, AND SERVICES

**Sales, Advertising,
Marketing Research,
Public Relations,
and Market-Oriented Planning**

THE TOTAL MARKETING DEPARTMENT ORGANIZATION, under the marketing concept in its simplest form, would provide three basic structural blocks in terms of the functions that have to be provided. How they are arranged depends on the needs, objectives, and policies of each organization. In this basic structural concept, the importance lies in the separation of services from operations in order to keep the manager with sales responsibilities directed at selling; the staff or service managers servicing and aiding those sales, and marketing management coordinating both for an integrated total effort. The contributions in this section show that these functions can be very effectively used in nonprofit organizations.

	Government	Education	Health	Religious and Charitable	Associations and Others
The Supersalesman at the Census Bureau Business Week	X				
Politics and Ad Men: A Sticky Mess Marketing Communications	X				
The Role of Marketing Research in Public Policy Decision Making William L. Wilkie and David M. Gardner	X				
Bridging the Public Relations Gap Between Hospital Provider and Consumer Lee F. Block and M. Elliott Taylor			X		
Should Hospitals Market? Robin E. MacStravic			X		
Using a Team Approach to Market-Oriented Planning Arnold Corbin	X	X	X	X	X

The Supersalesman at the Census Bureau

Vincent P. Barabba heads what he considers to be "the largest marketing research organization in the world": the Bureau of the Census. This year, his huge federal agency is budgeted at $120 million, will employ 10,400 people, and will generate more than 1,100 reports containing more than 200,000 pages of statistics, tables, graphs, charts, maps, and text—enough to fill nearly nine sets of Encyclopaedia Britannica. Yet for all this statistical wealth, the bureau feels that it is reaching only a small share of its potential corporate customers. As the youngest Census director in half a century and one with a strong marketing bent, the 39-year-old Barabba is determined to change that, and is now mapping the first phase of one of the biggest selling jobs of his career.

The problem, as he sees it, is not that Census Bureau data lack usefulness, but that they pour out in such an overwhelming flood and variety. "It's terribly easy to inundate people with data," says Barabba, who became director last August after a stint as president of Datamatics, Inc. "The real challenge is to distill that data into usable form." Only this way, he claims, can census information fill a key purpose for which it is collected: to tell the government, social planners, and businessmen where

Reprinted with permission from *Business Week,* March 23, 1974.

the economy is now, where it has been, and to provide some information necessary for them to plan rationally for the future.

"If you're going to have an open economic system such as ours," Barabba adds, "you need as much information as you can get, not only about the distribution of goods and services but also about the ultimate consumer. And here's where our system breaks down sometimes. It's not that we don't have the information. It's just that we don't use it as much as we could."

NEW PRESSURES

Current material shortages and inflation only multiply the pressure for this kind of information. "Things are beginning to come to a head," Barabba says of the economy and competitive climate. "As a manufacturer, I can no longer say to myself, 'I'll just make up a billion or so of these widgets, and then if they don't sell, add some bells and whistles and cut the price.' Now I've got to ask, 'Am I going to get enough raw materials to factor out this kind of miscalculation?' And the answer is, 'Probably not.'" Many manufacturers, of course, recognize this—and in the last five years alone, requests for census information have quadrupled. But Barabba feels the bureau's market should be expanding more rapidly.

From his office in the leafy, Washington, D.C. suburb of Suitland, Maryland, where the Census Bureau makes its headquarters, Barabba is confronting more than a simple marketing problem. Over the years, the Census Bureau—like most other federal agencies—has come in for more than its share of brickbats. Some critics accuse the bureau of generating too many esoteric facts or the wrong kinds of facts. Others claim that it often only duplicates the research of other agencies. Robert Eggert, vice-president for economics and marketing research at RCA Corp. and a leading customer of the bureau, is one of many who would like to see "a little more prompt release" of Census data.

Right now, that information comes in many forms—microfilm, computer tapes, punchcards, and regular printed reports—and covers a dizzying array of subjects. Some of it is highly specialized—population projections for West and East Pakistan (now Bangladesh) or the number of grocery stores in Orange County, Calif., for instance. Other reports include key basic statistics, such as sales and payroll information for more than 100 types of wholesale, retail, and service businesses; figures on virtually everything that is imported or exported; the number of housing starts; and the production and consumption of chemicals, rubber, plastics, ferrous and nonferrous metals, textiles, lumber, glass, and other vital raw materials.

Hundreds of "Current Industrial Reports" (CIR) cover production, inventories, and orders for 5,000 products, or about 40 percent of all U.S. manufacturing, and are published weekly, monthly, quarterly, and annually. There are 16 separate reports on textiles alone and another eight on apparel. A quarterly CIR covers construction machinery, a monthly CIR details plastic bottle production, and an annual CIR keeps customers up to date on electrical lighting fixtures.

SERVICES

Over the last ten years or so, a growing number of Census customers want more than simply Census reports. They also want access to the raw, often unpublished data in the form of computer tapes and other software. This way, they can prepare their own tabulations and analyses.

Sometimes customers even want the bureau to make the special tabulations for them. The cost for these ranges from $39,000 for a one-shot deal to $10 million or more. One of the bureau's biggest current projects is a $15-million survey of consumer spending to update the "market basket" of goods used by the Bureau of Labor Statistics to compute the Consumer Price Index.

To help meet the growing demand for computerized data, the Census Bureau organized the Data Users Service in 1966. In its last fiscal year, DUS brought in $46.2-million worth of business, or more than one-third of the bureau's $112.5-million operating budget. It now has 13,000 to 14,000 customers. However, only 30 percent of them are from business and industry—a figure Barabba hopes to raise by upgrading and actively promoting the DUS.

While some customers may have their individual gripes about Census data, nearly all are full of praise for the overall job that the bureau does.

KEYSTONE

"Census data are the keystones of all market research," says Arthur C. Nielsen, Jr., president of A. C. Nielsen Co., the big market research operation. For its Nielsen ratings that measure the size of television audiences, Nielsen draws on the Decennial Census for age, sex, income, education, and other demographic details for the entire population. These figures are updated monthly, using the Census' "Current Population Survey," a household income report that breaks down the population by race, family size, income, occupation, and education. As another updater, Nielsen also draws on the "Marital Status and Living Arrangement" report. This covers the age and relationship of respondents to the head of the household.

All these facts, along with the Census' population estimates by county and state, are massaged by the Nielsen computers to produce a detailed profile of the population. Based on the results, Nielsen randomly chooses the 1,500 households that will be his sample TV audience. "The whole thing," Nielsen marvels, "costs us about $30 a year."

Nielsen's company also offers a retail trade service, drawing on a wide variety of sources to measure the movement of different products and brands through various types of retail outlets. The five-year Economic Census and the monthly *Current Survey of the Retail Trades* round out his demographic needs. These are "vital," says Nielsen, because they are a way not only of keeping tabs on prices by product and brand, but also zeroing in on the supermarkets, drugstores, and other types of outlets that do the most business in a particular item. With this information in hand, Nielsen researchers set up a sample of 1,600 supermarkets and 750 drugstores, and then actually go in and audit some 8,000 different products.

DEMOGRAPHIC DATA

PepsiCo, Inc., another big customer of the Census, relies on the same type of demographic data. "This permits us to get the dimensions of our markets, and to determine the size of our 550 franchises in relation to the competition," says H. Naylor Fitzhugh, vice-president of special markets for the Pepsi-Cola division. Pepsi franchises are organized mainly by county or groups of counties, depending on population. For this type of data, Pepsi draws on the bureau's county population breakdowns, which cover income, race, age, and other factors. "These data are important because they determine how we market our product," says Barbara Miller, Pepsi's manager of marketing information. If, for instance, county population surveys and other demographic data indicate a heavy Spanish-speaking segment in one area, Pepsi might decide to advertise in that language. Income levels are important, too—even in the sale of soft drinks. "The price may be low," she notes, "but it is still a discretionary purchase. This can be a very important factor in times of inflation."

From the *Census of the Retail Trades,* part of the five-year Economic

Census, Pepsi can also pinpoint by county all of the gas stations, super-markets, drugstores, eating and drinking establishments, and other types of outlets that might logically sell soft drinks. "These data are relatively inexpensive, between $200 and $250 a year," she says. Occasionally, as in 1970, Pepsi runs up a bigger tab. That year, the company spent between $4,000 and $5,000 on a special rundown of the packaging industry col-lected during the Economic Census.

SIDE LINES

The bureau's newest class of customers—almost a small industry within itself—consists of service companies that buy raw Census data, correlate them with other statistics—local births, deaths, school enrollments, build-ing permits—and organize special marketing studies of their own. CACI, Inc., of New York, for instance, offers its own census information as up to date as 1973, and counts among its customers J. C. Penney, Allied Stores, Gulf Oil, and other companies that are looking for new store, plant, or service station locations.

The burgeoning market for Census data has even spawned at least one company that simply tells its 100-plus clients how others are using Census data. A nonprofit corporation organized in 1969 by four Census Bureau expatriates and funded in part by foundation grants, Clearing-house & Laboratory for Census Data, in Arlington, Va., puts out two publications: a quarterly *Review of Public Data Use* and a bimonthly news-letter called *Data Access News*. Their combined subscription price is $40 a year. CLCD also does some data processing itself. It uses the Census Bureau summary tapes and guides other individuals and organizations in the use of these data.

Barabba's marketing plan for building the Census customer list is now moving into its first and earliest stage. With the help of eight advisory committees representing various Census statistics users, the bureau has assembled a questionnaire designed to find out how business perceives and uses its data. This will go out to some 2,000 major companies, begin-ning next month, and will be followed up by intensive interviews probably conducted by senior staff members.

Like any other good marketer, Barabba first of all wants to get a fix on his market. "If you just hand somebody 4 billion pieces of information and say, 'Here, do what you want with it,' you're not doing him any favor," he says. "We've got to find out what information is most needed, cull that out, and then make it more graphic. That's what the survey is all about." That is also what the Census Bureau is all about—and what Barabba will soon begin selling.

Politics and Ad Men: A Sticky Mess

Discussions about the use of "the media" in political campaigns usually begin and end with television. So it will be in this section, although print and radio still remain important campaign tools.

Television is the medium without which no big-league politician can do—if he wants to win. And, unless he can dream up some dramatic and cost-free way to capture television's attention, he has to pay a fortune to use it.

Money and the manner in which the image-makers sell candidates have created controversy and problems—the magnitude of which are matched only by the power of television. Television itself has become a political issue.

In this chapter, four men take different looks at the picture.

Lawrence Laurent, TV-radio editor of The Washington Post, sets the scene with a brief historical look at the rise of television in politics and the development of controversy.

In the second piece, Frederic Papert, one of the founders of Papert, Koenig, Lois, Inc., assaults the notion that image-makers can work miracles with candidates.

Jay Weitzner, president of Broadcast Placement Co., follows Papert with suggestions for handling candidates on television and a call for extensive research.

The final chapter in this section is by Robert D. Squier, president of the Communications Company. Squier gives his views on the urgent need for campaign spending reform.

TELEVISION BECOMES A POLITICAL ISSUE

Lawrence Laurent, TV-radio editor, The Washington Post

The takeoff point for any discussion of "The Media and the New Politics" begins with the realization that television itself became a political issue in the 1970 campaign. I, for one, am surprised that it took so long.

To explain my surprise, I recall a panel discussion that took place four years ago at a seminar of the Federal Communications Bar Assn. in Williamsburg, Va. One of the panelists was Carroll Newton of the Batten, Barton, Durstine & Osborn advertising agency (BBDO), and he is usually credited with having introduced the political "spot" advertisement into national politics. He told the Communications Bar Assn. that when the one-minute commercials were made (in behalf of Gen. Dwight D. Eisenhower) in 1952, many of the television stations refused to broadcast such commercials. Their refusal was overcome, he said, only by bringing to bear the entire economic muscle of BBDO upon the stations.

Apparently, in broadcasting, a four-year span is long enough to create a "long established tradition," for by 1956 all argument over the merits of the brief TV political commercial had disappeared, and the form was being used by both the partisans for President Eisenhower and for Adlai Stevenson.

The 1956 campaign, by the way, brought the first real apocalyptic vision of where the TV political commercial would lead the American electorate. This vision came from a writer named John G. Schneider in his novel, "The Golden Kazoo" (New York: Rinehart & Co., Inc., 1956). He had a kind of monstrous science-fiction nightmare of a candidate who conducted a national television giveaway program to win votes. According to Schneider, television as "The Golden Kazoo" would dominate politics in 1960.

The second major phenomenon (the first being television itself, having become a campaign issue) is the overdue recognition that television is the main factor in escalating campaigning costs. This has led Federal Communications Commissioner Nicholas Johnson to suggest, "You can buy the whole damn country for $58 million."

One further historical note: at almost any annual convention of the American Society of Newspaper Editors (ASNE), you can be almost certain to hear at least three speakers quote from a letter that Thomas Jefferson wrote to his friend, Edward Carrington, on Jan. 16, 1787.

Here's what is usually quoted: "The basis of our government being the opinion of the people, the very first object should be to keep that right; and were it left to me to decide whether we should have a government without newspapers or newspapers without a government, I should not hesitate a moment to prefer the latter."

That is a lovely thought, but I suggest that it is absolutely and totally meaningless unless one quotes the sentence which Mr. Jefferson immediately added: "But I should mean that every man should receive those papers and be capable of reading them." [Paul Leicester Ford, ed., "The Writings of Jefferson," 10 volumes (New York: G. P. Putnam's Sons, 1892–1899), vol. 4, p. 370.]

And if one doesn't omit the rarely cited qualification, I would suggest that the possibility of attaining Mr. Jefferson's ideal didn't become realistic until the arrival in the 20th century of the new electronic media, capable of bypassing illiteracy and making possible the free flow of information to millions of citizens who would not, could not, or did not receive that information in print.

GOOD CANDIDATES MAKE ADVERTISING EXPERTS

Frederic Papert, president, Papert, Koenig, Lois, Inc.

I wish that this book had been written before 1970 and the unsuccessful Ted Sorensen and Charles Goodell campaigns in which we had a hand. For years we got a lot of mileage out of Jacob Javits's, Robert Kennedy's and George McGovern's victories; we spread the word that we had never been in a losing campaign, which, in fact, we had not; and let the political world attribute to us great political skill, hence power. A far more important truth, however, has always been that good candidates make political advertising experts. It simply is not the other way around.

I can't think of a more useless way to spend time than listening to political pundits whose specialty is advertising. Political advertising does not have a life of its own any more than political polls have a life of their own, and there is nothing more pathetic than the campaign year ritual of politicians and their staffs grubbing through the remnants of former campaigns looking for the pundit to lead them to office. What's sad is that they overlook the real key, which is the candidate himself, whose zeal and commitment are the qualities that make people want to vote for him.

To the extent that advertising can help illuminate those virtues, we can play a role. But the notion that we are able to "create" winners, or even to remove warts, is nonsense. We can only reveal. We can help show the candidate at his best; we can accentuate the positive. And we can even hide the candidate, as was done in Rockefeller's 1966 campaign, when the voters of New York were subjected to millions of dollars' worth of commercials in which the Governor was neither seen nor heard. But to an audience not unfamiliar with the techniques of television advertising, even *that* was revealing.

What we cannot do is create. We can't make the voters believe that a dummy is smart, a bent man straight, a follower a leader, a bad man good.

Winners have many advisers; losers do it on their own. Even though (in our defense) Papert, Koenig, Lois disclaimed credit, always arguing that our main talent lay in picking winners in the first place, our clients' victories led other potential clients to our doors. We were smart enough to turn down most of them.

We've tried to be good revealers. We've known enough not to get between the candidate and the voters, not to obfuscate the candidate's virtues with advertising techniques—old virtues. And because we believe it, we've always tried to concentrate on the candidate, to let him discuss the issues if there are issues, to talk about what he regards as important. By doing so, we've given the voter a close look at the man, eyeball to eyeball, and on the basis of that the chances of the right man's getting elected are improved.

Do we sound wise and professional and even brilliant? The most successful political television commercial we've ever done was for Robert Kennedy in his 1964 New York senatorial race. We arranged a question-answer session with several hundred Columbia University students. We encouraged them to give vent to their antagonism toward Kennedy (they were very antagonistic); and that, in turn, brought out Kennedy's real self, both in his answers and in his final five-minute, nonpartisan pep-talk/ lecture. We videotaped it all and put it on the air. One half-hour commercial included questions, answers and speech; another was the five-minute speech alone. And in the week they were on the air, what appeared to be a losing campaign (Kennedy's opponent had gone ahead in the polls and seemed to have momentum on his side) became a 400,000-vote victory.

We had tried other ways to capture the real Kennedy on tape or film for television: street corner conversations that had worked so well with Javits were no good for Kennedy—the crowds were mobs, cameras were jostled, no one could hear questions or answers; speeches into the camera at studios were disastrous, as they were with Javits—both men froze when lights went on; contemplative strolls through the garden were an even worse disaster—it takes an actor other-directed unreal fellow to pull it off (Reagan and Nixon come readily to mind). We were getting nowhere, until Ethel Kennedy suggested the students.

It was her idea. The agency saw to it that the cameras were in place, that the tape was edited to size, that the time buys were made, that the material got to the stations and on the air—and that's about as much as advertising experts can do.

My point is that I don't think there are any miracle workers in political advertising. I don't want to spoil Bob Squier's new business pitch to any potential candidates who may be here (if I were running for office, I would try to hire Bob to help run my campaign; he does what he does very well, indeed); but there are limits to what even Bob Squier can do. And if you work in politics and don't understand that, then you're going to get yourself in trouble.

Neither Squier nor Garth nor Guggenheim nor Papert ever elected anybody to anything, and we probably never will. The candidate gets himself elected. Sometimes we help; most of the time we make very little difference.

HANDLING THE CANDIDATE ON TELEVISION

Jay Weitzner, president, Broadcast Placement Co.

Acting as do believers in voodoo and witchcraft, critics of television's use in political campaigns have naively attributed all sorts of magical powers to the medium. Television in the hands of an unscrupulous candidate, they say, will bend the minds of the voters and send them glassy-eyed and mumbling his name to the polls. Recently the heads of some major advertising agencies voiced their fears of television commercials in politics. Of course, one is to forget the continual onslaught upon our ears and eyes by these selfsame spokesmen. How much veracity can be attributed to men responsible for dancing cigarette packs and green men suffering from giantism?

We must recognize one simple fact: television is a means of communication, albeit one way, in that I talk to you. It can present a point of view in the most stimulating manner, but it certainly cannot force me or you to do something against our will. Yes, an incompetent with a large war chest can inundate us with his commercials but that doesn't guarantee his election. He may make an overkill for name recognition but name recognition doesn't mean election, as we are all aware.

The television commercial serves only to match a message to basic attitudes already existing in the viewer's mind. It can create an impression either favorable or unfavorable, but it cannot make the voter cast his ballot one way or another. The commercial can only illustrate the personality of the candidate or provide him with a platform to raise issues.

Now to the original premise of this book—strategies in the new politics: strategy implies a course or plan of action. And there are three strategic periods of concentrated exposure for the candidate: predeclaration, declaration, and the campaign.

The predeclaration period gives the candidate the opportunity to present himself to the electorate on a somewhat informal basis. He has the opportunity to appear on a variety of entertainment and nonentertainment programs. The amount of free exposure time that is given to him by stations is not limited by equal time rulings of the FCC. The frequency with which he appears is limited only by the interest in the candidate and the story that he has to tell. It is our belief that during this phase the candidate should grasp any opportunity for exposure that is offered to him or is created by his staff. It is during this period that the candidate can take on a three-dimensional personality. He will be able to establish a more intimate relationship with the electorate by letting them see facets of his personality that will not come across during the actual campaign. He'll be able to satisfy that universal curiosity we all have about what goes on behind the scenes in the lives of our public officials. Depending on the type of program appearance, he will be able to tell a joke, play the piano, or go wherever his interest lies.

The declaration is a nonevent staged for the benefit of the news media. It is a nonevent because up until the big day the candidate has vigorously skirted a positive or negative statement regarding his candidacy, but back in our minds we know he's really going to run. The event is staged in that he will be talking to groups of his own supporters who will loudly cheer his every word. It is one of his big days, and possibly at no other time during the campaign will the news media be as kind to him. He is the star and will be treated as such. The scope of questions will run from, "Why are you a candidate?" "When did you make up your mind to run?" to the inevitable question asked of his wife, "Are you happy that he's running?" But that should end the honeymoon.

From then on, if the news media are doing their job, he will be on the spot every time a camera is focused on him or a microphone is held to his mouth. He will be on the offensive as well as the defensive. He is now a member of that uniquely American species—a candidate on the campaign trail.

Let's take a closer look at a prototype candidate. He should have one or more of those characteristics to which we all aspire—he should be attractive, dynamic, have the look of a winner, be likeable, warm, and human. Basically he should have all those preconceived traits that we expect our leaders to possess.

As a result of continual exposure to television, we have learned to project characteristics of our television heroes to our political heroes. We want them to be articulate and also look competent enough to handle the office they are seeking. They should exude confidence and assuredness, for it is the man we are looking at and not so much his message that is all important. We tend to like and judge people by their style and appearance. Our memories of words fade long before we forget the physical impression of an individual. We recall in terms of overall impressions.

I am not trying to create the impression that I advocate ignoring what the candidate has to say or even brushing it off, because words and their misuse can and do create negative images in our minds. The pompous verbalizer, the pedantic phrasing of an arm-waving candidate will almost immediately foster rejection in the minds of the electorate. I prefer candidates to use words that create pictures in the mind. Let him speak in short, nonlegalistic phrases. The taxpayer should be spoken about as a person and not as some faceless member of the constituency. Money should be talked about in terms of the individual and not in millions of dollars and the taxpayer in general. As a viewer I identify much more easily with a problem or an issue when it directly refers to someone I can identify with as a member of my own peer group.

One of the greatest problems facing the media specialist is that one candidate who just cannot come across the tube. He may have all the negative characteristics I mentioned before plus some of his own. What do you do in a situation like that? Keep him away from cameras, shoot stills, show only reaction shots? None of these is a solution. Try to enlighten the candidate and he will invariably answer, "Pompous, stiff . . . who, me?" The poor guy has been getting it from all quarters. Everyone in his personal or political family at one time or another has given him advice. For one appearance they've told him he was too uptight, and for the same appearance another guide and mentor will say he was too relaxed. So by the time the media specialist gets to him he has been so overwhelmed with advice that he even rejects the specialist's. It is at this point that the media man must call upon whatever psychological abilities he has in order to help the candidate display his strong qualities and suppress his weaker ones. The candidate will reject the concept of role playing in order to reach the electorate. But he must be convinced diplomatically that what he is doing is not creating a role as would an actor but, rather, enhancing his abilities to reach the electorate.

Extreme care should be taken with the candidate's physical appearance. For television, a competent make-up person should be on hand. And never let a news photographer within a mile of a candidate being made up. For the same reasons, don't allow retouching while he is on the studio floor unless it is a closed set. Lights should be checked—hopefully with a stand-in of the same height for all candidates but especially those wearing glasses or who have deep-set eyes or extremely white hair or bald spots.

The television commercial—and it may sound strange to hear this—is not intended to be seen or heard as a single entity existing just for its own sake. Rather, it is supposed to create an impression in the mind of the viewer by involving him in an event. Commercials do not sell; all they can do is create a favorable environment.

And this environment can only be created through the marriage of attitudinal research and the commercial. Therefore, it is to the advantage of the media specialist to work with attitudinal researchers to find those issues that the voter most readily accepts.

If we sit down and attempt to determine one specific formula that will create an impression in the mind of the electorate, we are only deluding ourselves. There is no one answer. And these multiple answers can only be found in the minds of the electorate. Only through extensive polling and researching can we learn if the voter believes that a political controversy exists or that the controversy is between political personalities. How else are we to learn the political and issue preconceptions of the voters? What is the voter like, and how can we reach him? Is the voter interested in the candidate as a human interest figure, a public interest figure, or as a political leader? Is our candidate trusted or distrusted? Does the candidate match those characteristics considered desirable by the voters?

It is from this information that we are able to develop themes and techniques that will present the candidate to the electorate. For as someone has said, we have gone from the era of the people seeking an audience with a leader to the leader seeking an audience with the people.

Not only are we dependent on attitudinal study for our themes but also for the very language that we must use in communicating with the voters. We must know what symbols should appear in our commercials that are most understood by those we are trying to reach.

Because of the increased sophistication and perhaps the jaded appetites of the voters, we believe that the era of commercials showing the candidate staring at the ocean, river, or lake with his jacket over his shoulder; playing tennis or basketball, or talking to the workers is over. What has defeated it is the fact that we can now direct commercials to specific audiences through the implementation of class and deep-level attitudinal studies. The class grouping or ethnic commercial offers a great potential in terms of its specific appeal, but it is a delicate thing to handle, as it can appear patronizing or even insulting to the audience if mishandled. The regional commercial provides somewhat more leeway in speaking to a specific audience, but it can also have a negative effect in those regions screening opposing commercials. With today's instant communications, one cannot say one thing in one region and then take an opposing stand in another.

By increasing our knowledge of the voter and his attitudes and beliefs, we will best be able to reach him with our messages.

LOWERING THE COST OF BUYING DEMOCRACY

Robert D. Squier, president, The Communications Company

Television has been largely responsible for moving politics from the back room to the living room. Unfortunately, in the process, it has also raised the costs of democracy.

There has been a good deal of controversy surrounding this phenomenon in the past several months, principally in connection with the 1970 campaigns and with the attempt to override the President's veto of a TV spending bill.

One must understand that the cost of broadcast time is what has caused the need for so much money in the first place; 60 cents of every campaign dollar must now be set aside for television and radio.

Why? The reason is very simple. Television has made it possible, for the first time, for a candidate to have direct and personal communication with every potential voter. That communication, however, is riddled with static. It is long on rhetoric and over-simplification and short on responsibility, but it is real, immediate, and a political fact of life—a fact of life we must deal with.

Two things require our immediate attention. First, we must clean up and improve that communication and, second, open it up so that a man or woman doesn't have to be rich to use it.

As the system now operates, candidates must pay a ransom to broadcasting stations to use the people's airwaves in order to transact the most important business of the democracy—elections. This is wrong. We, the people, own the medium and ought to be able to borrow it back from the broadcasters whenever it suits our public purpose.

The Campaign Broadcast Reform Act of 1970 was just vetoed by President Nixon, and the veto was sustained. This act would have gone a long way toward removing many of the inequities that now exist in the process of televised political communication.

The President, I cynically believe, proposed a broader campaign reform act at the last hour as a tactic for defeating the legislation. There is no task more important for all of us here to perform than to hold him to that promise I am sure he does not intend to keep. If we don't, we will be affirming a national elections system where an admission price is permanently fixed to the pursuit of public office. We will, by our silence, endorse Political Pay TV.

No campaign spending reform legislation will be complete without the three basic elements of the bill that was just vetoed. It must include:

1. A reasonable limitation on broadcast spending for candidates.
2. Reduction in rates to make candidates the most favored rather than the least favored of the broadcasters' clients.
3. Suspension of S.315 to permit debates between the two major-party presidential candidates.

I would add one final thought which has always served to keep our heads straight when forced to think about the impact of our work on the political system. It is a quote from Daniel Boorstin's book, "The Image":

"We can fabricate fame, we can at will (though usually at considerable expense) make a man or woman well known; but we cannot make him great. We can make a celebrity, but we can never make a hero. In a now-almost-forgotten sense, all heroes are self-made."

The Role of Marketing Research in Public Policy Decision Making

William L. Wilkie
David M. Gardner

Government agencies are making increasingly active attempts to assure and maintain a "fair competitive environment" for consumers. One important characteristic of these public policy activities has been an underutilization of the skills and insights of researchers in marketing and consumer behavior. This paper explores reasons for this underrepresentation and proposes means by which marketing research can contribute to future policy decisions.

Although many points made here can apply across government agencies, attention will focus on the Federal Trade Commission (FTC), where the authors recently completed extensive in-house consulting assignments for the purpose of effecting increased utilization of marketing research by the organization. This experience resulted in several significant conclusions:

Reprinted from *Journal of Marketing*, January 1974.

1. Public policy makers have a sincere interest in contributions from marketing and consumer behavior research.[1]
2. This interest is well founded—effective research could significantly improve many public policy decisions.
3. There is currently, however, a substantial gap between information needs and the nature of available research inputs.
4. Marketers are thus faced with the alternatives of either increased participation in enlightened policy making or continued reaction in the political arena. The research gap can be closed if the marketer is willing to understand and adapt to the exigencies of policy decisions. Marketers should recognize that public policy will continue to be created, with or without their research.

The above points are amplified in the sections which follow. First, a brief discussion of the background and decision processes of the FTC outlines information needs of the organization and highlights a crucial distinction in problem perspective between marketers and consumerists. Next, a detailed analysis of the research gap indicates necessary shifts in research emphasis that should be made by marketers if their research is to be useful to policy makers. The third section of the paper offers suggested areas of inquiry for future research.

A BRIEF PERSPECTIVE ON THE FTC

The Federal Trade Commission is broadly charged with the responsibility for providing a fair competitive environment for the nation's economic system. Its mandate, apart from administering several specific acts, is surprisingly vague. Section 5 of the Federal Trade Commission Act originally declared "unfair methods of competition in commerce" to be unlawful, and was later amended to include "unfair or deceptive acts or practices" in this category. These statements historically have been interpreted as assigning responsibility and authority in areas of industry structure (competition) and trade practices (consumer protection).

Critics have often questioned commission activities in both competition and consumer protection. Much of the FTC's recent activity can be attributed to charges leveled in 1969 studies by "Nader's Raiders"[2] and an American Bar Association committee commissioned by President Nixon.[3] The primary responses by the FTC under Chairmen Weinberger, Kirkpatrick, and Engman have been to make major internal changes in organization and staffing and to increase efforts to seek effective impacts externally.[4]

Figure 1. FTC decision stages.

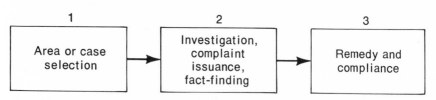

A brief overview of the FTC's decision process is useful in assessing the rationale for these shifts. As outlined in Figure 1, there are essentially three decision stages for the organization. Stage 1 requires the determination of program priorities and, within programs, selection of specific cases for further involvement. Stage 2 represents decision sequences in staff investigations, commission complaint procedures, consent negotiations, and formal adjudicatory procedures. Stage 3, remedy generation and compliance monitoring, determines the actual impact of commission activities.

Public criticisms by Nader and the ABA concerned FTC performance at each stage. Charges included too little activity and that what activity there was centered on trivial problems (Stage 1); excessive time delays (for example, four or more years) in Stage 2; and weak, ineffective remedies in Stage 3. The FTC has since attempted to improve performance within each decision sector. A new Office of Policy Planning and Evaluation was created to report directly to the commissioners on program planning and resource allocation. A management information system is being developed to streamline Stage 2, and power to seek preliminary injunctions has been requested. The search for more effective remedies at Stage 3, of course, has been the most obvious of all changes at the FTC. There are four areas of new remedies of particular interest to marketers:

1. Advertising substantiation.
2. Corrective advertising (affirmative disclosure by single firms).
3. Product information (affirmative disclosures by all firms within an industry).
4. Consumer education.

The much publicized advertising substantiation program was developed to provide public documentation of the basis for competitive copy claims. Corrective advertising reflects the dual concerns of rectifying "ill-gotten" competitive advantages and correcting the "residual effects" consumers may have received from deceptive advertising campaigns. Product information programs are aimed at providing consumers with information to help improve purchasing decisions, while consumer education is concerned with developing consumers' abilities to deal effectively with complex purchasing problems.

While these programs are open to, and have been receiving, legitimate criticisms on legal and economic grounds, the intent here is neither to advocate nor to disparage their value. The *concepts* are significant in that they reveal a shift by the FTC from *re*action to *pro*action. Rather than rely solely on rectifying isolated and recognizable abuses, the agency has begun an attempt to change the consumer environment so as to reduce the probability of abuses.

Two rationales can be advanced to account for this shift in FTC activity. The first follows from the above-mentioned charges of inefficiencies in internal procedures and external effects; the new remedies are clearly aimed at increasing impact per FTC resource dollar. The second is less obvious but more important in that it symbolizes a significantly different perspective of the consumer environment than that implicitly held by most marketers and researchers. Consumer advocates place primary emphasis on perceived shortcomings of the extant consumer environment as compared to a more desirable environment characterized by full information, quality and price competition, and rational purchasing. The current environment is attributed solely to marketers having exercised "marketing freedoms" in their own best interests. The marketing researcher should recognize the existence and implications of this viewpoint whether or not he chooses to accept it, for it appears to underlie much of the disagreement as to appropriate roles and tactics for government policy.

In summary, present research needs of the FTC can be identified with respect to its three decision points: program priorities, fact-finding, and development of equitable and effective remedies. A number of worthwhile suggestions for the incorporation of consumer research were advanced by Dorothy Cohen four years ago.[5] Despite the obvious insights that marketing research can offer the commission, little influence has yet been evidenced at the FTC. This situation can be traced to a basic gap in understanding between policy makers and consumer researchers.

THE CURRENT GAP

That a gap in understanding exists is obvious. Specification of the nature of the gap will aid both marketers and public policy makers to better understand the elements that they are trying to influence. The least understood element in the implicit models of competition used by the FTC staff seems to be consumer behavior. The following misconceptions are widespread in the agency among those who have not studied the behavioral sciences.

Economic Man Assumption

The study of consumer behavior has repeatedly shown that the economic man assumption in its purest form is not valid. Nonetheless, this assumption has certain intrinsic attractions to the policy maker who is trying to reduce a complex situation into a manageable one. In addition, there is little likelihood that there will be any educational experience in the background of the public policy maker to make him aware of the fallacies of an assumption that rests heavily on the further assumption of "all other things being equal." Consequently, it is common to find at least the following three ideas underlying much of the thinking of the FTC.

First, it seems that price, brand, store, advertising, and quality are often considered to be completely independent of each other and other factors. The idea that a person would be willing to pay more for a certain brand, even though the almost identical product is available at less cost, is thought by many to signal some flaw in the system and represent anticompetitive behavior on the part of some business firm. Likewise, advertising expenditures often are viewed with suspicion and in isolation.

Second, frequently it is assumed that the consumer has unlimited shopping time to make numerous comparisons and unlimited time to acquire the necessary information to achieve the lowest economic cost. This belief, unfortunately, ignores *total* economic cost.

Third, psychological needs of consumers are often ignored or, if included, are said to be the result of marketing and advertising practices. Incorporated here is the failure to recognize the relatively large amount of disposable income in the hands of consumers after "basic" needs have been satisfied.

Definition of Rationality

While the economist can use the theoretical results of pure or perfect competition to measure actual competitive organizations and strategies, no similar model of consumer behavior is widely accepted. In the absence of such a model, various normative models are applied. Unfortunately, these are often inductive models based mainly on personal experience and observation. They are not, therefore, representative and do not generalize beyond rather narrow limits.

Proxy Variables

Through experience, word-of-mouth information, and expectations, consumers learn to use certain aspects of the purchase situation as cues or proxy variables to provide them with information about products. The policy maker often acts as if information transmitted by price, brand name, and store is not related to the product itself. This can easily lead to the assumption that the consumer needs more information and would use it if available. Conversely, it may be maintained by some policy makers that in some situations one of the variables is so important that no other variable matters. Complaints that focus on a brand name, a price strategy, or a store name and purposely or otherwise ignore other variables represent this view.

Consumer Information Processing

The most serious misconception or assumption is the belief that the consumer is highly impressionable and that by saying the right words he will blindly obey what he is told by an advertisement or other source of product information. This is the belief that leads people to attribute great powers to advertising. It denies the concept of consumer information processing and, especially, selective perception. Three conclusions follow from this view of consumer information processing.

First, *more information is better*. The more information consumers have, the better decisions they can make. Little recognition is given to the actual needs of consumers, the environment in which the information is used, and accumulation of relevant information through product usage and word-of-mouth. Considerable consternation results when information provided to consumers is ignored. Likewise, the policy maker often does not understand the failure of education campaigns which try to provide customers with information to help them be better decision makers.

Closely related is the *lack of concern with the quality or content of the message*. The study of consumer information processing indicates a variety of factors necessary to insure that the consumer receives the same meaning from the communication as the communicator desires. However, there is an inherent belief that if you say something in plain English, it will be clearly understood in the intended manner by all.

The third idea is that *information is processed in a uniform manner by all consumers*. This idea ignores differential processing of information according to experience, anticipated use for the product, and the importance of the product. A related assumption is that most products are relatively important to customers.

Howard and Sheth suggest that decision making can be divided into three stages during which purchase criteria are crystallized and the range of alternatives is narrowed.[6] It is clear that the type of information desired and useful to the consumer varies from stage to stage. It also appears that information has a greater capacity to influence consumers who are in the earlier stages of search. These sorts of insights should be incorporated into policy decisions aimed at consumer utilization of information.

Corrective Advertising

To illustrate the problems that these misconceptions can cause, the relatively recent FTC program of corrective advertising is reviewed below. These comments in no way should be construed as value judgments, but only as observations. By presenting these observations, the authors hope to clarify the need for the incorporation of research into decision processes.

The primary goal of corrective advertising is to eradicate the "residual effects" of deceptive advertisements. An effective program of corrective advertising would seem to benefit consumers as well as honest competitors and provide a strong deterrent to deceptive advertising in general. It should be noted, however, that a number of difficult decisions are required of the FTC in order to create an effective program.[7]

First, it must be determined whether or not the advertisement at issue is deceptive. If deceptive, a second decision must be made as to the need for corrective advertising. This involves a determination of the extent and magnitude of the residual effects of the deception. If residual effects are held to exist, it is necessary to specify the best program by which to "correct" them. Such diverse concepts as media selection and scheduling, time period for correction, budget, and copy elements are included in this decision. Early corrective advertising orders have typically required that 25 percent of the brand's advertising budget be expended in normal media schedules for one year, with the corrective copy subject to FTC approval.

A failure to consider research perspectives and evidence raises several significant issues for the commission. While it may be reasonable to assert that advertising can have residual effects in general, how are these effects to be assessed in any particular case? This problem would seem to require both a precise definition of "residual effect" and an effort to obtain evidence on whether or not such effects are present in the minds of consumers.

Assuming that residual effects are present, how can they be eradicated? An important constraint in this regard is that FTC remedies cannot be punitive in intent. This suggests that considerable *precision* is required in the FTC's specifications for the corrective advertising order. Guidelines for corrective copy are surely required; research has shown that strong corrective copy can lead to negative brand attitudes, decreased intentions to purchase the brand, and unfavorable corporate and brand images.[8] These negative predispositions could be viewed as punitive and should be avoided through copy specifications focused on less affective dimensions of consumer information.

Delivery of the corrective message also requires precision. Consider the strong assumptions implicit in requiring that 25 percent of an advertising budget be devoted to corrective copy for a one-year period. It is much more logical to assume that each case will require its own budget formula and its own time frame if eradication is to be achieved without punitive effects upon the respondent firm.

In light of these problems, an alternative approach to the FTC's corrective advertising program has been advanced.[9] This approach requires, first, that the nature of "residual effects" be carefully defined in terms of consumer behavior. Second, evidence as to the existence and magnitude of the residual effect must be used to decide whether or not corrective advertising is needed in a given case. Finally, the FTC should withdraw from its new role as the public's advertising agency; it is simply not clear that legal training and expertise provide a basis for developing copy, budgeting, media, and timing decisions aimed at precision without punishment. Instead, the FTC's order would simply require that the previously defined and measured residual effects be reduced to a minimal baseline level. Respondents would retain flexibility in the manner by which this is accomplished. Failure to accomplish the eradication or to meet secondary measures of "good faith compliance" would constitute violation of the order and subject the respondent to the heavy penalties of violation.

The basis for such an approach lies in consumer research rather than intuition or introspection. Resistance to such a change is one characteristic of the current gap between consumer research and public policy.

Information Processing Constraints

Most policy makers received their formal academic training prior to the emphasis on the behavioral sciences. In addition, especially within the FTC, most policy makers are lawyers by training. With a few notable exceptions, there is little if any training in the behavioral sciences offered by present day law schools. Since policy makers are not familiar with the potential contributions of the behavioral sciences, they appear to be reluctant to incorporate the findings of behavioral science and incapable of understanding inferential research as it bears on their problem.

Even if the lawyer understands the scientific method and inferential research, he generally avoids the use of research findings if the design or conclusions can be attacked in any manner. Since all inferential research can be attacked, it is generally not used because any attack on evidence is apt to leave a negative halo effect that may carry over to other points of the case.

Lastly, the pressure is on the lawyer or policy maker to find a solution NOW! The difficulties of incorporating formal planning within a political environment contribute to a timing problem. Very seldom does the policy maker have the time to conduct an extensive research investigation. It is not uncommon for an attorney to have less than two months to gather his complete legal brief for a case to be heard before an administrative law judge. Yet carefully designed research projects typically take much longer and even then the lack of replication would open questions of reliability and validity.

But the gap is two-sided. While the lawyer may find it difficult to use information because of his training and inclinations, there is a serious problem with the type of information available to him.

Policy makers are decision makers. Generally, they are not interested in theory—they want practical, unambiguous information. In addition, they want "specific and absolute" proof. But what information is available to the policy maker? The immediate reply is: quite a bit. A closer look at this situation is warranted. The inspection is best handled by breaking existing research evidence into two categories: (1) consumer belief and attitude research, and (2) consumer decision-making research.

Consumer Belief and Attitude Research

The first category includes all research directed at demonstrating how consumer beliefs and attitudes are formed, organized, and used to give meaning to products and services. Much of what is known about this category comes from research carried on by social psychologists. While a great deal has been learned about motivation, personality, learning, socialization, and group interaction, careful assessment should be made as to whether what has been "learned" is readily usable by the policy maker.

The objectives of social psychology should not automatically be equated with the objectives of the study of consumer behavior. Since social psychology is primarily concerned with the social behavior of man in society, few of its findings or tools had as their genesis the need or desire to know about the consumer. While many of the findings from social psychology are indeed transferable to the study of consumer behavior, they have often been accepted with an uncritical attitude.

With the exception of those who specifically call themselves consumer psychologists, most social psychologists who study consumer behavior do not do so as an area of primary interest, but because such study might allow them to investigate a general phenomenon. It should also be noted that, for the most part, social psychologists are not concerned with external validity. Consequently, two difficulties arise when one tries to apply to public policy knowledge borrowed from the findings of social psychology about consumers. The first is that psychology is generally concerned with exploring a small aspect of behavior in a rigorous manner. The objective is often to increase knowledge simply for its own sake. The second difficulty is that certain problems which are basic to the understanding of consumer behavior have not been given adequate attention by social psychologists. The result of this gap in an understanding of consumer information is that one can only talk in generalities about the formation of consumer information. This level of knowledge is not sufficient for the implementation of public policy. Therefore, much of what the marketer claims to know about attitude and belief formation with regard to products and purchase situations is not readily applicable to the needs of the policy maker.

Consumer Decision-Making Research

The research evidence available to the policy maker on consumer decision making is more in line with his needs. Even so, this considerable amount of information about the consumer's use of unit pricing information, open dating, interest rate disclosure, and the availability of consumer product rating publications has hardly scratched the surface. The gaps in this area of research are not to be blamed on social psychology; rather, they represent the results of a piecemeal attack, often based on questionable or nonexistent theoretical foundations.

The major deficiency is that many studies attempt only to describe consumer behavior rather than explain it. For example, many studies on brand loyalty, unit pricing, price/quality and advertising/sales relationships present quite simplistic explanations for the behavior described. Marketers have perceptual maps of many products and have seen canonical correlation and discriminant analysis applied to many problems. But why are these developments not directly useful to the policy maker?

The reasons are complex, of course, but the major components are an implicit marketing management orientation, a strong interest in techniques, and a lack of research programming.

An implicit marketing management orientation is not to deny the high quality of research useful to marketing managers. As just two examples, the body of research dealing with market segmentation and that dealing with market share analysis make fine contributions to the body of knowledge needed to be a successful marketing manager. However, these two areas, as well as most research in marketing, deal only indirectly with how consumers process information. This research is focused on controllable decisions of marketing management, while little attention has been given to controllable decisions of public policy makers. The latter orientation might begin, for example, by carefully considering the scope and character of a desirable consumer environment.

There is a very understandable interest in developing techniques associated with consumer behavior. The unidimensional techniques used for many years simply are not appropriate for the complex, multidimensional world of the consumer. Likewise, the development of techniques is often a very rewarding experience personally. But the application of these techniques to the study of consumer behavior lags many years behind their development. Marketers must ask themselves serious questions about the value of devoting increasingly greater resources to development and refinement of new techniques as opposed to encouraging the use of existing techniques to develop information about consumers for the policy maker.

Within the field of consumer behavior, no research traditions apart from short-lived interest areas have emerged. The net result is that *no research programming exists*. Three major models have been proposed: Nicosia in 1966;[10] Engel, Kollat, and Blackwell in 1968;[11] and Howard and Sheth in 1969.[12] Although interesting and sometimes controversial attacks have been directed at components of these models, no comprehensive program is yet in sight. Academic researchers are often too ready to blame the lack of funding for this deficiency. The interest in small "doable" pieces of research because of the need to "publish or perish," coupled with the absence of any organized groups of researchers, may go further toward explaining the absence of a coordinated, comprehensive approach.

If research on consumer behavior is to have an impact on public policy, it must be useful and available to the policy maker. Therefore, it is imperative that marketing researchers examine their strong interest in research techniques, reconsider their biases, and start pooling their talents and research efforts in comprehensive programs.

The Negative Halo Effect of Business-Sponsored Research

A final basic constraint is that research conducted or sponsored by business firms and organizations of business firms is often subject to suspicion by policy makers. Since policy makers typically are not sophisticated in research design and analysis, they are apt to rely on the assumption that the only reason a business firm would sponsor research would be to support the firm's position. Unfortunately, there is some validity to this general assumption of the policy maker. Therefore, any research directed at the policy maker must be conducted in such a manner as to allow him to completely remove these suspicions.

IMPLICATIONS FOR FUTURE RESEARCH

A significant increase in the use and effectiveness of research in public policy is likely to occur when researchers begin to anticipate future information needs and make insights available when they are needed. A primary objective for interested researchers should thus be to *lead rather than lag* public policy issues.

Future decision needs of the FTC and marketers concerned with public policy and consumer protection offer challenging topics for research. As noted earlier in this article, recent activities of the FTC indicate a willingness both to challenge the quality of the existing consumer environment and to effect changes in it. It seems highly appropriate that businessmen and researchers add their insights to this decision process. The authors' impressions of the most prominent topics are listed in Table 1.

Program Priorities

The most important and complex decisions made by the FTC involve choices concerning areas of activity. While philosophical disagreements will occur as to the appropriate scope of governmental regulation, it is hoped that most marketers will choose to participate in this process rather

Table 1. Topics for future research.

Program priorities	Response research
Consumer environment descriptions	Product information
Models for resource allocation	Consumer education
Social cost-benefit measurements	*Product and segment research*
Structural versus trade practice remedy	Special markets
Stimulus research	Specific products and services
Advertising effects	
Personal selling and promotion	
Pricing	
Product quality	
Guarantee and warranty	

than ignore it entirely. Four decision areas in particular require research on priorities: description of consumer environments, resource allocation models, social cost/benefit measures, and remedy approaches.

Consumer environment descriptions refer to measures of the state of the consumer world, both present and future. While considerable information on aggregate consumer behavior currently exists, interpretation is difficult without bases for comparison. Such bases might include aggregate models of an "optimal" consumer environment or individual data on problems and satisfactions with existing conditions. Either form of information could be used to measure "deviations" indicative of program needs.

Models for resource allocation should include explicit considerations of nonregulatory remedies such as industry self-regulation or consumer education. While internal costs might be accurately predicted for these models, major work is clearly needed to obtain external program costs and social benefits. Improved methods of measuring or analyzing nonquantifiable costs and benefits are also required for these models. *Social cost/benefit measures,* in addition to acting as model inputs, could also serve as performance indicators for the FTC and the macro-marketing system.

Structural versus trade practice remedy issues concern the alternative means by which consumer benefits can be gained, ranging from forced divestitures in concentrated industries; through limitations on, or prohibitions of, certain marketing activities; to case approaches of single problems. Marketer and consumer behavior are key elements in predicting the effects of these alternatives; yet they are often subject to simplistic assumptions in such analyses.

Stimulus Research

Much of the recent activity of the FTC has been directed at stimuli created and disseminated by brand-competitive marketers. Concern with the nature of such stimuli as they foster or impede brand comparisons is evident. Interest in stimulus research and experience was exemplified by the FTC advertising hearings held in 1971. One major benefit which resulted from marketer testimony at these hearings has been an increasing recognition by the FTC of stimulus complexity and appreciation of the need for advanced forms of stimulus research. It should also be noted, however, that some slight reorientation is required for stimulus research to fit public policy decisions. The essence of this orientation reflects needs for aggregate or macro-analysis, research standards or protocols, and generalizable constructs around which useful FTC programs can be developed. Many of the issues discussed in this section can be viewed in this regard.

Advertising effects have received the greatest attention recently and thus present many significant research topics. Can advertising deception be behaviorally defined and measured? Should advertising be more informative? Are brand comparison advertisements likely to improve consumers' choices? What are the role and effects of emotional copy themes? Are testimonials particularly susceptible to deception? Is advertising substantiation a desirable program? Does advertising really have little or no lagged effect? Is repetition actually more important than advertising copy? Does advertising lead to increased or decreased prices; does this effect depend upon industry conditions and analysis mode? Is industry self-regulation a viable alternative to further government involvement? Is there a need for corrective advertising and can it be expected to meet its nonpunitive objectives? Note the simplistic phrasing of these questions; given that answers will differ as a function of conditions, the present need is for careful identification of such conditions by researchers.

Personal selling and other promotional forms are subject to many of the above questions but have as yet received little focused research attention. Although there are likely to be increased difficulties in investigation and evidence, plus compliance monitoring by the FTC, the sheer size and nature of these activities indicate major effects on social welfare. Remedies are likely to require considerable research due to probable choices between seller requirements or consumer education. Research and analysis may be most efficiently accomplished when conducted on a product- or service-specific basis, with particular attention paid to high-ticket, infrequent purchases utilizing product as well as brand demand stimulation. Topic areas might include door-to-door sales, games and sweepstakes, cents-off coupons, "free" trips, or arrangements between suppliers and salesmen.

Pricing and product quality, in addition to relating to issues discussed above, present important topics for further research. Findings by Morris and Bronson, for example, show low correlations between list prices and quality ratings presented in *Consumer Reports.* [13] Is it desirable that high correlations exist? What are the implications of consumer research on imputed price-quality relationships? Does price competition actually exist in many industries? With respect to quality, is it possible to assess accurately psychic value in addition to functional performance? Should more attention to quality improvements be given at the expense of promotional stress? Are consumers presently concerned with these issues and, if so, in which industries?

Guarantee and warranty issues also involve questions of promotion, performance, and consumer expectations. Are there certain products or services which do not deliver expected performance due to weak or nonexistent service arrangements? Are standards or guidelines for guarantee desirable, or is this a promotable product differentiation variable? Do consumers presently use guarantees as brand differentiators? Is this area susceptible to complex payoff analysis by marketers?

Response Research

The explicit distinction between stimulus and response research points to the differences which arise when attempting to research potential rather than past or present stimuli. The distinction follows from the aforementioned orientation of public agencies to effect new environments for the consumer. This in essence places these agencies in the role of *stimulus generators* and requires that they recognize the responsibilities and difficulties of this role. Problems exist in developing criteria for stimulus generation, implementing and evaluating communication vehicles, and determining audience segments and topic areas. There are, in addition, critical decisions as to appropriate public agency participation in programs which could potentially be handled by the private sector. The value of consumer research is becoming increasingly evident as simplistic models of the "rational" consumer or "helpless" consumer continue to prove unrealistic.

Product information provides particularly interesting examples of consumer research needs. It is commonly agreed that few, if any, consumers use comparative product information to reach optimal purchase decisions. It is also agreed that such information is not readily available in many product categories and that, in some of these (for example, high-ticket, infrequently purchased goods which are difficult to evaluate) decision costs can be high. It is not clear, however, whether such information can be effectively gathered and communicated.

Difficult problems in developing standards for measurement can be anticipated in at least some product categories. The major difficulties lie, however, in deciding how much and what kinds of information should be made available and the means by which such information should be communicated.

Much of the required input must come from researchers, and at present it is not clear that either this information or the methods for obtaining it are available. For example, two basic criteria for public information programs might be (1) effectiveness and (2) neutrality with respect to directing choice. Experience and expertise in marketing, however, have been developed in providing effective nonneutral, persuasive communications. Are there adaptable evaluation methods for neutral information? Is behavior change an appropriate objective? Are consumer self-reports of usage or satisfaction sufficient, or is information-processing research the key to this question?

Within information processing, is it true that consumers typically operate in few dimensions—that relatively low cognitive capacity limits the quantity of information that can be communicated? If so, what are the implications for neutral disclosure of full information on complex products? How can potential segment differences be anticipated and provided for? In what form should information be provided, by whom, and with which vehicles?

Consumer education offers many of the same researchable topics but is distinct in that criteria and methods may differ substantially. The focus is less likely to be on particular brand information, with more attention paid to hints for the decision process. Neutrality is a less significant criterion but no less a problem for public agencies. Evaluation appears especially difficult in that both criteria and the "market" are less well defined. Marketing research methods can potentially offer great benefits to this activity, but only by moving into new territories.

Product and Segment Research

Issues in this area reflect public policy concern with special topics, and can provide data and focus for pursuit of research in the areas discussed above: program priorities, stimulus research, and response research.

Special markets reflect attention on those segments of the population who appear least able to deal effectively with certain aspects of the consumer environment. Children, the poor, those with little education, and the elderly are some of these markets. Children's television, ghetto prices and fraud, vocational school deceptions, home repairs, and retirement residencies are examples of topics which have been attacked. Possible remedial actions range from criminal charges to consumer education. Investigation, remedy, and compliance are complex, but involved program research is needed.

Specific products and services are often stressed due to either high social costs or conditions of consumer inability to adequately evaluate alternatives and anticipate effects. Health and safety provide a number of possible topics, including nutrition, fire hazards, OTC drugs, and medical care. Purchasing power issues include consumer credit practices, insurance, encyclopedias, and self-improvement products.

CONCLUSION

Public policy regarding consumer behavior is going to be made, with or without research evidence. If marketers feel that public policy regarding consumer behavior could benefit from research evidence, it behooves them to recognize the weakness of present research and to conduct studies that are more relevant to public policy decision making.

Unfortunately, researchers operate at severe disadvantages in providing information that will be used by public policy makers. For the purposes of this discussion, no distinction is made between legislative, regulatory, and judicial policy makers and policy making. However, one thing must be clearly understood: policy makers are decision makers. They are not interested in theory; they want practical, useful information.

The most severe disadvantage researchers must overcome is that most public policy makers have neither training nor experience in the use of research evidence. Public policy makers with legal training and backgrounds may not include working knowledge of the scientific method among their skills. Legal practice often avoids the use of research findings if the design or conclusions can be attacked in some manner. Instead, reliance is placed on the use of qualitative statements by "experts." Meehl suggests that "legislators and judges have relied upon the 'fireside inductions' (common sense, anecdotal, introspective, and culturally transmitted beliefs about human behavior) in making and enforcing law as a mode of social control."[14]

The second disadvantage researchers face is that many public policy makers desire "specific and absolute" proof. They are not comfortable with the use of probability statements and, furthermore, they want the evidence to be directly relevant to the specific topic, not some "similar" topic.

Not all policy makers, fortunately, are reluctant to use research evidence. Two encouraging trends are evident. First, many law schools are now giving their students some exposure to research as a component of the legal process. The research tradition of "sociology of law" is receiving increasing attention in these schools. Second, there is an increasing tendency among firms to introduce research as evidence in proceedings instigated by government agencies. This practice will force more people to become aware of the value of research evidence and how it can be used.

What should be the posture of researchers interested in doing research on consumer behavior relevant to public policy making?

1. Recognize the inadequacies of research based on untested assumptions, conducted on nonrepresentative samples, and oriented too specifically toward marketing management.
2. Tailor the study to the needs of the policy maker. This requires that the research also have a forward orientation. Therefore, *it is absolutely imperative* that the researcher be in constant touch with policy makers to learn what their problems are and what types of research are most appropriate. As those researchers who have done otherwise will testify, an impeccable piece of research has little or no value unless the policy maker sees its value and it fits into his perceived set of needs.
3. Since research is somewhat foreign to many policy makers, it behooves the researcher to do more than just present his study and the results. The concept of research must be sold along with the findings.
4. Researchers might usefully segment their market for research. There are public agencies such as the National Science Foundation whose mission is to promote basic research. Most government agencies, however, deal in policy decisions and require research applied to their policy environment. Policy makers are not using existing consumer research because it does not answer their questions.

Will the FTC use marketing research in the future? An educated guess is a definite yes. Open systems theory would predict a positive response and a few limited, but hesitant, steps have been taken by the

FTC.[15] The question yet to be answered, however, is the willingness and readiness of market researchers to be adaptive.

ACKNOWLEDGMENT

The authors wish to acknowledge the assistance of Professor Murray Silverman of San Francisco State University in conceptualizing the potential contributions of marketing research to public policy decisions.

REFERENCES

1. Comments by FTC Commissioner Mary Gardiner Jones are especially relevant; see Mary Gardiner Jones, "The FTC's Need for Social Science Research," in *Proceedings of the 2nd Annual Conference, Association for Consumer Research,* edited by David Gardner (College Park, Md., 1971), pp. 1–9.
2. E. Cox, R. Fellmeth, and J. Schultz, *The Nader Report on the Federal Trade Commission* (New York: Richard W. Baron, 1969).
3. *Report of the American Bar Association Commission to Study the Federal Trade Commission,* committee print, September 15, 1969.
4. A summary of important changes is presented in R. E. Freer, "The Federal Trade Commission—A Study in Survival," *The Business Lawyer,* July 1971, pp. 15–5–1526.
5. Dorothy Cohen, "The Federal Trade Commission and the Regulation of Advertising in the Consumer Interest," *Journal of Marketing,* January 1969, pp. 40–44.
6. John A. Howard and Jagdish N. Sheth, *The Theory of Buyer Behavior* (New York: John Wiley & Sons, 1969).
7. A detailed discussion of these issues is given in W. L. Wilkie, "Research on Counter and Corrective Advertising," paper delivered to the American Marketing Association Conference on Advertising and the Public Interest, Washington, D.C., May 9–11, 1973.
8. Ibid., p. 11.
9. Ibid., p. 11.
10. Francesco M. Nicosia, *Consumer Decision Processes* (Englewood Cliffs, N.J.: Prentice-Hall, 1966).
11. James F. Engel, David T. Kollat, and Roger D. Blackwell, *Consumer Behavior* (New York: Holt, Rinehart & Winston, 1968).
12. Op. cit.

13. R. T. Morris and C. S. Bronson, "The Chaos of Competition Indicated by Consumer Reports," *Journal of Marketing*, July 1969, pp. 26–34.
14. Paul E. Meehl, "Law and the Fireside Inductions: Some Reflections of a Clinical Psychologist," *Journal of Social Issues*, Vol. 27, No. 4, 1971, pp. 65–100.
15. David M. Gardner, "Dynamic Hemostasis: Behavioral Research and the FTC," paper presented at the 4th Annual Conference of the Association for Consumer Research, Boston, November 9–11, 1973.

Bridging the Public Relations Gap Between Hospital Provider and Consumer

Lee F. Block
M. Elliott Taylor

If we've heard the question once, we've heard it a thousand times—why does a hospital need an organized public relations function? The very fact that the question is raised so often suggests part of the reason why the hospital needs such a function, because it demonstrates the lack of understanding not only of the function of public relations but also of the hospital's role in relationship to the public.

If our interpretation of the question is correct, it assumes that business uses public relations as an adjunct to the selling, advertising, and acceptance of its products. Hospitals do not sell a product, ergo they do not need public relations. Well, yes and no. Hospitals do indeed "sell a product" in the sense that they, perhaps more than any other socio-political entity, are required to continually justify their existence to the public in order to continue to serve that public.

This fact of life imposes upon the hospital not only the desirability of public relations as a management function, but the necessity of an organized public relations activity in order to fulfill its obligation to the community.

Despite the vital service that the hospital provides to the health care consumer, the relationship of hospital provider and health care consumer is unlike that of any other provider–consumer relationship. The health care consumer is, in effect, a captive consumer. Although he pays the bill, either directly or indirectly, he in fact does not choose to buy the hospital product. He does not choose to be sick and when he is sick, it is not he who decides when or how much, or how or where he should be treated. Nor is he asked how much he is willing to pay.

And the hospital provider is in a sense a "captive provider" in that it does not control the design and distribution of its "product." The hospital can neither fully anticipate nor control the demand for its services, nor can it even assure that its product, once delivered, will be paid for.

Between hospital provider and health care consumer stand layer upon layer of intermediaries—physicians, insurers, government agencies at every level—who in fact control the choices, exercise the options, and make the decisions that in virtually any other consumer–provider exchange are accomplished on a one-to-one basis. Certainly some information exchange must be provided both to arm the consumer with the ability to assess the value of the choices made in his behalf, and to equip the provider with an understanding of the expectations that govern the potential demand for its product.

AN ESSENTIAL ROLE

Public relations in hospitals, than, could be seen not only as an adjunct to the promotion and sale of a product or service, as in industry, but in an even more essential role: As a pivotal intermediary in the process of exchange between consumer and provider. If the public relations practitioner in industry can be said to act as the advocate for industry, then the public relations practitioner in the hospital can—or *should*—act as the advocate for the consumer.

In a sense, hospital public relations can be considered a sales function in that it can provide the marketing service of assessing and interpreting demand of the provider while explaining the product to the consumer, making him aware of its availability and educating him to its proper use, its value, and—a corollary function—its cost, so that he is better able to ascertain whether value in terms of health maintenance and service has been received for the dollars he has spent.

The question, then, it seems to us, should not be whether or not hospitals need a public relations function, but whether hospitals are equipped to do the vital job of information exchange that their responsibility to the public dictates must be done.

Yet if the art of public relations in industry can be said just now to be coming to maturity, the art of hospital public relations has to be considered as just having entered advanced adolescence. The emergence of hospital public relations as a cohesive social science is the offshoot of the development of a hospital industry that itself has come to maturity largely after World War II when medical technology turned the corner that brought hospitals from their historic role as hostels for the sick to their modern role as repositories for the enormously expanded armament of medical science. With that development came a geometric increase in demand for hospital services and a concomitant increase in hospital costs that led in turn to a series of increasingly more complex payment arrangements.

The simple job of providing bed and board to patients to facilitate the physician's efforts had now become a complex task of organizing multifaceted facilities, services, and arrangements, and of justifying the effectiveness of that organization.

With the increased sophistication of the institution came more sophisticated management. By the end of World War II, the job of running the hospital had been transferred, in most instances, from the nursing supervisor or the superintendent to a professional trained in management techniques, an administrator who frequently could understand in an at least rudimentary fashion his hospital's communications needs and who looked to industry for direction in how to meet those needs.

What he saw often led to an episode of what we think of as the "get-a-guy" syndrome—that desperate recognition that he had to get someone, anyone, to do something, anything.

And so, recognizing the need for someone to perform the public relations function he saw as answering industry's needs, he "got a guy"—or, in most instances—a girl, from the secretarial pool, from the hospital's volunteer force, from among the community's school teachers, from newspaper news desks. It was small wonder that these raw recruits, employed to direct a complex function, all too often disappointed those who had looked to them as simple answers to complex questions.

AN INDUSTRY IN CRISIS

Those of us in the health care field have heard countless times in recent years from critics on the outside that our health care system, of which hospitals are a critical element, is in crisis. We know all too well of the weaknesses of the system, but we also are aware of what has been done and, perhaps more importantly, of what is proposed and could be done to strengthen the system. Our too-frequent failures to communicate those possibilities, as well as to create realistic expectations among the consumer public, may be the price we have had to pay for the false economies of those early "get-a-guy" years.

As an industry, health care has before it now two immediate and practical problems, in addition to the continuing problem of providing for the information exchange between the hospital and the consumer. One has to do with a phenomenon of the past several years—the emergent role of government, especially federal and state government, as an active participant in health care.

This role was initiated with the establishment of a major federally funded hospital construction program immediately following World War II. It was solidified during the years of the Johnson Administration with a bumper crop of new Federal health care programs, the most familiar of which are Medicare and Medicaid. That trend is certain to continue, with increased government involvement in health care as absolute certainty, especially when national health insurance in some form is enacted.

As a by-product of that increased government interest, hospitals are being forced to act together in the national arena, and must develop the expertise needed to facilitate communications among themselves in order to develop the consensus that will allow them to speak nationally with one voice.

The second problem also relates to a trend in government, a trend away from providing the kind of massive economic support for research that we have had in the past. This trend also will call for a major infusion of public relations expertise as it inevitably forces hospitals to go to the public sector to raise increasing percentages of funds to continue these important efforts.

As pressures for change mount both internally and externally, hospitals are faced with the challenge of laying the foundation of public understanding on which a more effective health care system can be built. We at the national association level must now assure ourselves and our constituents that we have the public relations expertise to do so.

STUDY MEMBERSHIP

As a beginning, the American Hospital Association-affiliated American Society for Hospital Public Relations Directors last year sent questionnaires to its 800-plus membership from which it hoped to develop a profile of its membership, what they are doing, and what they are capable of getting done. Questionnaires were returned by about half of the society's membership. The responses indicated that although hospital public relations still trails behind industrial public relations in terms of professional maturity, the gap is beginning to close, and there are solid signs that there is the potential to close it completely in the foreseeable future.

Just how new the awareness of the importance of public relations is in hospitals was indicated by the finding that a substantial majority of those who answered our questionnaire had been employed in their present positions for five years or less. In fact, almost a third of those hospitals represented by the respondents had only established public relations departments within the past five years.

Perhaps the most gratifying finding was that more than half of those who responded indicated that they had been in the public relations field prior to coming to their present jobs, a long step forward from the "get-a-guy" expediency.

Fewer than one-quarter of those answering had held another position in the same hospital prior to their present positions. In addition to the more than half who had come to hospital public relations from other public relations assignments, the ranks of hospital public relations personnel were drawn from such disciplines as journalism, fund raising, hospital administration, teaching, personnel work, advertising, editing, and sales.

Almost half indicated that they had previously worked for newspapers, while significant numbers had been employed by public relations firms or advertising agencies, by magazines, in radio or television, or as fund raisers.

They demonstrated solid academic backgrounds as well, with almost three-quarters indicating that they had had at least four years of college and one-third indicating that they had had graduate level education. Fewer than a third, however, said that they had taken college level courses in public relations.

Although a handful of the respondents still apparently had been drawn from the secretarial or volunteer pools, many hospitals clearly have learned the importance of finding people who already have performed in a public relations or related capacity.

And they are beginning to pay them accordingly. Almost two-thirds indicated that their annual salaries were $12,000 or more and almost half that number earned over $15,000 a year. While we do not have statistical data on salaries paid hospital public relations practitioners in the past, it would undoubtedly be safe to assume that these figures would have been significantly lower as few as five years ago.

The findings indicating how the skills of these individuals were used were disappointing, however. Although our statistical selection was too small to develop a definitive profile of how hospital public relations personnel spend their time, the overall outlines indicate a heavy emphasis on quantifiable production—writing and placing news releases, developing internal publications and brochures, fund-raising, and such miscellaneous tasks as tour conducting and working with volunteer groups.

We also asked our respondents to indicate how they believe the time of the public relations department should be allocated to make the public relations effort most effective. Interestingly, despite slight shifts, the overall pattern of time allocations remained essentially the same, with only minor variations from the actual way in which time was said to be spent. Clearly, a large task that we have ahead of us is an internal education job.

It is at this point and with this information that we in hospital public relations face the future, with an awareness of what hospital public relations not only can be but what it *must* be to assure that our hospitals are fulfilling the role that society is demanding of them, with a recently awakened but not fully developed awareness of the potential of public relations to help accomplish that task, and with at least a nucleus of individuals prepared to develop that potential to realization.

Nevertheless, hospital public relations remains hampered in its development by the attitudes and modes of thought that are traditional to the not-for-profit hospital field. Earlier we spoke of hospital public relations as being capable of providing the marketing functions needed to promote and sell the hospital "product." But that concept would be a difficult one to communicate to a field which traditionally, historically, and on principle has resisted any analogy between its situation and that of for-profit business.

The resistance is understandable in an industry which, subject to close and continual public scrutiny, is forced to zealously defend itself against any hint of profit-making interests. Interpreting the concept to our own field is yet another of the responsibilities we must assume. We must dispel the lingering suspicion that dollars spent on public relations are questionable expenditures by demonstrating that the function can indeed directly serve the patient's interest.

A SIMILAR PROBLEM

Our situation is not unlike that which formerly plagued industrial public relations in that we suffer from the popular confusion between the terms "public relations" and "press agentry." But while industrial public relations has generally been allowed a trial period under the guise of press agentry in which to prove its greater capabilities, we must, in effect, prove ourselves before we will even be allowed our trial. The problem is circuitous. We must create a break in the cycle.

Our approach must be two-pronged. First, we must build the professionalism of those already involved with hospital public relations. More important, we must reach that key individual, the chief administrative officer of the institution, and make him aware of what his public relations dollar *should* be buying. It has been said that one of the reasons public relations in hospitals has been slow to receive acceptance is because it deals with intangibles, that it cannot provide quantifiable results to the administrator who is required to be strictly accountable for every hospital function. Perhaps those same circumstances may account for the fact that while we are now seeing a growing acceptance of the *idea* of public relations in hospitals, we have yet to see it even begin to approach any realization of its full potential.

Our administrators are allocating resources to public relations and they are finding better qualified individuals to staff their public relations departments. Yet at the same time, married to the quantifiable result as the sole measure of accomplishment, they have yet to set an expectation high enough to encourage the development of public relations in hospitals to the level it can and ought to attain.

Our task in hospital public relations may be a unique one. Perhaps we can best serve our profession and the public, not by assuring our employers of the effectiveness of the job we are doing, but by encouraging their discontent, a discontent that will lead them to demand that we do the job that we know must be done. We must create a new cycle, a cycle of demand. We must educate the hospital administrator to expect more of public relations so that he no longer will be satisfied with merely the production of newsletters and brochures by his public relations staff.

He must demand more in order to attract the calibre of public relations professional who can produce more.

At the same time, we must arm the hospital administrator with new criteria against which to measure the effectiveness of his public relations department. Rejecting the old measurements is not enough, especially when we are dealing with the hospital administrator and board of trustees who are held both morally and legally accountable for the efficient use of the dollars they spend on behalf of their institution. We must be self-critical and self-policing rather than self-justifying.

It is a job we are only now beginning to undertake.

Should Hospitals Market?

Robin E. MacStravic

In order to understand why hospitals should even consider marketing, it is first necessary to define the term. In its broadest sense, marketing means planning and managing exchange relationships.[1] These exchange relationships, or transactions, involve any situation in which some person or organization does or gives something to the hospital, presumably in exchange for some tangible or symbolic value. Such relationships include employing workers, recruiting physicians, securing members for a board of trustees, attracting patients, obtaining zoning approval for expansion, and securing certificate-of-need approval for purchase of new equipment.[2]

Any trade or donation of something the hospital wants or needs to survive and prosper is worth planning and managing well. Marketing is a discipline that was primarily developed within the framework of managing the buying and selling of goods and services to consumers. During this process, information-gathering and analytical techniques have been developed and tested that have a potential for serving hospitals in manag-

Reprinted with permission from *Hospital Progress,* August 1977. Copyright © 1977 by the Catholic Hospital Association.

ing exchanges with patients. These techniques, as well as basic marketing concepts and principles, are available for use.

A number of recent developments suggest that hospitals may have to become increasingly familiar with and adept at marketing their services to patients. Traditionally, managing exchanges with patients (use of inpatient and outpatient care) has been accomplished indirectly through physicians. As long as a hospital has the right number and mix of physicians on its staff, referrals of patients tend to follow naturally. As a result, hospitals have to manage their medical staff exchanges (memberships, service on committees, referral of patients) by making things as comfortable and convenient for the physicians as possible. Purchase of the latest equipment, special parking areas, on-site office facilities, and so forth, have been used to attract and keep medical staff.

At least the prospect exists of a change in this situation from a seller's to a buyer's market for physicians. Although shortages have been traditional in the past, there may soon be not only a sufficiency but even a surplus of physicians. Their number per 10,000 population is projected to increase from 15.9 in 1970 to 19.7 in 1980 and 23.7 in 1990, an increase of 50 percent.[3] Thus it may be that physicians will have to begin offering more in order to obtain staff membership, rather than hospitals offering more to maintain adequate staff.

Exacerbating this trend are the efforts, just beginning, to limit and even reduce the supply of hospital beds. If the ratio of beds to population drops from the current 4.5 beds per 1,000 population to 4.0[4] or even 3.5,[5] as has been suggested, more physicians will depend on fewer beds for their patients. While this may produce some shift in the power of hospital administrators and trustees relative to physicians, it does not improve the patient utilization situation.

Increasingly, hospitals face having their reimbursement linked to required utilization levels.[6] Those hospitals unable to maintain the occupancy standards used in calculating reimbursement rates will end up either operating at a deficit or seriously cutting services. When the time comes to select which hospitals to close in reducing surplus beds,[7] those with lowest occupancy are likely to be considered first. With reimbursement and even survival linked to maintaining high occupancy[8] and with utilization review and regulatory efforts aimed at minimizing inpatient utilization, the hospital will become increasingly dependent on the patient.

As the number of physicians per 10,000 population increases, people will have a wider choice of physicians and, subsequently, of sources for inpatient care. As hospitals move to expand their service population by offering primary care,[9] they enter an area in which the patient decides whether, when, and where to seek care. Thus, the hospital itself must find effective ways to plan and manage exchange relationships with (or utilization by) patients.

USING MARKETING TO SOLVE UTILIZATION PROBLEMS

If current utilization is simply too low, marketing can be used to increase it by increasing penetration of existing markets, adding new markets, or both. If utilization is too high or misdirected (for example, emergency room use for routine medical needs), marketing can be used to reduce or redirect patterns of use.[10] Alternatively, utilization may simply fluctuate too much, causing low occupancy on weekends, holidays, and during the summer, despite high fixed costs the year around.

If it is true that people use more inpatient care than is necessary, then marketing concepts and techniques can be used to reduce such overutilization. By analyzing what physicians and patients gain through overuse and by adjusting either what they get or what they have to give for such abuse, overutilization of inpatient care may be reduced. For example, if patients or physicians were forced to pay for unnecessarily extended stays or if it were made easier and more convenient for patients to leave earlier, extended stays might well be reduced. Manipulation of either side of an exchange (what people get or what they give) may alter the amount or rate of transactions.

Marketing can influence utilization patterns by managing the components of the exchange relationship. Briefly, these components include:

1. Product, the service itself, as perceived by patients in terms of what good it does them.
2. Place, the mechanism used to get the service to patients or patients to the service; this includes referral network, outreach, and transportation arrangements.
3. Price, the cost to patients of using the service, not just out-of-pocket payment but whatever pain, discomfort, or indignity is involved.
4. Promotion, the information patients get about the nature of the service and its availability and benefit.

By viewing the hospital's services in terms of these four components and from the perspective of patients, marketing can identify which aspects can be manipulated to improve utilization. Marketing techniques can be used to measure the perceived needs and attitudes of current or prospective patients and to test the usefulness of alternative means of promoting services.

The hospital must always analyze possible changes in utilization from its perspective also: What must it pay to achieve such changes, and are they worth this cost? Which alternative approach is most suitable and likely to be effective?

CONSIDERING ETHICS OF MARKETING HEALTH CARE

It is not possible in this paper to cover the various concepts and techniques which have been used for years successfully (and sometimes unsuccessfully) outside the health care field. It is possible, however, to mention some of the major issues and common objections raised by health care organizations in terms of marketing. Typically, these concerns express doubts about the ethics of marketing: Is what's right for the auto industry or retail merchandising equally appropriate for hospitals?

One specific issue can be raised: the ethics of advertising. Should hospitals promote themselves and their services? The American Hospital Association has recently discussed establishing a policy toward advertising that frowns on comparative promotion (claiming to be newer, better, or otherwise superior). A related issue is the question of advertising costs: How much can a hospital spend, ethically speaking, to blow its own horn?

Promoting services and communicating with prospective patients need not be limited to or even involve formal advertising. Hospitals can communicate via satisfied customers and news stories without resorting to paid promotion. On the other hand, where communication is geared to informing the public about methods for securing specific services and the benefits these services provide, then the advantage to the public should override any rigid prohibition of advertising. Parent education classes, preadmission visits for children, etc., are certainly legitimate ways of acquainting prospective patients with the hospital, though they entail some cost.

One major objection to advertising is that it smacks of competition. Any attempt to alter use of some specific hospital service must be made with recognition that other sources of such services are likely to be affected. While certificates of need and attempts to reduce bed supplies will reduce competition, they won't eliminate it. The question, then, is whether a hospital should seek to expand its market and increase inpatient utilization of its services at the expense of another hospital.

EXAMINING AN INAPPROPRIATE MARKETING EFFORT

Perhaps an obvious example of inappropriate marketing aimed at changing hospital utilization is that of a hospital in Las Vegas that promoted weekend admissions through a giveaway program. According to a recent article this hospital offered patients who chose to be admitted on Friday or Saturday a chance for a two-week cruise.[11] From the hospital's viewpoint, this promotion was probably worth its cost, since the result will even out utilization and spread fixed costs over more days. From the community perspective, however, the program is definitely inflationary. A recent study in Michigan clearly suggests that people who are admitted to hospitals on Friday or Saturday end up staying an average of two days more than people admitted during the week.[12] Thus the hospital benefits by increasing and smoothing utilization, but the community foots the bill for unnecessary days in the hospital.

Another objection to both promotion and competition is that they may lead to unnecessary utilization. One might argue that medical care in general has already been oversold to the public, with the result that people seek medical care when they should have guarded their own health better or when they could have simply endured a minor condition. Additionally, promotion of any one hospital's service may lead to greater interest in such services and thus to increased demand. And if one hospital's promotion efforts are successful at the expense of another hospital, then the other will be forced to promote its services, increasing only the costs of care.

A major concern to hospitals in any case, but especially in view of current attempts to control hospital costs, must be the question of whether marketing will inflate hospital costs. No simple answer to this question can be given, since inflationary effects would depend on the object and means of any marketing effort. If a hospital de-markets excessive length of stay by expanding its discharge-planning program, the costs of such expansion may be inflationary and may increase costs per patient day. On the other hand, if length of stay is reduced, costs to the community for hospital care will be less. Whether a marketing effort will increase costs or not will vary with the situation. Competitive marketing, in which a number of hospitals try to add patient or physician amenities to increase their shares of the same inpatient market, will most likely be inflationary.

In some overbedded communities, hospitals have already begun competitive marketing. In order to attract patients, some hospitals in Florida have offered discount coupons to local residents and have agreed to pay either ambulance costs for patients delivered to their emergency rooms or Medicare deductibles. While these efforts certainly affect hospital costs, they may not adversely affect total health expenditures by the community. With a "Carter cap" on revenues, however, any increase in hospital expenditures must be viewed with alarm.

If marketing efforts smooth out census levels without increasing patient days, and if the hospital can reduce its staffing and standby costs as a result, then the costs of marketing activities may be offset by savings elsewhere. If hospitals develop and market a new product, such as ambulatory surgery, this may well decrease community health costs. Whether marketing is inflationary in practice will depend on what expenses are necessary in altering exchange relationships and what impact that alteration has. This will also depend on what is used as a measure of costs: hospital costs per patient day, total operating costs, or total cost to the community for health care.

A final issue may be the question of manipulation. As more is understood about the conscious and unconscious factors which govern people's behavior, that understanding can be used to manipulate behavior. In the past, marketing has been linked to subliminal advertising, overpackaging of dubious or noninnovative products, and other techniques aimed at meeting organizational goals but producing no public benefit. The hospital must be more concerned with the right of patients to make informed choices; the principle of caveat emptor has no place in medical care.

These issues complicate, but do not prohibit, the effective use of marketing concepts and techniques by hospitals. They do require that marketing principles be adapted to the unique aspects of hospital care, rather than merely adopted from commercial uses. Marketing challenges hospitals to understand and to respond to what makes patients seek or avoid care: their needs, attitudes, awarenesses, and perceptions of the risks and benefits of specific services. Marketing also asks a hospital to understand and to be willing to alter its own capacity in order to achieve more successful exchange transactions with patients and, ultimately, more effective achievement of its own goals.

To implement a marketing program, hospital personnel must understand marketing concepts and be familiar with marketing techniques. In some cases it may be necessary either to hire full-time marketing specialists or to use consultants.[13] In addition to marketing competence, however, the hospital must first adopt a marketing perspective: an awareness of and sensitivity to the exchange relationships it depends on for its very existence. Marketing provides ways to manage such transactions (see Table 1) to the benefit of the hospital and of the community it serves.

Hospitals are beginning to show evidence of substantial interest in marketing. Previous use of marketing has tended to be restricted to health

Table 1. Hospital Transactions.

MARKET = WITH WHOM MIGHT TRANSACTIONS OCCUR?		EXCHANGE = WHAT DOES HOSPITAL GIVE, AND WHAT DOES IT GET IN RETURN?
External entities	Suppliers	Money for goods and services
	Supporters	Prestige or warm feeling for services or money
	Regulators	Approval for promised or real behavior
Internal entities	Trustees	Prestige or warm feeling for time and effort
	Employees	Money and feeling of accomplishment for time and effort
	Physicians	Equipment or prestige for patient referrals
	Volunteers	Fellowship and feeling of accomplishment for time and effort
Client entities	Patients	Care and relief of pain and anxiety for money
	Community	Access to services and protection for money
	Other clients	Lab testing for money
	Professionals in training	Education for services
Colleagues	Other hospitals	Sharing for economies of scale
	Ambulatory centers	Support services for referrals

Note: The possible markets and types of exchanges are for illustration only. Most transactions are far more complex than can be described in this table and vary from one situation to another.

maintenance organization development,[14] family planning promotion,[15] or preventive health services.[16] Recently, however, articles on marketing for hospitals have been written by both a hospital administrator[17] and an academician.[18] This awareness of the potential for marketing in hospitals should be welcomed by hospitals and by the public at large. Marketing is a tool—one that can serve the community well or ill depending on how it is used.

REFERENCES

1. Philip Kotler, "A Generic Concept of Marketing," *Journal of Marketing,* April 1972, p. 46.

2. R. E. MacStravic, *Marketing Health Care,* Aspen Systems Corp., Germantown, Md., 1977, Chap. 2.

3. U.S. Department of Health, Education, and Welfare, *The Current and Projected Supply of Health Manpower,* Health Resources Administration Report, 75-17, Washington, D.C., July 1974.

4. Institute of Medicine, *Controlling the Supply of Hospital Beds,* National Academy of Sciences, Washington, D.C., October 1976.

5. Walter McClure, *Reducing Excess Hospital Capacity,* National Technical Information Service HRP-0015199, Springfield, Va., October 1976.

6. R. E. MacStravic, "Should We Link Occupancy and Reimbursement?" *Hospital Financial Management,* July 1977, pp. 18–21.

7. McClure, Op. cit., p. iii.

8. B. C. Vladeck, "Why Non-Profits Go Broke," *The Public Interest,* Winter 1976, pp. 86–101.

9. J. H. Bryant, et al., "The Present Role of the Community Hospital in Primary Ambulatory Care," *Community Hospitals and Primary Care,* Ballinger Publishing Co., Philadelphia, 1975.

10. Philip Kotler and S. J. Levy, "Demarketing, Yes, Demarketing," *Harvard Business Review,* November 1971, pp. 74–80.

11. Christy Marshall, "Ethics Aspects of Advertising Debated," *Modern Healthcare,* April 1977, p. 48.

12. *The Ryan Advisory,* Ryan Advisors, Inc., Washington, D.C., 1977, p. 5.

13. J. A. McLaren, "Marketing for Hospitals," *Modern Healthcare,* April 1977, p. 6.

14. R. Burke, *Guidelines for HMO Marketing,* InterStudy, Minneapolis, 1973.

15. A. I. El-Ansary and O. E. Kramer, Jr., "Social Marketing: The Family Planning Experience," *Journal of Marketing,* July 1973, p. 3.

16. P. D. Cooper, "Consumer Behavior Aspects of Preventive Health Care," *Southern Marketing Association Proceedings,* November 1976.

17. R. D. O'Hallaron, et al., "Marketing Your Hospital," *Hospital Progress,* December 1976, pp. 68–71.

18. S. L. Tucker, "Introducing Marketing as a Planning and Management Tool," *Hospital and Health Services Administration,* Winter 1977, pp. 37–44.

Using a Team Approach to Market-Oriented Planning

Arnold Corbin

Total business planning should focus on the marketplace, with customers and consumers, not on the manufacturing plant. Inputs from the marketplace are essential to both marketing planning and strategic corporate or business planning. It logically follows, therefore, that the marketing plan should become the keystone element in the total business plan.

To be effective, however, marketing planning, implementation, and control require close cooperation, coordination, and exchange of ideas and information among all the major functional groups involved in the business. There must be agreement among all members of management that the marketplace is the integrative basis for planning throughout the company (though with full recognition for the role of technological innovation in the process).

But the spotlight of this approach to unified, market-oriented planning falls on marketing as the prime integrative force. And in this central role, marketing should attempt to secure the full involvement and com-

Reprinted by permission of *Management Review*, June 1977. Copyright © 1977 by AMACOM, a division of American Management Associations.

mitment of the other main "resource owners" of the business, namely, the people in production, R&D, engineering, finance, and legal, as well as strategic planning. The best results are obtained when all work together as a team to develop the marketing plan—which then becomes the basis for the R&D plan, the production plan, and the financial plan. These individual functional plans are then integrated into a master plan for the whole business, which, of course, should be consonant with a clear-cut, pre-agreed definition of the business the company or other organizational unit is in or desires to be in.

TOTAL BUSINESS PLANNING

a non-profit business

Here are some examples of how the team approach provides opportunities for cooperation among major functions of the business.

1. The product planning and development process offers a fine proving ground for the application of the interfunctional approach at the interface between marketing and R&D. In companies subscribing to this concept, the idea of continuing interaction and communication between the product side and the market side is paramount as the development evolves.

Team planning not only encourages effective cross-functional integration of marketing and R&D but also helps underwrite a strong market orientation. As a full and equal partner in the business of planning, the marketing manager can take the leadership in focusing the energies of his or her peers on finding market opportunities and marshalling the resources they represent (especially technology) to take full advantage of them. Full expression of the customer point of view is thus ensured at a stage early enough in the planning cycle to influence the thinking of the team members representing the technological side of the business.

Conversely, as equal partners in planning, the other team members can temper the marketing view with important, pertinent technological considerations. In the process, the team can, it is hoped, hammer out an optimum, innovative, synergistic approach that builds on both marketing and technology.

2. The team approach can also do much to forge a strong bond of reciprocal interdependence between the marketing and financial functions.

The marketing concept clearly assigns a profit responsibility to the marketing organization. Since management is primarily interested in results, marketing executives must be managers of money as well as marketers of goods and services. To implement the concept effectively, therefore, marketing people require a steady flow of profit-oriented information from financial people to help them make sound planning and control decisions and understand the financial implications of their decisions. Even more importantly, they need professional guidance in the application of the newest financial and accounting concepts and techniques, such as breakeven analysis, contribution, payback period, return on investment, discounted cash flow, direct costing versus absorption costing, and so on. Concepts such as these should be in the daily lexicon of marketing people. But how will this come to pass if we do not organize and operate to ensure that such knowledge is imparted to marketers by financially sophisticated people?

Conversely, financial people, traditionally more manufacturing-oriented than marketing-oriented, need to know much more about the marketing concept, the financial information and decision-making needs of the revenue producers (marketing), and how marketing decisions affect the financial results of operations—receivables, inventory, profit, and so on. The problem is essentially one of inducing a free two-way flow of communication between the marketing and control functions.

The organizational response to this clearly implied need for closer liaison should be the appointment of a marketing "controller," who could be a member of the controller's staff, but would be physically located in the marketing department with line responsibility to marketing management and a close working relationship with the controller. In addition to good training in accounting and control work, the marketing controller ideally should also have some practical sales and marketing experience. In effect, the marketing controller would be an in-house accountant in the marketing department.

Several companies already have adopted this pioneering organizational concept with substantial success. The incumbents are sometimes called "profit managers" or "marketing cost consultants"—but the objective is the same: to ensure profit maximization for the total company by helping marketing managers take full advantage of the best and newest financial and accounting techniques to improve their decisions, plan and control their operations, and ensure maximum return on investment for the company as a whole.

STRATEGIC MARKETING PLAN

The "marketing plan" is more than a single plan; it is a series of plans that, when integrated, constitute an organization's overall marketing plan. Thus, there may be a basic strategic or master plan, a product or brand plan, a market plan by segment, and individual functional plans—for advertising, sales promotion, sales, and so on. The basic strategic plan, however, is the keystone element in the marketing plans system because it sets out the major objectives and strategies for marketing for the particular period being planned.

In the development of this master plan for marketing, inputs should flow from the basic strategic plan for the business, particularly in terms of the markets and products that will provide the basis for closing the gap between the so-called momentum line and the plan line. In other words, basic decisions taken with respect to the directions in which the entire business will be moving, particularly in terms of overall strategies and objectives, should provide pertinent guidelines to those charged with preparation of the basic marketing plan. Furthermore, information developed in the process of preparing the strategic business plan, such as the environmental analysis, should also provide valuable inputs to the basic marketing plan.

Just as the master marketing plan should receive valuable inputs from, and be tuned to, the strategic business plan, there should be a complementary flow of information in the opposite direction. Marketing personnel can and should make useful inputs to the strategic planning process as members of the total business team. In principle, the marketing manager, with the other key managers (finance, manufacturing, R&D, and so on) should participate in the total strategic business planning process. His experience and knowledge put him in a position to provide important inputs and make achievable commitments to his teammates. As a result, the strategic plans that emerge should be realistically market-oriented. Furthermore, by his involvement in the overall planning effort, the marketing manager is then obviously in a much better position to guide his own marketing associates as they develop and build the basic strategic marketing plan.

In the development of the strategic marketing plan, the marketing manager acts as the team captain, or prime mover, of a group that might typically include product managers or product planners and the managers of sales, advertising, sales promotion, and marketing research.

OTHER MARKETING PLANS

The various types of marketing subplans should closely interlock and be consistent with one another and with the strategic marketing plan so that the best use is made of time, effort, resources, and money in running the business. For example, in an organization that operates with product managers, each product manager may find it useful to enlist the cooperation of the key functional managers in the marketing organization (advertising, sales promotion, marketing research, and so on) as team members to participate in the deliberations, contribute information and ideas, and make commitments to ensure the development of the final product plan. Since these *functional* managers participate in building all the product plans, they are then in a position to develop realistic plans for their own functions by integrating the commitments in the individual product plans. Thus, the advertising plan becomes a unified, coordinated summation of the advertising components of all the individual product plans.

Flexibility in terms of interchangeability of roles is the key requirement. Sometimes it may be useful to set up special task forces, or teams, with a captain or project leader in charge to accomplish the planning for specific objectives or projects.

The use of the team approach in developing the various marketing subplans helps minimize the danger of suboptimizing, or causing disruptions, resulting from the plans being out of synchronization in timing or resource development. It helps ensure that the subplans will be integrated into a master plan that makes the best sense for the operation as a whole. Furthermore, it is far better to get all the inconsistencies and "pulls" on resources straightened out in the planning stage rather than letting them happen in the action stage.

Another virtue of the team approach is that it capitalizes on the fact that functional managers may be experienced "businessmen," as well as specialists in their own fields. They may have valuable ideas to contribute that go far beyond their particular functional interests. When these managers actively participate as members of a planning team, looking for new opportunities in the marketplace and deciding on the broad objectives and strategies with which to capitalize on them, they put on their businessmen hats. But when they go back to prepare their own functional subplans for, say, sales or advertising, each puts on his sales or advertising hat. Having had a voice in making the key decisions of the master plan, they are more likely to come up with subplans far better than if they had not been consulted, but had simply been "told" to make them.

The same principle of duality (wearing two hats) applies equally to the marketing research function. The marketing research manager should be a fully accredited member of the marketing team. He should be considered not only as a research specialist who can make useful inputs to the information base for planning but also as a marketing generalist who can contribute to the decision making of the marketing team in formulating objectives, strategies, and action programs.

Far more effective research planning will result if the research manager is regarded as a marketing person as well as a researcher. (This, of course, implies that he possesses the necessary credentials and competence for such recognition.) Through participation in the decision making of the marketing operation, he can gain a truly first-hand appreciation of what is going on in the marketplace, with customers and their marketing people, with customers' customers, and so on down the line.

Operating at these grass-roots levels, he will be stimulated to generate his own research projects to meet the needs of the operation as he detects them, on the basis of his own first-hand evidence, instead of waiting for second-hand requests from others. His role in initiating research thus changes from passive to active. He thereby gains greater insight into research needs and opportunities, and can plan and program research activities with greater realism and effectiveness.

SOME IMPLEMENTAL GUIDELINES

If team planning is to be effective, the process must be organized, systematic, and continuous. Planning must be planned; it cannot be done on a one-time, hit-or-miss basis, wedged in when people are not doing "more important" things. It requires dedication to the proposition that team planning is just as important as team operating. Team members must receive adequate time to plan together on a regular predetermined schedule, put their team-designed plan into operation, and revise it, if necessary, as feedback indicates variances are occurring.

The modus operandi of team planning is a series of team sessions, one at each of the principal stages in the evolution of the plan. Although the purpose of each meeting will normally vary, the motivating philosophy is to secure commitment, based upon a sense of involvement and a healthy interchange of views, among the key people who can make or break a particular project. Team sessions are not concluded until divergent views are reconciled and a consensus emerges.

Because we must operate increasingly with scarce resources, particularly management talent, planning operations that have been most successful have benefited by designating someone who will be responsible for scheduling the use of available resources optimally in the planning process. This person would, in effect, help design the master plan for planning, including the scheduling of team sessions to avoid duplication, conflicts, and overlapping requests for common resources. In essence, his job would not involve planning, but he would be responsible for seeing that all the planning gets done most efficiently.

A skillful blending of top-down strategic guidelines and bottom-up grass-roots inputs is essential to achieve the best results from the planning effort. Either alone is not sufficient. Strategic conceptions may sometimes have to be tempered to meet the hard realities of the marketplace; conversely, empirical inputs from the grass roots should normally be evaluated in the light of a sound strategic frame of reference.

A MODEL PLANNING CYCLE

To facilitate and implement the team approach to planning, a model planning cycle should be constructed in matrix form. Figure 1 is an abbreviated version of such a form. Details of participating personnel have been omitted for reasons of brevity and convenience and because tremendous variations in organizational structures and position titles make it impractical to design a universally applicable membership designation for each plan step for each plan team. Also, only the first of 17 planning steps is spelled out in the illustration; all of the steps in the suggested planning cycle are listed in the box on the page opposite the matrix illustration.

This generalized model of an "ideal" marketing planning cycle is presented here as a basic frame of reference. It should be regarded as a statement of normative principles for integrating, in an optimum manner, the steps in the planning process, with the personnel participating in each step by type of plan. However, it is flexible enough to be adapted to actual circumstances and requirements of individual organizations.

PLANNING CYCLE GUIDELINES

Here are some general guidelines and observations that may be of value in implementing the planning cycle:

Step 1 calls for each echelon above the one doing the actual planning to provide the latter with a statement of basic objectives and strategies to be used as a frame of reference. This is an extremely important first step to ensure that the planners themselves receive appropriate guidelines within which to do their planning. The objective is to prevent wasted time and effort in the generation of plans which, while well designed, may not be consistent with the basic aims of the next higher echelon of the busi-

Figure 1. The marketing planning cycle.

Steps in Planning Process	Participating Personnel, by Type of Plan					
	Master (Strategic) A	Product B	Market C	Advertising D	Sales Promotion E	Sales/ Distribution F
1. Prepare and disseminate guidelines for planning; provide statement of basic objectives and strategies. (Responsibility of the echelon(s) above each of the echelons developing the actual plans)	Division or operation manager, based on guidance and concurrence of higher echelon(s)	Marketing manager based on guidance and concurrence of division or operation manager and higher echelon(s)	Same	Same as B	Same as B	Same as B

ness. The risk lies in the possibility of concentrating on "doing the thing right" (that is, developing a plan), rather than "doing the right thing" (doing planning consonant with predetermined overall objectives and strategies). In other words, one must be careful to avoid "planning myopia." The macro guidelines from the echelon above are essential to ensure that the micro plans that emerge make sense in terms of the frame of reference of the people who will be reviewing and approving the plans.

Step 2 should involve all the relevant resource owners or functional personnel whose factual contributions and analytical judgments are required for each type of plan.

Step 3 requires the synthesis of all the data, assumptions, and other assessments produced in Step 2. It is an integrating step, best delegated to one person; in many cases, the task is performed by the marketing research manager or his designee.

Steps 4–8 should normally be treated as a single step in constructing the cell for each type of plan. The basic reason for grouping these five closely related steps is that the participating personnel within any one type of plan should usually be the same for all five of these steps.

These five steps also should be taken at a single session of the respective teams responsible for particular activities of the business. After the individual members of a planning and operating team have done their homework as individuals (studied their respective information base/ situation reviews), they assemble as a team for the next series of major steps in the planning process. Thus, at this meeting, they identify and agree on the key opportunities and problems, set objectives, develop alternative strategies, select the optimum strategy, and finally identify the resource groups necessary to implement this strategy.

Certain other points are worth noting in connection with the accomplishment of these five steps as a unit in the planning process. As indicated earlier, it is felt that the best plans emerge when they are based on both "bottom-up" and "top-down" participation. Thus, in the sales/ distribution plan, designated representatives from the field sales force could be considered an integral part of the planning team. Similarly, the advertising agency could play a contributive role at this stage in the development of advertising plans. Participation in these kinds of decisions should help later in generating more meaningful and more effective advertising plans and programs.

Step 9 is a critical step that calls for review and approval of what has been accomplished up to this point in the team planning process. Thus the opportunities, objectives, and strategies set out in the master marketing plan would be checked by the general manager. Similarly, these same elements in the other five types of plans would undergo evaluation by the marketing manager.

There seems to be much wisdom in providing an opportunity for the echelon above to offer its comments and make any additional inputs, including suggested modifications, at this stage. It is certainly far better to get the thinking and opinion of the next higher echelon(s) regarding opportunities, objectives, and strategies at this point, rather than working out the entire plan, including action programs and subplans, and then submitting it for review and approval. By this method, any suggested revisions in the basic fundamentals of a plan can be incorporated before the details are spelled out. While this step undoubtedly requires some additional time, it offers the offsetting advantage of ensuring that the effort devoted to subsequent steps will have a higher payout in the sense that it will be focused on the correct things. In other words, providing this intermediate review and approval step increases the probabilities that the final plan will be on target. Furthermore, it will simplify the work to be done in Step 14— review and approval of the final plan. This is because such evaluation will be essentially confined to the actions taken in Steps 10 through 13, covering the detailed implementation of the previously approved objectives and strategies in terms of tactical action programs and subplans.

Steps 10 and 11 should be closely integrated. They are team activities and are accomplished by the same teams as those involved in Steps 4–8.

This is indeed quite logical under the team approach. After having originally met in a team session to accomplish Steps 4 through 8, the team members then proceed to develop the action programs for the necessary subplans and other details of tactical implementation, including control and review procedures (Step 10). Once these subplans have been prepared, the teams work out the adjustments necessary to arrive at the optimum arrangement (Step 11).

Step 12 calls for some close interfunctional cooperation between marketing and financial personnel in working out the financial implications of the proposed marketing plans. Joint efforts are also necessary to be sure that the financial data appearing in marketing plans tie in with those appearing in budgets.

Step 13 is an assembly function, and responsibility for it should be with the prime movers for each type of plan.

Step 14 is performed by the respective next higher echelons.

Steps 15, 16, and 17 are characterized by identity of responsibility for performance; that is, all three are accomplished by the prime mover for each type of plan.

These steps are summarized in Figure 2.

Figure 2. Steps in the planning process.

1. Prepare and disseminate guidelines for planning; provide statement of basic objectives and strategies.
2. Obtain information and make inputs to information base situation review. State assumptions where data are incomplete or not available. Audit capabilities, strengths, weaknesses, "faults," "threats," opportunities.
3. Prepare information base/situation review.
4. Identify opportunities to be exploited and weaknesses to be overcome.
5. Set objectives of the plan.
6. Develop alternative strategies to achieve objectives.
7. Select optimum strategy.
8. Identify resource groups necessary for implementation of this strategy.
9. Review, recommend modifications, and approve plan (objectives and strategies).
10. Prepare action programs (tactics): subplans for each participating resource, including subobjectives, substrategies, action schedules, and timetables (who is to do what by when). Key tasks, people responsible, deadline dates, dollar and manpower effort required. Include implementation, control, and review procedures.
11. Analyze and modify all subplans; make harmonizing adjustments to arrive at optimum plan.
12. Prepare relevant financial analyses, including pro forma contribution statements, return on investment, and so on.
13. Prepare "final" total plan, integrating modified subplans, action schedules, and financial analyses.
14. Review, modify, and approve final plan.
15. Put plan into operation.
16. Review performance against plan; analyze variances; take corrective action.
17. Make appropriate modifications and revisions in plan.

ADVANTAGES AND BENEFITS

The team approach offers a significant array of constructive advantages and synergistic plusses to organizations that implement it effectively:

1. It "pools" the best brainpower in the company, and concentrates it on how to plan and run the business better. Nobody has a monopoly on brains.

2. By actively involving functional heads in the planning process right from the beginning, by giving them the opportunity to contribute their ideas to the broad major decisions on opportunities, objectives, and strategies, they develop a strong sense of mutual commitment as functional specialists. They accept a deep personal responsibility for the successful implementation of their particular subplan.

3. The consultations among the various functional managers, marketing and nonmarketing, increase the likelihood that all are pointed in the same direction.

4. As a corollary advantage, participation in the team-planning effort lessens the tendency for some functional managers to regard their own spheres of operation as "islands"—that is, as being somewhat separate and apart from the other functions.

5. Because planning is now a team affair, based on mutual respect and understanding, the last step in the planning process, namely, fitting the individual functional subplans into the overall master plan, becomes a much easier task. It is accomplished by the team working to harmonize inconsistencies and the commitment of resources in the interest of developing the best possible total plan from the point of view of the business as a whole.

6. Finally, nothing succeeds like success. Once team planning gets started and begins to generate plans that achieve good results, a strong esprit de corps develops and grows among people in the organization because they know *where* they are going and *how* they are going to get there.

Part 5

MARKETING . . .

. . . The Performing Arts
. . . The Museum
. . . The City of New York

THIS SECTION IS ORGANIZED DIFFERENTLY from the preceding sections. Parts 2, 3, and 4 discuss various considerations and aspects of marketing under the marketing concept as they are being applied in a mix of organizations. The contributions in this section focus on special non-profit organizations not heavily covered in earlier sections. These special kinds of organizations appear to be unique because of special characteristics associated with them. Articles on these organizations have been highlighted and singled out because of their emphasis on particular problems of marketing in that sector or organization.

	Government	Education	Health	Religious and Charitable	Associations and Others
BAM Grows in Brooklyn Brendan Gill					X
Museums Find a New Patron: The Retail Market Business Week					X
A Sales Pitch for New York Michael Sterne	X				X

BAM Grows in Brooklyn

Brendan Gill

Connoisseurs of city planning have reason to be grateful to the Brooklyn Academy of Music. So have connoisseurs of drama, dance, song, chamber music, movies, children's theater and almost any other category of the performing arts that one may wish to name. For the Academy, familiarly known as BAM,* is a veritable Vesuvius of incessant cultural activity, lighting up the sky over Flatbush Avenue in a fashion readily visible even from myopic Manhattan. Daily and nightly throughout most of the year—the volcano is permitted to slumber for a few weeks each summer—something exceptionally lively is sure to be going on in one or another of the several theater spaces that flourish in ingeniously isolated and soundproofed propinquity within the stout walls of the Academy.

Reprinted from *The New York Times Magazine,* October 24, 1976.

* I admire everything about the Academy of Music except the acronym by which it chooses to be known. To me, BAM has the unwelcome sound of a blow in the face, but I admit that to most people it amounts to an affectionate diminutive, not unlike "Honey" or "Babe." So BAM be it, alas!

A few years ago, the Academy was nearly extinct; today it blazes and bubbles with life. In the 60's, its audiences were dwindling away into the hundreds; now they amount to well over a quarter of a million people a year. Subscriptions to Academy programs have doubled in the course of the past 12 months alone, and another formidable increase is expected to be achieved this year. What is going on here? How does it come about that what is probably the oldest performing-arts center in the country— the Academy was incorporated in 1859 and opened in its own grand Gothic auditorium on Brooklyn Heights in 1861—has become one of the most youthful-seeming centers in the country, as well as one of the strongest? Why is BAM not only a house of smash hits (many of which, like "Candide," "Yentl," and "The Royal Family," subsequently leap over the East River onto Broadway for extended runs) but itself, as an institution, a smash hit?

I put connoisseurs of city planning first on the list of those who have reason to be grateful to BAM because BAM is a well-nigh perfect example of how a failing cultural enterprise can be restored to life and, with energy and imagination, be made to prosper in its old age even more splendidly than it did in its youth. BAM is also a model of how to deal with an increasingly common urban problem: the architecturally distinguished landmark building that, having fallen on hard times, is threatened with destruction.

The present Academy was designed in the early 1900s by the architectural firm of Herts & Tallant, which was then among the most celebrated designers of theaters in the country (the Lyceum Theatre on West 45th Street in Manhattan, generally held to be the oldest active legitimate theater in the city, is a characteristic specimen of the firm's work). Neo-Renaissance in style, the Academy is of exceptional size—its facade is over 360 feet long—but it has been scaled with such care that it doesn't feel oppressive. Henry James once said that, everything else being equal, a building that sits is more pleasing than a building that stands, and BAM sits with grace and confidence on its immense site, welcoming audiences without tyrannizing over them.

When a landmark like the Academy goes, much of the close-knit fabric of buildings surrounding it is likely to go as well, and we have learned at long last that this fabric, once torn apart, is almost impossible to reweave. Not only in New York, but in innumerable cities from coast to coast, many a tarnished embodiment of civic pride has been ruthlessly thrown down in recent years because it was deemed to have outlived its usefulness. In the name of urban renewal, a ritual disembowelment of our cities has leveled respected landmarks and the often-cherished neighborhoods around them and has opened up in their stead immense vistas of paved plazas and grim parking lots—deserts of inhuman empty spaces, as dead as Carthage.

Now, some such fate might well have befallen BAM, and all the more so because its present home is not the Victorian ornament erected long ago on elegant Brooklyn Heights—that building was destroyed by fire in 1903—but a twentieth-century building on Lafayette Avenue, in a commercial district characteristically subject to the creeping decay that afflicts so large a number of our inner cities. (When cities are healthy, there is little talk of "outer" or "inner"; the healthy city is a seamless web.) Brooklyn Heights is a well-preserved and much reverenced historic landmark district, protected by law and with plenty of inhabitants ready to defend it, but Lafayette Avenue and its environs have long been in jeopardy and have found few champions willing to attempt to impose new order on old disarray. Of these few, the most successful has been Harvey Lichtenstein of BAM.

In 1967, Lichtenstein came to Brooklyn to assume the post of executive director of BAM. (A few months ago, he was elevated to the presidency of BAM, mostly for organizational reasons. As an admiring friend has said, "Harvey is the 'I am' of BAM, whatever his title.") From the beginning, Lichtenstein perceived that if the Academy was ever to regain its place in the sun, the neighborhood around it must be a part of the venture. If the venture prospered, so would the neighborhood. For the arts are not only nourishing to the soul; they are nourishing financially as well.

Lichtenstein is eloquent upon this topic; he has been studying it at close range for many years, not only in Brooklyn but throughout the city. One might think, he says, that the connection between the cultural activities of a community and its economic life is an obvious one, but no—it has been a connective largely ignored even by sophisticated urbanologists and entirely ignored by politicians and bureaucrats. A year or so ago, a committee under the chairmanship of Martin E. Segal, a New York financier and patron of the arts, undertook to discover, in actual dollars and cents, the size of the economic contribution to New York City by all the activities that can be gathered together under the rubric of Culture. It was a time when the city administration, hard pressed for funds, was eager to slash the already small sum that it ordinarily budgets for cultural activities—those scores of institutions that many members of the administration have been accustomed to dismiss as "luxuries," "unnecessary frills," and the like.

To almost universal astonishment, the Segal committee was able to demonstrate that the arts in New York are big business. More than 50,000 people are employed here in cultural activities of one sort or another, and these activities generate an income of more than 13 billion a year. Crassly put, Culture is one of the biggest industries in town; moreover, unlike many other local industries, it is a growing one, indispensable to the city's economic health. It is also a terrific bargain. Indeed, it can be argued not only that Culture costs the city nothing, but also that it returns a sizable profit on the city's small investment in it. The city grudgingly grants one-fiftieth of 1 percent of its budget to Culture; for every dollar that Culture receives from the city it gives back $4 in the form of taxes. Culture's indirect benefits to the city are no less impressive, though harder to appraise. A few seasons ago, the Metropolitan Opera took the trouble to examine the fiscal consequences of the occasion on which Beverly Sills sang in the Metropolitan's production of "The Siege of Corinth." There were 4,000 people in the audience that evening; they came from 27 states, and they are estimated to have spent a total of $185,000 in local restaurants, hotels, garages and department stores. That sum is far in excess of the sum that the city contributes to the Metropolitan Opera during the course of an entire year.

When Lichtenstein, backed by a brave board of directors, undertook the rehabilitation of BAM, his first task was to induce the media to pay attention to it. For generations, it has been famously difficult to make newspapers and magazines, to say nothing of the public at large, regard with seriousness events taking place in far-off, vaguely comical Brooklyn. Thomas Wolfe wrote a celebrated short story called "Only the Dead Know Brooklyn," and sometimes this grim apothegm appears to be true, especially when it comes to the arts. Even the august, world-famous Brooklyn Museum finds it hard to draw visitors from across the river to its superb exhibitions; how much harder then, in the late 1960s, for the faded Academy to persuade critics, reviewers and patrons of the performing arts to find their way to an obscure corner of mysterious downtown Brooklyn.

Lichtenstein lured the media moguls to BAM by the most straightforward and old-fashioned means imaginable—he offered them programs that proved literally irresistible. In dance, for example, Eliot Feld, Merce Cunningham (with whom Lichtenstein himself once studied), Alvin Ailey, Maurice Bejart, Twyla Tharp, Trisha Brown, and the Pennsylvania Ballet; in theater, Grotowski's Polish Laboratory Theater, Peter Brook's International Center for Theatre Research, the Royal Shakespeare Company, the Young Vic, the Chelsea Theater Center, and the experimental stage works of Robert Wilson. The Brooklyn Philharmonia, under the direction of Lukas Foss, took up residence in BAM; so did the Brooklyn Boys Chorus, under the direction of James McCarthy. Impossible for the media to ignore such an array of delectable attractions; soon the sourest of Manhattan taxi drivers were beginning to confess that there were bridges over the East River and a tunnel under it, and that BAM was every bit as real as Borough Hall and Gage & Tollner.

First the critics, then the crowds. Well, not exactly (in the world of theater, there are plenty of times when the critics rave and the crowds go elsewhere), but no matter—Lichtenstein and his staff were eager to attract audiences that, with or without the lure of smash hits, would develop a loyalty to the Academy itself. To that end, they devised a marketing technique that combined unusually low prices with subscriptions to several events in a single package. One advantage of these packages is that they encourage people to attend what BAM thinks of as "crossover" events; if someone habitually goes to the dance, an inexpensive package subscription may seduce him into taking a chance on an occasional movie or play. Furthermore, the Academy has made a strenuous effort to build an audience with a substantial local base. In 1973, it sold some 6,000 subscriptions, of which more were purchased by residents of Manhattan than by residents of Brooklyn. In 1975, BAM sold well over 40,000 subscriptions, and Brooklynites made up the majority of subscribers.

To strengthen the effectiveness of the Academy as a neighborhood activity, BAM operates what amounts to a mini-restaurant without walls, serving shrimp cocktails, quiche Lorraine, fruits, cheeses, and wine and beer, before performances and during intermissions. It also runs a number of inexpensive attended parking lots and a system of express buses to and from major events. BAM's indefatigable pursuit of patrons has caused the number of seats filled to rise from less than 30 percent of capacity a few years ago to 85 percent of capacity today. And a continuous renovation of the actual structure of the Academy has been keeping abreast of the increase in audiences. In 1973, for example, the shell of a long-unused ballroom was transformed into the crisp, brick-walled Lepercq Space, holding an audience of around 600 and named for Paul Lepercq, the French-born investment banker who was, until recently, chairman of the board of directors of the Academy. During the past year, under the direction of James Stewart Polshek, dean of the school of architecture at Columbia, the former Music Hall has been remodeled into the Playhouse, a superbly equipped legitimate theater, seating approximately 1,100 people. The Opera House, the largest of the four auditoriums under the roof of the Academy, seats around 2,200 people, while the Chelsea Theater, the smallest of the auditoriums, seats around 200 people. These four spaces, as varied in appearance as they are in purpose, are rarely idle.

With confidence in its programming and with pride in its refurbished plant, the Academy has been able of late to give more attention to the long-range problem of urban renewal in downtown Brooklyn. For one thing, it has helped to form the Brooklyn Educational and Cultural Alliance (BECA, for short), which includes, along with BAM, the Brooklyn Museum, Long Island University, St. Francis College, St. Joseph's College, Polytechnic Institute of New York, Pratt Institute, the Brooklyn Public Library, and the Long Island Historical Society. These bodies all share a profound concern with the economic good health of Brooklyn; they cannot hope to perform their cultural tasks successfully if the neighborhoods around them are dying. BAM believes in forming the closest possible ties between cultural groups, business groups, and government groups. "In the old days," Lichtenstein says, "people used to think that those groups had nothing in common. Each kept his distance from the others. Now we understand that we're all facing a single enormous problem—nothing less than the survival of the city. We understand that we must work together to find a solution to that problem. No more luxury of aloneness!"

Connoisseurs of city planning have reason to be grateful to BAM precisely because Lichtenstein and his associates assume, as a matter of course, responsibility for the preservation and enhancement of their community. The Academy has been an important presence on Lafayette Avenue for almost 70 years; now proudly restored to life, it will serve as a model for other communities throughout the city. For never again in this century will we observe on the part of government agencies and private real-estate developers the wanton knocking down of individual buildings and whole neighborhoods that appear to have outlasted their prime. Instead, we will observe how those buildings and neighborhoods can be sympathetically reused and given a second, third, or fourth chance at life. Inevitably, neighborhoods will continue to change, for better or worse, but in future our efforts and our money will be spent on turning worse into better and not on murderous obliteration.

A busy, handsomely redecorated old building like the Academy becomes an island of health in a more or less ailing community; little by little, the community renews itself, drawing on sources of energy long-neglected. Currents of eager connection flow from one island of health to the next and then to the next; month by month, year by year, the grievously injured fabric of the city is stitched together and made as strong as when it was new—with luck and skill and love, stronger than when it was new. This is easy to document in the case of BAM. In the course of the past few years, a dozen new enterprises have opened their doors in the neighborhood—bars, restaurants, and even a flower shop, which occupies a corner of the parking lot that BAM operates across the street from its building. A restaurant called the Camperdown Elm (its charming name is taken from an ancient elm in Prospect Park) attributes much of its prosperity to BAM. It opened a couple of years ago and quickly found that when BAM was at its busiest so was the restaurant, drawing customers from Connecticut, New Jersey, and far out on Long Island. Proprietors of other restaurants, including the venerable Gage & Tollner, tell the same story: a hit at BAM has an immediate, measurable impact on the economic life of all its neighbors.

Donald E. Moore, president of the Downtown Brooklyn Development Association, is a close student of this process of civic symbiosis. He points out that the terminus of the Long Island Railroad in Brooklyn is practically next-door to the Academy. The terminus is physically in very bad shape, and the Metropolitan Transportation Authority has been contemplating the expenditure of some $20 million on its improvement. "Maybe 10,000 people a day are currently using the terminus as a change-over point from train to subway on their way into Manhattan," Mr. Moore says. "If the terminus is improved, this number will greatly increase. Many of the people using the terminus will be good potential members of Academy audiences. But if the Academy weren't already drawing crowds, the MTA might be much less interested in saving the terminus and so upgrading the whole neighborhood. In the best possible way, one hand washes the other."

In a classic example of how, given sufficient impetus, the fabric of a city reweaves itself, the Brooklyn Union Gas Company has taken a considerable interest in the popular Brooklyn practice of restoring nineteenth-century brownstones. Utility companies are eager to find new customers, and where a utility company steps in, banks and insurance companies are usually quick to follow, granting construction loans and mortgages in areas that previously may have been, whether openly or covertly, red-lined. Under the rubric of "Cinderella Project," Brooklyn Union Gas has worked closely with homeowners in Boerum Hill, Park Slope, and half a dozen other flourishing communities; now it is casting a hopeful eye on the Academy area, which lies roughly between Fort Greene to the north and the downtown district of Brooklyn to the northwest and, except for the presence of the Academy, would have been an unlikely candidate for rehabilitation. The Brooklyn Union Gas Company arranged for the purchase of a number of dilapidated old houses on St. Felix Street, which runs along the east front of the Academy building, and they will be put back into apple-pie order. According to present plans, the houses will be opened to the public and will serve as models for further redevelopment in the neighborhood.

The Brownstone Revival Committee, which was founded by Brooklynites, has some 2,000 members scattered throughout the country. The original president of the committee, Everett H. Ortner, is an ardent supporter of the Academy, and his wife, Evelyn, an interior designer, is a member of the board of directors. "More and more young people are coming to Brooklyn to live," Ortner says. "They all seem to want the same thing—a nice old house with a nice garden and plenty of sky to look at. Well, we can still offer them such things in Brooklyn. And we can offer them culture as well. Thanks to BAM, there isn't much in the line of the performing arts that they need to do without. There's a lot of enthusiasm being generated in Brooklyn; you can feel it in the air. We've put together something called the Brooklyn Brownstone Conference, which is a number of organizations with the same purpose—the preservation and enhancement of Brooklyn. We staged a fair on Montague Street last fall. Some Jeremiahs said that nobody would show up. Well, 15,000 people showed up. We had a wonderful time."

Museums Find a New Patron: The Retail Market

As Egypt's "Treasures of Tutankhamun" exhibit winds its way through a tour of leading museums in the U.S., it is leaving a trail of staggering attendance figures—and equally eyepopping sales figures for the line of merchandise that accompanies it. During its first six months on tour, nearly 2 million people have seen the show, and a good proportion of them have contributed to the $3 million spent on the 400-item line of reproductions, ranging from $5 hieroglyphic charms to 18-carat gold statues of Tut that sell for $1,500.

The success of the Tut-inspired reproductions spotlights the push that many museums are making into the retail arena. Now, with Christmas approaching, once-stuffy institutions are busily advertising their wares in shops, mail-order catalogs, and tie-ins with leading department stores. Surveys indicate a wide potential audience: A 1975 Louis Harris poll found that 78 million Americans age 16 and over had visited a museum at least once a year, up from 68 million in 1973. With soaring operating costs and pinched funding from endowments and public sources, museums are elevating their former "sales desks"—once devoted to postcards and

Reprinted from January 5, 1978 issue of *Business Week* by special permission. Copyright © 1978 by McGraw-Hill, Inc.

guide books—into full-fledged retail stores offering a wide array of goods ranging from reproductions of treasures to T-shirts and tote bags.

"The day of the great patron is diminishing," says David Collins, merchandise manager of the two retail shops at New York's Museum of Modern Art, which have gross revenues of $1.5 million. "Museums have to look at every possible device to be self-sustaining," Collins adds. Yet, he concedes, "we're not sure how far a museum can get into merchandising without becoming a bazaar that compromises its image."

This is indeed a sore point. So is the problem of protecting a museum's tax-exempt status, while selling goods that must have a wide appeal. The Internal Revenue Service has ruled that profits from a museum's retail sales can be taxed as unrelated business income if the goods are not artistic or educational. That broad ruling has allowed the Museum of Modern Art to sell with success Italian-designed toilet brushes and ice cream scoops. The Smithsonian Institution's eight retail shops and its catalog sales gross some $5.5 million for items that range from ties and umbrellas to lightweight metallic luggage made of material similar to that used in an astronaut's flight suit.

Is this educational? "It's fun," shrugs Richard Griesel, the Smithsonian's business manager. "We try to avoid being commercial," he says, pointing out that such items are a way of expanding the institution beyond its walls. But the "educational" dictum is so vague that many institutions are leery of publicity. In fact, the Museum of Science & Industry in Chicago refused to talk with *Business Week,* lest publicity bring inquiries from the IRS.

"I would prefer to see a purist museum shop," says Gudmund Vigtel, director of Atlanta's High Museum of Art, which recently added glass sculptures, candelabra, European toys and clothes, jewelry, and bridge score cards to its usual inventory of books, cards, and original art pieces. "But unless you can make up the income in other ways, most are forced into this business of trying to sell things for a profit." Until Vigtel broadened the shop's scope in 1976, it was operating at a loss. "Now sales are booming," he says. Still, he wants to soft-pedal his success. "Museum shops in almost every city are being criticized by retailers because we're tax-exempt yet competing with them in the marketplace." So, he concludes, "we don't advertise because we don't want to rub it in too much."

That line of reasoning evokes little sympathy at the Metropolitan Museum of Art in New York, which has pioneered in retailing since it first opened in 1870. Competitors alternately look upon the Met with envy and cattily refer to it as "Bloomingdale's North."

SURVIVAL FACTOR

Last year the Met's retail shop and mail-order division grossed $10.4 million, up from $7 million in 1975, and contributed over one-third of the museum's overall income. This year sales are expected to bring in some $12.5 million, with three-quarters of that originating from its four catalog mailings to 1 million households.

"Retailing is why the museum is surviving and able to mount shows and pay its employees a halfway decent wage," says Joanne Lyman, production manager for three-dimensional products. Lyman canvases the Met's permanent and visiting collections with a curator to decide what pieces can be reproduced or adapted—and sold—most readily.

This year the Met's 114-page Christmas catalog features Egyptian tote bags at $22.50, bellflower pitchers for $45, and a T'ang dynasty ladle available in sterling silver for $250, as well as the usual cards and tree ornaments. Lyman says that the Met's goods may cost more, "but people like to shop here because they feel that they're doing something to help the museum survive."

Museums are banking on that feeling being widespread. Universe Books has just published a 176-page *Shopper's Guide to Museum Stores,* which includes some 700 products from museums across the country. The book was compiled by Shelley M. Hodupp, executive director of merchandising services for the Philadelphia Museum of Art, which recently expanded its own retail facilities and began accepting credit-card purchases.

MERCHANDISING TRICKS

In Boston, the Museum of Fine Arts expanded its space and product line in the past year, pushing its sales beyond $1 million for the first time. Similar results are being toted up at the Los Angeles County Art Museum, which last year added more selling space and began a mail-order operation. Sales hit $800,000 for the year ended in June, up from $350,000 two years earlier, and officials expect more than $1 million this year. Profits usually run about 15% of sales.

Beyond expanding product lines, museums are learning other tricks, such as shop placement and price inducements. The Chicago Art Institute's retail efforts brought in $1.2 million last year, up 17% from 1975, and net profits rose by 52% to $243,000. Ralph Weil, the museum's shop director, credits much of the gain to discounts for members, "plus our location near downtown office buildings." In fact, says Weil, "people don't even have to go through the museum to get to the shop; they can walk in right off the street."

COLLABORATION

If museum shops are learning from major merchandisers, the reverse is also true. "A lot of stores are interested in museum goods because the articles connote a certain reassurance about quality to customers," says Brian Rushton, head of publications and marketing services at the Brooklyn (N.Y.) Museum, which recently collaborated on an Egyptian project with Bloomingdale's and Block China Corp. Called the "Brooklyn Museum Collection," the dinnerware and gift items come complete with a back stamp and educational brochures. "It's met with pretty good response," says Block China President Jay Block, who is now working with the Philadelphia Museum, the Carnegie Institute, and the Baltimore Museum to develop goods for sale through department stores. The return for a museum can be alluring. Typically, it receives a royalty of 2% to 8% on all items sold.

Still, some in the cultural community fear that museums may soon plan shows with an eye to promotional tie-ins. "We all react against being in the souvenir business," says Brooklyn's Rushton. And right now, he says, "it's hard to tell if the tail is wagging the dog. After all, it's a museum first—and it could get to look the other way."

A Sales Pitch for New York

Michael Sterne

It's not exactly a salesman's dream. The product is flawed, the competition is intense, the customers are wary—and the payoff doesn't come until years after the sale. Yet last year, New York City (the product) was host to more conventions (834) and more convention visitors (1,213,960) than at any time since the World's Fair of 1964–65. And this year is expected to be as good as, or better than, last year.

The salesman (the New York City Convention and Visitors Bureau) cannot afford to rest on his laurels, however. The lag between sale and convention dates is too long. The National Association of Realtors meeting is a case in point.

Back in 1966 the realtors, 12,000 strong, convened in New York. Some of the hotels where they were registered refused to honor their reservations. The realtors have not been back since. But next month the bureau will make a sales pitch to the association's board of directors.

How will the bureau handle the memories of 1966? Martin Gray, the vice president for convention sales, takes this line: "Those were the days when reservations were handled manually. Since 1972, New York hotels have been using computers for bookings. The system now is highly accurate, and we'll be making that point strongly."

Getting the realtors' convention for 1983 or 1984 is a major goal of the bureau sales staff for 1978.

Some 30,000 conventions took place in the nation last year, and the numbers are growing. Studies commissioned by Meetings & Conventions, a trade publication that reaches the managers of most of the 5,000 major conventions, showed an increase of 12 percent a year since 1973.

Direct spending by sponsoring organizations and delegates is estimated at more than $4 billion a year, with New York City's take thought to be about $600 million. The statistics of the convention business are uncertain at best, but experts agree that New York ranks second to the Second City, Chicago, which brings in more than 1,000 meetings a year.

In another kind of ranking, however—one very dear to the salesman's heart—New York is currently in 17th place. Only $500,000 of public funds are spent to build convention and tourist business in the city. That sum is supplemented by $750,000 contributed by hotels, restaurants, and other organizations that profit from visitors. But even with those private funds added, the New York bureau receipts rank far behind the likes of Las Vegas ($3.3 million) and Miami ($2 million).

The bureau operates with a staff of 45, led by its generally optimistic president, Charles Gillett. "I'm sure we could do better," he says, "but we can't do the job without greater resources. In this business, like any other business, you get what you pay for."

Mr. Gillett, 62 years old, has been with the bureau for 30 years, and his hair is gray, but there is a youthful dash to his well-cut suits and carefully chosen ties. A gold apple pin, reminder of the city's "Big Apple" campaign, is never absent from his lapel. Most of his career with the bureau has been in promotion, and he is a tireless booster of the city.

The operation he runs, however, specializes more in footslogging salesmanship than in promotional coups. Like Fuller brush men who methodically ring every doorbell in their territory twice a year and then go back over it again to catch the housewives they missed, the bureau's salesmen relentlessly pursue the association officers and convention managers who decide where conventions are to be held.

Recently that approach worked handsomely for Chris Paskalides, a convention salesman who has been with the bureau since 1961. For many years he has been talking up New York to the manager of the joint annual convention of the American Pediatric Society and the Society for Pediatric Research. This April convention attracts 3,000 people, and New York, because of its concentration of practitioners and medical facilities, would seem to be a logical site. Yet Mr. Paskalides had never been able to sign it up.

Last month the groups' file was pulled in accordance with a regular schedule, and Mr. Paskalides telephoned the manager to remind her that New York still wanted the pediatric societies. An hour later the manager learned that her Atlantic City hotel booking for 1978 had been canceled because the hotel was being remodeled. She immediately called Mr. Paskalides back, and he was able to sign her up for the New York Hilton.

"It was a very nice piece of business," he says, "and I probably never would have gotten it if I hadn't made that call."

Through information exchanges with other bureaus, the New York agency has put together files on all 5,000 major conventions, indicating where their previous meetings have been held, where their next ones are to be, what kinds of facilities they need, how much they can spend on hotels, exhibit space, and services, and who the current officers are.

The files also contain confidential information the bureau does not share about who actually makes the decisions as to where conventions are held, what those people think about New York, and what problems may have kept them out of New York in the past.

"The heart of our work" is how Mr. Gillett describes the files. "We update them constantly. We mine them every day, and we can tell from them almost instantly if a group is a likely candidate."

The work is done by five salaried convention sales representatives—four men and one woman, all recruited from the meeting sales departments of hotels. The load breaks down to about 1,000 organizations for each to contact at least once a year. Though they have secretarial and clerical help, they are spread pretty thin. Selling a single convention can involve weeks of research on costs, space availabilities, and services.

For example, several weeks of intensive work done in April 1974 paid off last month when 6,000 members of the National Council of Teachers of English came to New York for a Thanksgiving Week convention. Their last visit had been in 1955.

Mr. Gray told how it was done: "I had been talking to this group off and on for two and a half years, and I knew that the man we had to convince was Bob Hanley, the convention director. His recommendations carried great weight with the small executive committee that made the decision."

The bureau's research showed that all of the council's conventions on the East Coast had been successful, drawing large numbers of teachers. It also showed that, in the council's sectional rotation of convention sites, the East Coast was due for another one in 1977 and that the group had held recent conventions in Baltimore, Atlanta, Philadelphia, Miami, and Washington.

"It seemed to me that 1977 was the right year for New York, and I put it to Hanley. He had nothing against New York, he said, but he didn't think we had the facilities, and he thought our prices for rooms, meals and entertainment were too high for people living on teachers' salaries. But he left the door open and said he was willing to be convinced."

Mr. Gray started gathering ammunition. The council uses 50 to 60 meeting rooms simultaneously during its convention. The bureau was able to line up 80 in three hotels—the Americana, the Hilton, and the Park Sheraton, all within three blocks of each other.

The council required 3,500 to 4,000 rooms, all moderately priced. Mr. Gray found that the Thanksgiving week date for the convention was a very slow time for New York hotels and that the hotel managers were willing to cut their rates to get a big chunk of business.

He gathered information on New York's many free or low-cost attractions—its museums, exotic neighborhoods, gardens, zoos, and parks. He prepared a list of Broadway shows that were offering two tickets for the price of one. He selected a group of interesting but moderately priced restaurants from the guide the bureau publishes every six months.

"When I had it all put together, I went out to Urbana, Illinois, where the council has its offices, and four hotel representatives went with me. Hanley went over everything we told him line by line. He asked a lot of questions and he bargained hard, but we were able to make our point: New York could handle this convention and do it at a price the teachers were willing to pay."

After meeting for five hours with the New Yorkers, Mr. Hanley took their case to his executive committee, and the next day he called Mr. Gray with their decision: It would be New York for the English teachers in 1977.

Every convention has its own special needs, and the bureau tailors its presentations to address those needs. But it also has films, slide shows, guides, and brochures that point out New York's attractions and put a gloss on some of its flaws.

As a not-for-profit private corporation, the bureau is able to use sales techniques a public agency could not. It may spend funds to entertain prospects, and the bureau does so, on what it calls a modest scale. This year, for example, it staged "blitzes" to woo convention officers in Chicago, Washington and New York.

Every person in those cities who could pick a convention site for a major organization was interviewed individually. Then they were brought together for luncheons and screenings of the bureau's "Big Apple" film. And the day following the luncheons, each guest was sent a red plastic "Big Apple" ice bucket. "The ice buckets cost only $3.50, but they made a big impression," Mr. Gillett says.

The bureau also promotes tourism by courting travel agents, sending out visitors' guides and encouraging newspaper, magazine, radio, and television features on New York. Roughly half of its budget is spent on selling conventions and the rest on attracting vacation visitors.

What the bureau does not do, and would like most to do if it could get the money, is to advertise New York heavily. "We badly need some offset to the bad press and bad television New York continues to get in many parts of the country," Mr. Gillett says.

But the single sales aid the bureau most covets is a new convention center. It estimates such a center could attract as many as 60 additional large conventions a year.

Help of another kind is coming, however. This year, reversing a policy that had scanted the tourist promotion budget of the State Department of Commerce, the Legislature granted $4 million to the department for an advertising campaign. Some $900,000 of this sum was set aside to advertise weekend tour packages for New York City, a campaign that is to begin on Valentine's Day. The slogan: "I love New York."

Biographical Notes

BATES, DON is executive director of the National Communication Council for Human Services, Inc., known until January 1, 1976 as the National Public Relations Council of Health & Welfare Services, Inc. (New York City).

BERRY, LEONARD L. is professor of marketing and chairman of the Department of Marketing at Georgia State University, Atlanta, Georgia. He received his DBA in marketing from the University of Denver in 1965 and holds a BA in behavioral sciences. Mr. Berry has published numerous articles and books on business, marketing, and banking. He is an active member of the Bank Marketing Association and the World Future Society.

BLOCK, LEE F. is president of Lee F. Block & Partners, Inc., Chicago, a consulting service to the health industry. He holds a BA and MA in English literature from the University of Pittsburgh. He is an accredited member of the Public Relations Society of America, executive director of the Academy of Hospital Public Relations, and a member of the National Association of Science Writers.

BOGART, LEO is an executive vice-president and general manager of the Newspaper Advertising Bureau, Inc. He has taught at the Illinois Institute of Technology, New York University, and Columbia University, and holds a doctorate in sociology from the University of Chicago. A director of the Advertising Research Foundation, he is also on the editorial board of *The Public Opinion*

Quarterly, and has received the AAPOR award for distinguished contributions to public opinion research. Mr. Bogart was a member of President Kennedy's 1960 task force on U.S. information policy and has served on the board of the National Safety Council.

BYBEE, H. MALCOLM is a vice-president and account supervisor on new and established household products for the Colgate-Palmolive account at Kenyon & Eckhardt Advertising, Inc., New York. He holds a master of arts degree in communications and a bachelor in journalism degree from the University of Texas.

CHIAMPA, PAUL was a graduate student at the University of Virginia School of Business Administration in December 1976 (at the time this article appeared in *Hospital Progress*).

CORBIN, ARNOLD is professor emeritus of marketing at the New York University Graduate School of Business Administration, does marketing and management educational consulting, is coauthor of a half-dozen books on marketing subjects, and has written many articles for professional and trade publications. He is presently a partner in Corbin Associates, a marketing and management consulting firm, Rockville Centre, New York. He has served as the author's mentor in marketing for the past fifteen years, and many of the concepts embodied in this book have been learned from him.

GARDNER, DAVID M. is professor of business administration at the University of Illinois, College of Commerce and Business Administration. He holds a Ph.D. in business administration from the University of Minnesota and a BSC in marketing from the University of Iowa.

GEORGE, WILLIAM R. is assistant professor in the Department of Marketing, School of Business, Virginia Commonwealth University, Richmond, Virginia. He holds a Ph.D. in business administration from the University of Georgia, an MBA from the University of Pittsburgh, and an AB in economics from Thiel College.

GILL, BRENDAN was drama critic of *The New Yorker Magazine,* author of *Here at the New Yorker,* and is chairman of the board of Municipal Art Society and Landmarks Conservancy of New York. He is a drama critic and architectural enthusiast.

GUTMAN, EVELYN is associate director for Cancer Center Planning at New York University Medical Center. Her contribution is based on her MBA thesis project entitled "Effective Marketing of a Cancer Screening Service," which was completed at New York University's Graduate School of Business Administration in May 1977. At graduation she was awarded the Hector Lazo Memorial Award for achievement and scholarship. She has also done consulting work for cancer programs in New Jersey.

IHLANDFELDT, WILLIAM is dean of admissions and financial aid at Northwestern University, Rebecca Crown Center, Evanston, Illinois. He holds a Ph.D. in education from Northwestern University.

IRELAND, RICHARD C. is president of the Ireland Educational Corp., Littleton, Colorado.

KOTLER, PHILIP is Harold T. Martin Professor of marketing at Northwestern University. He holds a Ph.D. in economics from Massachusetts Institute of Technology. He is an active consultant to many companies on marketing planning and information systems.

LEVY, SIDNEY J. is professor of marketing at Northwestern University and also teaches behavioral science. He holds a Ph.D. in psychology from the University of Chicago. Dr. Levy is the author of many articles and books.

LUSTERMAN, SEYMOUR is senior research associate of public affairs research at the National Industrial Conference Board. He was senior vice-president of marketing and media services at Gumbinner North Advertising from 1963 to 1968. He holds a BA in economics from New York University and an MA in economics from Columbia University. He has authored several publications.

MACSTRAVIC, ROBIN E., Ph.D. is associate director, Program in Health Administration and Planning at the University of Washington, Seattle, Washington. He holds a Ph.D. degree.

MINDAK, WILLIAM A. is with the University of Texas at Austin, Department of Advertising, Austin, Texas.

O'HALLARON, RICHARD D. is executive director of St. Mary's Hospital, Richmond, Virginia.

SHAPIRO, BENSON P. is associate professor of business administration at the Harvard Business School. His recent article entitled "Can Marketing and Manufacturing Coexist?" appeared in the September-October 1977 issue of the *Harvard Business Review*.

STAPLES, JEFFREY is director of fiscal services of St. Mary's Hospital, Richmond, Virginia.

STERNE, MICHAEL was formerly with the London Bureau of *The New York Times* and is now on the local staff responsible for reporting on the economy of New York and the metropolitan region.

TAYLOR, M. ELLIOTT is director of public affairs for the Greenville Hospital System, Greenville, S.C., and past president of Carolina Hospital Public Relations Society (CHPRS).

VERTINSKY, ILAN is professor of management science, policy analyses, and animal ecology at the University of British Columbia, Vancouver, Canada. He has published more than 60 articles in such journals as *Management Science, Operations Research, Review of Economic Studies,* and *Administrative Science.* He holds a Ph.D. in business administration from the University of California at Berkeley.

WAGNER, PAUL is president of the NPO Task Force in New York City, a Hill & Knowlton associate. It serves the nonprofit organizational field with special emphasis on universities, foundations, and national professional organizations. Dr. Wagner has had extensive experience as public relations counsel for the American Bar Association, National Education Association, and the National Association of Health, Physical Education and Recreation. An accredited member of PRSA, he has worked in the media for such organizations as *The Chicago Daily News* and *Newsweek*.

WASEM, GEORGE is president of Commercial National Management Consulting Company of Commercial National Corporations, Peoria, Illinois.

WILKIE, WILLIAM L. is associate professor of marketing at the University of Florida. He also teaches behavioral science. He holds a Ph.D. in business administration from Stanford University, an MBA in marketing from Stanford University, and a BBA in marketing from the University of Notre Dame.

ZALTMAN, GERALD is professor of marketing and teaches behavioral science at the University of Pittsburgh. He received his doctorate in sociology from Johns Hopkins University, an MBA in marketing from the University of Chicago, and an AB in government from Bates College. Dr. Zaltman is advisor to numerous public and private health agencies in Central America.

WOOTERS, J. DUKES, JR. has been president of Cotton Incorporated since its founding in 1971, an association that conducts worldwide research and marketing activities on behalf of approximately 100,000 cotton producers in 19 states. Mr. Wooters was previously in the sales and international operations divisions of *Readers Digest*.

Index